Islam
and Political
the
Discourse of
Modernity

INTERNATIONAL POLITICS OF THE MIDDLE EAST SERIES

Islam
and **Political**
the
Discourse
of
Modernity

Armando Salvatore

ISLAM AND THE POLITICAL DISCOURSE OF MODERNITY

Ithaca Press is an imprint of Garnet Publishing Limited

Published by
Garnet Publishing Limited
8 Southern Court
South Street
Reading
RG1 4QS
UK

First edition 1997
First paperback edition 1999

ISBN 0 86372 273 3

British Library Cataloguing-in-Publication Data
A catalogue record for this book is available from the British Library

Jacket design by Neil Collier
Typeset by Samantha Abley

Printed in Lebanon

TABLE OF CONTENTS

———

PART I
ORDER AND DISCOURSE

To my parents

This book is partly based on my Ph.D. dissertation, *The Making (and Unmaking) of "Political Islam"*, which I defended in March 1994 at the European University Institute (EUI) in Florence, Italy. This unique institution, that hosts and harmoniously merges various European and other academic cultures, provided an ideal environment to explore a new research path into the historical and contemporary relationship between Islam and politics from a global cultural viewpoint. I began work on this project at the EUI in the fall of 1990 with my supportive supervisor, Klaus Eder. I would like to thank him for his invaluable advice on matters of theory and method, for the encouragement and trust that he gave me, and especially for the genuine enthusiasm for a subject related to the transcultural politics of Islam.

However, the first seeds of the project had already been planted during my previous period of study at the University of Bonn, Germany, where Stefan Wild, and especially Reinhard Schulze, who later acted as external supervisor for my Ph.D. thesis at the EUI, provided me with orientation and stimulation, and imparted to me a sense of openness in the search for new ground in the cross-disciplinary problematization of contemporary developments in Arab Muslim societies. My indebtedness to Reinhard Schulze is so evident throughout the book that it needs no further emphasis here.

At the EUI, I met two other scholars who influenced, from different perspectives, my course of investigation no less than my appointed supervisors. Nazih Ayubi was helpful in providing insights into the historical and empirical basis of the phenomenon called "political Islam". Meanwhile, Arpad Szakolczai helped me to think of the phenomenon differently, by developing a genealogical approach that became the methodological hub of the book. Nazih and I agreed how to transform my Ph.D. thesis into a book. He proposed to publish the work in the present series at Ithaca Press, which he directed until his tragic and premature death in November 1995. Between summer 1994 and summer 1995 we were in constant contact in order to give the book its present shape. Without him, this book, born an orphan, would not have been.

Very special thanks are due to Clifford Geertz and Alessandro Pizzorno, two social scientists of unique experience, versatility and insight whose comments on my thesis enriched the work before and during its defence as a Ph.D. dissertation.

Turning the thesis into a book was no easy enterprise, in spite of the encouragement from winning the Malcolm H. Kerr Dissertation Award in the Social Sciences of the Middle East Studies Association of North America (MESA) in November 1994. I spent additional time first at the EUI and later in Berlin – where I began to work at Humboldt University in July 1995 – in completely rewriting the first half of the work (Parts I and II). This was necessary in order to redress the theoretical, comparative and historical profiles still unclear and underdeveloped in the thesis. More in general, I felt motivated to couch my arguments in a style that could reach the non-specialist and help him to place the current flood of publications on Islam and politics within a proper historical and conceptual context. However, the effort itself to re-evaluate genealogically the relationship between the hermeneutics of Islam and the political discourse of modernity implied tackling crucial (because either controversial or still largely unproblematized) issues in the theory of religion, the intellectual foundations of the Enlightenment, the genesis of sociology, the immanent rules of public spheres and, as a result, the long-term processes of "subjectification" and "objectification–reification" of religious and intellectual cultures.

Correspondingly, the simplification of language and argument in Part I has faced limits intrinsic to the theoretical complexity of the subject matter and the vocabulary and argument in use, largely shaped according to what we can call a "continental" conceptual austerity. Nonetheless, this part can be skipped by the reader less interested in these theoretical problems: the core thesis of the work, and the reconstruction of the salient passages in the dialectic between the hermeneutics of Islam and the political discourse of modernity, are elaborated in the remaining three-quarters of the study, from Parts II to IV. In particular, the narrative device of presenting the complex interpretive contentions about Islam and politics in the form of a hermeneutic chain formed by seven circles (and represented by seven authors), has also been intended to facilitate the orientation of the reader with the diachrony and synchrony of the interpretive shifts.

During the whole period of work on this book, before and after receiving my Ph.D., I engaged in fruitful exchanges and discussions of both my ideas and of written material – in formal frameworks such as workshops or seminars, or in more informal conversations – with a number of scholars belonging to different disciplines and generations. I am able here to mention but a representative sample of them, though my debts of gratitude certainly encompass a larger number of people: Mohammed Arkoun, Dale Eickelman, Bernhard Giesen, Monica Greco, Bruce Lawrence, James Piscatori, Martin Riesebrodt, Emilio Santoro and Jeff Weintraub.

I am particularly grateful to Raymond Stock of the University of Pennsylvania in Philadelphia and the American Research Center in Egypt (Cairo) for copy-editing the manuscript with sensitivity and insight. But I also would like to thank my research assistants Wael El-Gayar, Jeanette Jouili and Muna Naddaf, who, at the beginning of their collaboration on a new research project at Humboldt University in Berlin, have spent precious hours helping me to reorder the bibliographic references.

With few exceptions quotations from foreign language sources have been translated by me, even when published English versions are available. The transliteration system employed in the book is a simplified version of that suggested by the *International Journal of Middle East Studies*, in that it avoids diacritics and long vowels.

Armando Salvatore
Berlin, winter 1995 – Cairo, summer 1996

A genealogical approach to "political Islam" and political modernity

Islam and modernity, modernity and Islam: different approaches in historiography and the social sciences attempt to find a significant connection between these two, allegedly separate, certainly distinct, "forces of history". The option of seeing both entities as plural in an ultimate effort to de-essentialize them (see al-Azmeh, 1993), is not itself sufficient to overcome the tension inherent in their juxtaposition. Yet unbiased attempts to view both Islam and modernity in their historical, hermeneutic and discursive components animate several studies which, like most on these subjects, cannot escape an essentialist reduction of the two terms. It is often the case that de-essentializing Islam results in re-essentializing modernity, on the basis of some oversimplified – whether explicitly or implicitly – Kantian definition of the latter.

The present work is from the outset methodologically committed to analysing Islam as the plural hermeneutics of a complex civilization and the flexible medium of a collective identity centred on *one* Koranic keyword (*islam*). On the other hand, modernity is conceived as the sort of politically relevant discourse mediated by intellectuals once the idea of rationality is recognized as embodied in society, no longer confined to a transcendent *logos*. Both definitions are consciously only halfway down a de-essentializing path of which I dare not go the whole length, as this would either be impossible, or would not do justice to the way Islam and modernity have constituted themselves historically as intellectual traditions. An uncompromising deconstructionism would diminish both the historical depth and social-scientific systematicity of any attempt at dealing with the unsolved question of the relationship between Islam and the political discourse of modernity. An analysis of their conditions of existence and evolution, as well as of their social and intellectual functions, should heed the questions of how and why they have been constructed, and which are the changing range and typology of discourses that are permitted within the sphere where the hermeneutics of Islam and the political discourse of modernity intersect and fertilize each other.

My strategy to account for these trajectories, and the major shifts within them, is articulated as follows. Part I is a theoretically informed treatment, in comparative perspective, of the historical background that conditions

– mediated by the two, "Axial" and "modern", breakthroughs – both the hermeneutics of Islam and the political discourse of modernity. Part II dwells on the formation and interaction of the categories of the "West" and "Islam" within learned discourses in both "Western" and "Arab–Islamic" settings, and on the consequent emergence of a sort of transcultural dynamics of public communication. Parts III and IV are devoted to the analysis of a representative hermeneutic chain unfolding during the last thirty-five years in both contexts again: in the Western one, where it has been dramatically shaped by the concept of "political Islam", and in the Arab–Islamic one, where it departs from a similar notion but ultimately engenders new, methodologically conscious attempts to reconceive the relationship between Islam and the political discourse of modernity through visions unbound by a too immediate dependence on the actual political agenda in contemporary Arab Muslim societies.

The present work does not approach the social basis of such phenomena as "Islamic politics" or "political Islam" directly, but through an analysis of the historically given conditions of existence of such categories in the discourses of the social group responsible for formulating the common good and the paths to truth: the stratum represented by the legitimate holders of the keys to sound knowledge and politics, the so-called intellectuals.

By following this research path, we will be confronted with a twofold and tense intellectual phenomenon, consisting of the extent to which the Western political discourses of modernity have intervened in the constructions of Islam, and the definitions of Islam have contributed to shape political discourses of modernity both in the West and in the "Arab–Islamic world". The guiding thread of the more empirical, discourse-analytic portion of the work (Parts III and IV) is spun through an inquiry into how this tension has produced, by way of successive interpretive breaks, the catchcategory of "political Islam",[1] as well as into how this concept provides a tempting, though analytically fragile, solution to the tension.

The quite recent conceptual construction of political Islam has superimposed the more ancient, long-term process of objectification of Koranic *din* (having a meaning close to "religion": see Chapter 1) in the form of *islam*, a word not central in the Koran, signifying the Faithful's act of commitment to the only God. "Islam" is a keyword that has acquired over time first the social power of an ethical path, and later – through the Orientalist intervention – has been defined as a "civilization" in principle comparable with the Western Christian one. Finally, it has acted as the instrument for defining an "Islamic" communal reference that is complementary or surrogatory to national consciousness within Arab societies.

These processes have been discursively sustained by the constraint to predicate Islam in terms of its alleged societal and political dimensions, up to the formation, during the 1970s, of what I will call the "hermeneutic field of political Islam". This is the terrain of interpretive contentions on the relationship beween Islam and politics, a field governed by the emerging image of an "Islam in movement". This image represents the antithesis of the persuasive strength of a public discourse that appeals to the citizens' rationality of judgement typified in Jürgen Habermas's model of the public sphere (see Habermas, 1992a) as the epitome of Western political modernity.

The choice of postulating the existence of an interpretive field of political Islam as the common semantic background of attempts to make sense of the so-called politicization of Islam under modern conditions, has no ontological pretension but rather an heuristic function. The hermeneutic field is here intended as the area of intellectual production and competition dominated by a strong vision condensing in a family of similar, though not always overlapping, definitions. The central one in our case is "political Islam" itself, which retranslates or reformulates the lowest common denominator of all other binary expressions like "Islamic fundamentalism", "radical Islam", "Islamic revival" and the like. All of these terms associate Islam with a political impulse not considered, at least at first glance, conducive to public rational debate and deliberation, but instead to societal turmoil. Their common assumption is that the politicization of Islam occurs by virtue "of an excess of zeal rather than with clearly defined goals" (Piscatori, 1983, p. 1).

The urge to undertake such a project resulted from observing the widespread unease of scholars engaged in studying phenomena of Islam's politicization, a feeling intensified by the alleged crisis of Orientalism as the Western study of Islam. This embarrassment has particularly gripped the new generation of Middle East historians. As one of them has written:

> The epistemological ground on which studies of popular political action in Islamic societies is situated is notoriously spongy and subject to periodic cave-ins. Not only is it difficult to spot a trend except by hindsight, because of the extent to which we are all prisoners of present ways of thinking, but it is also perilous to advance an explication of the so-called Islamic revival without reproducing the concerns of the ambient political culture of our own society, with its deeply grounded fears and phantasms about Islam. The discourse on the Other, especially the Muslim Other, is politically saturated (Burke III, 1988, p. 18).

A scholarly contribution to politically desaturating the study of Muslim politics in Arab societies in the context of the so-called "Islamic revival" was as urgent as it was difficult, due to the methodological deadlock resulting from the compartmentalized view of all categories at stake: Islam, politics, modernity. What aggravated the stalemate – but in the end concealed a methodological key for overcoming it – was the epistemic break in Western culture and self-consciousness at large, which has matured since the late 1960s, and which has been accompanied by the rising influence of simplifying interpretive patterns of the political role of Islam propagated by mass media.

The crucial juncture in this process is represented by the 1973 crisis characterized by the Arab–Israeli October War and the ensuing oil embargo and huge leap in the price of crude oil. This was the "meaning event" that forced the Arabs on the attention of the wider Western public, so paving the way for a consideration of the Middle East, the hub of the "world of Islam", as an area of permanent and multiple crisis. The impact of the Islamic revolution of Iran in 1979 on the formation of this concern can be understood only through the 1973 crisis, which laid the basic foundations for a theorem that envisaged a region of turmoil with the Arabs at its centre, a source of constant threats to Western welfare and security. Through this process, it has been gradually established that the force behind this crisis is "Islam" – not, however, the Islam "as such" of Orientalists, but the impression and image of an Islam in movement, where the movement is prompted by basically irrational impulses to turn "religion" into "politics". This image began to influence virtually all attempts to interpret what was seen as a politicization of Islam. Anyone aspiring to be a critical observer had to start with this same vision in shaping any sort of counter-theorem. In this way, an interpretive field governed by the image of an "Islam in movement" superseded the older hermeneutics of "Islam as such" (see Chapter 8).

Significantly in the very moment that political Islam began to be treated as an autonomous and actual problematic, it settled into an interpretive and conceptual "solution" which has precluded new paths of problematization for most of the voices – both scholarly and non-scholarly, Western and "Oriental", Orientalist and social-scientific – intervening in the hermeneutic field. The symbolic force of the image of an Islam in movement, which is Western in origin but has been almost simultaneously matched by an equivalent self-image with Islamic features (note the similarity between the Western "Islamic resurgence" and the Arab *al-sahwa al-islamiyya*, "Islamic awakening"), suppresses the problematic potentialities of the object and makes a consolidated "phenomenon" out of it. This suppression relies on a snap judgement on the necessary conflation between faith and politics "in Islam", which any attempt at producing a deconflation is only partially capable of challenging, in so far as it tends, more often than not, merely to reverse the "conflationist" scheme without restoring the problematic dimension of the relationship. The dynamics of the interpretive field of political Islam and of its historical antecedents have been dominated by this pendular movement between "conflationist" and "deconflationist" models.

Due to the subjective contamination of the knowledge of phenomena affecting Islam and politics, the Western growth industry flourishing within the hermeneutic field of political Islam should be analytically considered in the same interpretive context with the massive waves of literature produced by the "Islamic revivalists", the alleged object of inquiry of the former. The joint consideration of the two categories of literature (Haddad, 1991a) should be guided by the need to question the distinction between the Western, or Western-centred (or guided by Western methods), "external" observer, and the "object", the "phenomenon" to be explained. A major assumption of this study is that both sets of interpretive production are interrelated in ways which the conventional subject–object dichotomy is only partly able to capture.

By examining the multiple paths of this relationship, I realized that in order to elucidate the making and unmaking of political Islam, and contribute to the desirable political desaturation of the study of social phenomena variably related to Islam, the relevant unities of discourse should not be seen as two solid formations facing each other, but rather as more contingent, smaller sub-formations. These unities, which I have called "circles", span the transcultural space between the areas of intellectual production that have acquired, over time, the ambiguous labels of "West" and "Islam". The hermeneutic circles which I will analyse basically take their concepts from the main discursive formations historically charged with the hermeneutics of Islam (Orientalism, Islamic sciences with jurisprudence – fiqh – at its centre, classic sociology of religion and new political sociology).

Unlike the universe of traditionally consolidated discursive formations, the high stability of these sub-formations seems compatible with the possibility of a combination between, and mobility among, different interpretive circles. This fluidity is given by the variability of what is at stake in the hermeneutic struggle at a given historical conjuncture (see Fairclough, 1992, p. 34), and it is clear that a particularly wide gap in the motivational background is recognizable by crossing the transcultural divide, within the hermeneutic field of political Islam, that cleaves the "West" and "Islam".

The adoption of a conceptual apparatus and vocabulary that includes such formulas as "circles", "transcultural space" or "hermeneutic field", which will be analytically defined in due time, should not be misunderstood as a void exercise in sociometaphysics. The use of spatial-geometric images is intended as a convenient strategy for the modelling and visualization of phenomena that are certainly much more dispersed in themselves (or "complex", as social scientists often prefer to say in such situations). This strategy of reduction is strictly tied to the reproblematizing perspective that animates the entire work. The terms here used, however inflexible they may sound, are always intended as soft devices for allowing the reader to recognize the central thread of my narrative. This thread consists of diachronic concatenations and synchronic interactions between different models of constructing or deconstructing political Islam. I try to fulfil this task on the basis of both a theoretical awareness of the supposedly universal laws of this type of hermeneutic production (Chapters 1 and 2), and of the consideration of historical and cultural contingencies determining shifts and major discontinuities (Chapters 2, 3, 4, 5 and 6).

The basic claim underlying the postulation of a single interpretive field is that one "truth game" has been played, since about the mid-1970s, on the how and why – and not, or only marginally, on the whether! – of the politicization of Islam, among several categories of specialized authors. As "intellectuals", these are defined as the modern producers of publicly relevant meaning, who invoke scholarly traditions often constructed for the task of the moment. Their role as players within the hermeneutic field of political Islam does not exclude their participation, at the same time, in more circumscribed truth games, delimited by boundaries of discipline or specialization. My focus, however, is on the grand transcultural game where such mega-constructs as the "West" and "Islam" play a crucial role and are themselves at stake.

Even if not couched directly in the language of the analysis of international politics, the present work attempts to throw light on the very conditions of transnational communication between the West and Islam. This is intended as a contribution that meets the mostly unheeded plea for the necessity of cultural analysis in the study of international relations (see Walker, 1990), on the grounds that intellectual cultures and discourses are the most immediate driving force in the expressive dimension of what we call the realm of politics. These expressions have to be analysed in their genesis, self-legitimation and concatenations, a step that logically precedes any evaluation of their political impact (which belongs to the realm of political science proper).

However, I will pay attention to the most immediate political impact of the hermeneutic outputs produced by the intellectual circles analysed, consisting of their acting as the source of legitimation for discourses and practices at a more broadly social, "sub-intellectual" level. Their claims to seriousness (variably justified and legitimized), are what enable them to perform this function. However, the modalities of reception, creative appropriation, manipulation or rejection of such discourses at the level of social agency cannot be the subject of this work. This is a task that probably transcends the investigative capacities of social sciences at large, that are themselves, in their short history, perennially damned to discount at the outset the existence of a gap between the "intellectual" and the "social", as their own genesis owes much to the need of "intellectual distinction" (see Chapter 2).

It is probably useful to outline briefly the suggested sequence of circles within the hermeneutic chain, to which the second half of this study is devoted (Parts III and IV). The formation of the first two circles precedes the rise of the interpretive field of political Islam proper. These are not only Western-centred, but solidly dominated by Western authors, the first (representing the model of conflation of "late-classic Orientalism") even more than the second (consisting of the deconflationist response by US-centred Middle East Studies inspired by modernization theory). All the other circles are immediately involved in the hermeneutic field of political Islam. The third and the fourth, although still Western-centred and taking an "externalist-observational" position, encompass several Arab authors, some of whom occupy leading positions within them. From the third circle on, I will examine exclusively authors of Arab origin. The third circle represents a reconflation carried out under the banner of formulas like of "Islamic revival" or "reislamization", while the fourth circle tries to propose a new, more energetic deconflation through appealing to the inevitable modernity of Islam's politicization.

Starting from the other end of the interpretive chain, the seventh to the fifth circles are locally based and characterized by an "internalist–normative" perspective. Most authors examined in Part IV (like those addressed in Chapter 5 concerning the historical emergence of "Arab–Islamic" public discourse) are located in Egypt. Yet due to that country's enduring political and intellectual centrality their argumentative models enjoy a wider Arab notoriety and are also objects of attention on the Western side of the trans-cultural space. The seventh circle expresses the standard Islamist conflation between the *din* and the *dawla* (whose translation as "religion" and "state" is not entirely correct, as we will see), wheras the sixth circle objects to the conflation in similar scripturalist terms by claiming the historical contingency of the *dawla* towards Koranic *din,* whilst maintaining and emphasizing the validity of Islam as an ethical blueprint and a framework of communal reference. The fifth circle, the least defined and stable in the whole hermeneutic chain, attempts to fulfil the crucial function of bridging the gulf between the Western and the Arab–Islamic sides of the interpretive field, through taking up the challenge of the Western-based, political discourse of modernity for redesigning an autonomous Islamic path to it. Within the orbit of the fifth circle, which will receive special attention, the alternative between conflationism and deconflationism seems to lose its relevance.

While concentration on the last two decades is sufficient to highlight the statics and dynamics of the hermeneutic field of political Islam, its genesis is much older. So we must go back further in order to identify the most critical phases and discursive loci in the intellectual history of this century during which the construction of relations between categories as broad as Islam and modernity (or of other categories strictly associated with these) acquired new shapes and were given fresh directions. This unearthing of the deeper historical terrain requires a genealogy of the statement according to which "Islam is a basically political religion", up to the historical juncture when it coheres into the concept of political Islam. Two elements constrain the genealogy: the reification of Islam as influenced by a Western concept of religion, and the definition of the rules governing the public sphere of politics. The attribution to Islam of an inherently political dimension states the degree of the divergence of this religion from the assumed normality, and the degree of the divergence of the "Islamic" polity from a normal concept and practice of politics.

I will look for several possible beginnings, more than for an illusory single point of origin, and explore, on both shores of the transcultural space, parts of the work of authors as distant as ʿAli ʿAbd-al-Raziq (Chapter 5) and Max Weber (Chapter 6). These represent the most crucial "points of no return" in the long-term genesis of the problematic here at stake, in the sense that their contributions to the definition of Islam have decisively impinged upon the legitimate ways of thinking about the relationship between Islam and the political sphere.

What I have said until now may be sufficient to introduce this work, expound its structure and logic, and suggest where its novelty might lie in addressing the topic of *Islam and the political discourse of modernity*. However, this is probably not sufficient to illustrate the genealogical approach and why such a method is adopted to attain the goal of the investigation. What follows is an illustration of the methodological perspective of the work, which some readers might consider unnecessarily sophisticated, but that can be useful to gain a deeper understanding of the relationship between method and subject matter. First, I opted for an approach that unveils the "wills to power" at stake in the hermeneutics of political Islam, as well as the almost technical constraints that ground the intellectual claims to truth. It is typical of the modern social-scientific mind to posit "explanation" as the superordinate form of the common process of attributing sense to something happening, of solving a puzzle, a form distinct from the narrower "interpretation", and which represents its scientific upgrading. It will not be my intention to question the value of a given theory or explanatory model of the alleged politicization of Islam for the purpose of scholarly exchange. I hope just to highlight which kind of cognitive practice, belonging to which intellectual setting, any theory serves, and to show the impossible innocence, on a political level, of the claim to truth reflected by any circle.

Second, rather than embarking on a reconstruction of the entire hermeneutic field of political Islam, I will identify a crucial chain linking circles of interpretation. In fulfilling this task, I will privilege the dynamic dimension of the relationship between circles instead of engaging in a static work of typification. This dynamic results from the analysis of the model adopted by a circle in framing the question of the politicization of Islam. The analysis will concentrate on the tension between the posing of the problem and the crafting of a solution to it. I will try to show how, through the breaches opened in a discourse aimed at solving the problem, another framing model, a new circle, takes shape. This, in turn, will be analysed according to the same criteria.

My assumption has been that "solution" in discourse is inherently volatile, since thought is primarily characterized by an intrinsic, hermeneutic impulse towards framing problems. It is difficult to say to what extent problem-posing is made for the sake of problem-solving, although it is undeniable that knowledge is incomplete without the latter. What discourse analysis has called "frames" indicates the way a solution is approached: the resulting "issues" lie in fact halfway between the problem and the solution, but are projected towards the latter. An issue is a problem metabolized, reduced and framed for the sake of winning a public game. The analysis will pay particular attention to the necessary reduction of hermeneutic "problematization" (the process through which thought steps back from action and questions "its meaning, its conditions, and its goals": Foucault, 1984a, p. 388)[2] to discursive practice.

It is by now evident that the methodological orientation of the present work cannot be assessed as purely exegetical. Statements will be analysed in their "materiality" as tools of power contentions, which depends on their having a formative status within particular institutional practices (Fairclough, 1992, p. 49). The seeming transparency and innocence of a text has to be checked against the full weight that its inevitable ambiguities and its playing with rhetorical devices has had, and continues to have, within the settings delimiting what can be said. One major implication of this approach is that the principle of author-centrism should be thoroughly re-evaluated (cf. Chapter 2). A useful guideline, beyond the rather metaphysical claim of the author's disappearance, is to "follow the distribution of gaps and breaches" (Foucault, [1969] 1984b, p. 105) which are precisely the product of what one can call the author's retreat, his functional self-reduction to technician and sometimes strategist within consolidated sub-formations or circles. The logic of the analysis will inevitably lead us to focus on those authors whose works reveal in the most cogent way the articulation of the problem that influences the discourse of a circle.

According to this logic, references to the authors made object of analysis, in their biblio-biographical individuality, will be contained to the minimum necessary to situate them in the context of their own circle, and to illustrate the relations they enjoy with other circles relevant to their position. Reference to the "work", as a unity surrogating the missing author, will also be reduced. Thus, the analysis will primarily address one circle's framing and argumentative model at crucial historical junctures, as these frames are revealed through excerpts from particularly significant texts written by well-known, "representative" authors. Criteria of representativeness here are not, however, based on the influence of an author as such, but instead follow the genealogical principle of searching for a "line of descent" highlighting the concatenation among propositions within the genesis and evolution of the interpretive field of political Islam.

The general orientation of the methodological branch called "discourse analysis" meets the needs of the perspective adopted by this study better than any generic "critique of ideologies", in that the former stresses the fragility, rather than the compactness, of mental constructs suited to public communication. The concept of "discourse" points to the dialogical character of the text considered, a character which, though not dependent on the intention of the writer, is inherent in the volatile nature of communication, which is in turn a consequence of the hermeneutic tension between problem-posing and problem-solving.

In this sense, the examination of discourse is a good "method for historical analyses" (Fairclough, 1992, p. 9), since "discourse is studied historically and dynamically, in terms of shifting configurations of discourse types" (p. 35). Yet the historicity of such a type of "intellectual history" (cf.

Kelley, 1990) must conform to specific conditions. As Foucault wrote in the late 1960s:

> the analysis of statements . . . is a historical analysis, but one that avoids all interpretation: it does not question things said as to what they are hiding, what they are "really" saying, in spite of themselves, the unspoken elements that they contain . . . ; but, on the contrary, it questions them as to their mode of existence . . . what it means for them to have appeared when and where they did – they and no others (Foucault, [1969] 1972, p. 109, quoted in Dreyfus and Rabinow, 1982, p. 51).

The claim to "serious meaning" of intellectual constructions will not be taken at face value, but will provide clues for reconstructing the formal context of the intended relevance of specific contents. For the analyst, the seriousness and meaningfulness of the statements analysed is given by the difference they want to make. This clarifies the extent to which the approach of the present study, apart from the original assumption about the hermeneutic-problematizing foundation of thinking, is *not* "hermeneutic". I am conscious, however, that the attempt to transcend a generically interpretive approach may lead to a curious reproposition of positivism. Dreyfus and Rabinow have shown, by reference to the "archaeologist" Foucault, the paradox inherent in such a pretension: "the doubly detached ultimate phenomenologist can thus locate what is serious and meaningful to an age, without its being serious and meaningful to him." (Dreyfus and Rabinow, 1982, p. 52). This is not to polemicize with positivism as such, but to highlight how an archaeological work thus defined, and the corresponding fiction of the "ultimate phenomenologist", would contradict the reasoning that led to the present research.

For if it is true that "there can be no statement that in one way or another does not reactualize others" (Foucault, [1969] 1972, p. 98, quoted in Fairclough, 1992, pp. 46–7), then it is undeniable that the statements produced by the analyst or archaeologist of discourse are themselves a form of reactualization, however *sui generis*. Since each history is dependent on the impositions of concatenations, and even more so a "history of thought" or "intellectual history", the identification of such concatenations, or, in a social-scientific mood, the making of "dependencies", involves the position, or the self-positioning, of the analyst, his concern and patterns of "problematization", or even a problematization of the (intellectual) self.

A way to break the methodological deadlock entailed by the analytical-archaeological perspective (in spite of the evidence that this is already an improvement of any objectivist short cut) is to capitalize on the subjective awareness of one's own problematization, in order to make it the hub of the work of reconstruction. This implies a passage from "archaeology" to "genealogy", or at least an effort to complement the former with the latter (see Szakolczai, 1993a). The adoption of a genealogical perspective, which I do not consider as a fully-fledged method, but as a powerful instrument for disciplining the research effort and enhancing its transparency on the subjective side (whereas positivistic social sciences are only concerned with transparency of the "object"), entails the following criteria:

a. the act of taking a distance from an alleged "phenomenon", of "losing familiarity" with it (I have illustrated above how this happened to me in the case of "political Islam"), considering it as an "effect";
b. the postponement of a first formulation of the problem to the moment when the historical analysis of displacements in problematization patterns has helped to dissolve the subjective impression of the "effect" (these first two operations belong to the stage of problem-posing and are logically antecedent to the actual analysis);
c. the search for the conditions for the problem to emerge, by renouncing the illusory quest for a unique "point of origin", and identifying, instead, a plurality of "beginnings" (this principle is all the more important if one tackles a problem of transcultural relevance);
d. finally, the identification of a "line of descent" out of the chain of unstable patterns of discourse: it is through the logic unveiled behind this concatenation of dependencies that the analyst-genealogist attains the final formulation of the problem.

The identification of a "line of descent" as the main clue for formulating the problem will imply, in the present work, an attempt to transcend the original effect represented by the image of an Islam in movement. In following such a genealogical perspective, a solution can be attained only through the final reformulation of the problem, which should help it to be thought out differently. This reformulation, however, is not an individual creation of the author-genealogist. It is not by chance that the genealogy of political Islam ends up at a point where it meets a sort of self-genealogy of some Arab authors who attempt to free themselves from the transcultural weight of essentialism.

The result is a recognition of the fact that there has been and is a trajectory of political discourse of modernity in the Arab world which can be expressed in terms that are not imitative of the Western experience. This claim cannot be sustained, however, by the invocation of an autochthonous tradition of modernity relying on a solid appropriation of history, since the West's colonial impact in the course of the nineteenth century progressively eroded the viability of endogenous lines of intellectual tradition. The tension between a proud and vehement reassertion of a right to citizenship within modernity and the consciousness of an ineluctable loss of intellectual assets is evident in the Arab–Islamic discourse revolving around the category of "cultural heritage" (*turath*), that constitutes at the same time the culmination of, and the exit point from, the hermeneutic chain of political Islam. This point indicates a possible consensus on the necessary search for – and authentication of – an allegedly indigenous, an "Arab–Islamic" constructed heritage or tradition, but also makes manifest how fragile and desperate is the enterprise to define this heritage in any credibly dynamic historical form, where imposed continuities interweave with subjectively well-mastered discontinuities.

NOTES

1   From now on, I will dispense with using quotation marks when referring to "political Islam" as a category, though I will keep considering it first and foremost as a conceptual and symbolic construct, and never as an unproblematic description of a clear phenomenon.
2   The word used in the printed version of the interview conducted by Paul Rabinow shortly before the death of Foucault in 1984 is "problemization". However, "problematization" appears in the transcription of a seminar that Foucault taught in 1983 at Berkeley.

ORDER AND DISCOURSE

CHAPTER 1

Communicative systems and the specialized quest for order

The first step in this inquiry has to be a definition of different dimensions of "religion", both because Islam is predicated as being first of all a religion, and because the political discourse of modernity cannot be understood without reference to specifically modern patterns of conceptualization of what religion is or should be. This step can be grounded on the notion of "symbolic-communicative system", here used as a theoretical device to account for "communication", a phenomenon stemming from the human competence in using and manipulating symbols.

General definitions of religion are not very helpful in disentangling the grass roots "structural" and the specialized "constructed" dimensions of order implied by the concept. Nonetheless Peter Berger provides us with a first platform to relate religion to order and communication: "Religion is cosmization in a sacred mode . . . The sacred cosmos is confronted by man as an immensely powerful reality other than himself. Yet this reality addresses itself to him and locates his life in ultimately meaningful order." (Berger, 1969, p. 26, quoted in Turner, [1983] 1991, p. 244). The kernel of religion is seen in a generalized quest for order or *cosmos*. I prefer to distinguish between the general emergence of order through the functioning of symbolic-communicative systems, and the shaping of religion as an enterprise requiring special hermeneutic tools. The following examination of the relationship between communicative systems and the specialized quest for order is necessary to place the hermeneutics of Islam in an adequate comparative and historical perspective. It will also help to understand the hermeneutic platform for the emergence of the political discourse of modernity.

We should distinguish between two different meanings of symbols. In a first approximation, they are signs providing the medium of communication not only in the sense of externalizing meaning, but as the vehicle for a connection, or a set of connections, within the very realm of signifiers (cf. Asad, 1993, p. 31). The elementary function of a symbol is to allow a sender to communicate with a receiver. However, to convey a meaning is also to perform an act which modifies the consciousness of the receiver and possibly his behaviour, so expanding or limiting the abilities of both the receiver and the sender. At this elementary level, communication has both a performative and disposition-engendering strength. This communicative function of symbols has been best highlighted by Edmund Leach (1976). If there is any meaningful and yet sufficiently general definition of "culture", it is a symbolically mediated communicative system. In this sense, culture is dependent on mechanisms of communication, but has an inherent performative dimension (Lawson and McCauley, 1990, pp. 32–44).

Within symbolic-communicative systems, what one calls "religious symbols" are those expressing the involvement of superhuman agents, thereby expanding the communicative field beyond the range of everyday practice. It is preferable not to consider these particular symbols as constituting a system of their own called "religion". We will see in the following chapter (cf. Asad, 1993, pp. 27–54) that this view is not analytically acceptable, as it is dependent on processes of intellectual specialization in modern Western history (see Chapters 2 and 3). "Religious symbols" cannot be understood in their highly functional nature only in terms of a particular "experience of the sacred",[1] i.e. without reference to more encompassing patterns of symbolic production and communication. Their original property is to induce particular dispositions, mostly through ritualized patterns of behaviour and communication: dispositions which have an impact on life conduct without being induced by pratical motivations.

It is incorrect to conceive of a symbolically mediated pattern of behaviour and communication as representing something else in an encoded form, either a hidden meaning or a hidden rationality. The perspective of looking at representations and assuming the existence of a hidden meaning or essence behind them is the product of the concatenation of two major breakthroughs in the specialization of codes, first the Axial-civilizational (illustrated in this chapter) and then the modern-intellectual one (see Chapter 2). Social sciences obviously reproduce this cognitive attitude as they move from a narrowly hermeneutic perspective to a quest for explanation of social phenomena. A structuralist perspective constitutes at the same time the completion of this search for the hidden and its reduction to the minimum needed by the modern social-scientific mind. It looks for a "structure" of the apprehension of the world and in particular for its systematic form. It is this form, more than a hidden meaning or rationality, which has to be discovered. The concept of symbol itself is thereby reduced to a functional minimum, and along with it the idea of meaning is dereified and dynamized.[2]

However, a structuralist approach can cause us to overlook the fact that, as stressed by Daniel Sperber (1985), at the root of symbolic-communicative systems there are "human mental abilities" which supply the competence to act as a sender and as a receiver, and are obviously subject to individual variations. Any participant in a symbolic-communicative system has to reconstruct, albeit with immediacy and minimal reflection, the rules governing the system (Lawson and McCauley, 1990, p. 68). This is the beginning of what we might call hermeneutic dispersion. However, symbolic-communicative systems in their purest, non-specialized form are not based on a work of "proper interpretation" that depends "upon breaking an underlying code" (p. 69). At this level, symbols only function in their performative embeddedness in the system. The functioning of symbolic-communicative systems is strictly associated with the production of particular dispositions among the actors. This is especially the case through those particular ordering and communicative performances that are called rituals, structured around sacred or religious symbols. For the participant, there is no disjunction between "outer behaviour" and "inner motive" (Asad, 1993, p. 63).

A participant can reflectively reconstruct his experience of the ritual without producing any kind of disembedded meaning, but simply by reference to the dispositions engendered in him by his partaking in the collective act. In the consciousness of participants, a symbolic-communicative system functions holistically. Symbols are not *per se* the engine of the process, but rather in their property to cohere into systems. What compels us to conceive of symbols as elementary units is the reductionist and dualizing constraint of social sciences at large. This points to the second meaning of symbol, no longer a sign establishing external and internal connections, but the vehicle carrying a hidden meaning that *has to be discovered*. Producing interpretations of the symbols is the function of a specialized discourse. This specialized activity can be defined as the transformation of regulative codes into semantic ones (p. 62).

The passage from "instant" communication rooted in practice and practical reason to hermeneutic dispersion is embedded in every social situation and can be theorized as the passage from common, everyday communication to specialized fixation of meaning. I will first provide a general account of the mechanism of this passage and then try to discuss the historical turn which has marked the beginning of the specialized search for truth: a breakthrough that is immediately relevant for the genesis of Islam and indirectly impinges upon the formation of a political discourse of modernity, as we will also see in the next chapter.

Constructing representations by means of words (or numbers) is the necessary basis for a rational enterprise, including its scientific variant, but is also grounded on the general linguistic competence of humans. The use of language entails some paradoxes that can turn into assets. First, there is an inherent fragility of language that can be defined as "the tendency of whatever we put into words to get away from us and to throw what is said into questions." (Bruns, 1987, p. 239). This peculiarity constitutes the basis for the almost technical constraint of language to "transcend". Before that imagined projection, transcendence is a potentiality of language. This points to the metaphorical foundation of logical thinking and of written language, if metaphor is used "in its original . . . sense of transferring the strange into the familiar in order to make sense of it, where the alternative to such transference is not anything literal or proper (something in itself) but, on the contrary, nothing at all (no 'sense' of any sort)" (p. 248). The ever more specialized use of language depends on a consciousness of its inherently negative dimension, given by the tension incorporated in the artificial insulation of logical constructs, which makes them different from or opposite to others, the negation of these others. This tension is due to their being overloaded with an individualizing capacity which they scarcely possess in their original, symbolic-systemic shape. Every sort of "doctrine" or "science" can be described as originating from this very tension between dispersing impulses and the compulsion to resystematize.[3]

Moreover, the "idea of nothing" implicit in language can shift into the "idea of *no!*" The performative dimension of symbolic-communicative action can be reconstructed as depending on the mechanism by which one converts descriptive into normative utterances (cf. Habermas, 1981, I). A very special development in human history is the enhancement of the idea of *no!* to its ultimatively normative sense, i.e. to the idea of the source itself of moral imperatives (remember the Biblical "Thou shalt not . . ."). This pattern of generalization is best exemplified by Platonic dialectics, where the progression towards ever more abstract terms ends with the Supreme Good or Divine. In the process of anchoring within a doctrine the potentialities of negation and generalization, language itself is enhanced to *logos*, as the engine of the *cosmos* (see Burke, [1961] 1970).

Thus, we should carefully distinguish between the communicative function of symbols in creating an intersubjective order, and the professional job of the formulator of the order. The first order is merely "practical", whereas the second order, endowed with the authority of speaking the truth, reacts on the former and imposes on it a cosmological framework of strong, crafted symbols. The specialist of this operation can be called a virtuoso of the Word. Among a set of possible virtuosities based on communicative systems and rituals, the virtuosity of the Word represents one very special development that surrogates other charismatic forms of specialization that we subsume under the label of saintliness.

This process of meaning-disembedding has, however, its origin in the development itself of symbolic-communicative systems and in particular in their highest moments of actualization, the rituals, as these become dependent on formalized conceptual systems which mediate between the performance and some abstract scheme. To the extent that rituals are dependent on such schemes they become meaningful. And this may concern an increasing number of participants, as the "spontaneous" reconstruction, by a simple participant, of what a ritual is about, is no longer impervious to a "specialized" attribution of meaning. Differentiation among members of a community opens up spaces for different models of such a reconstruction. The logical phenomenon of hermeneutic dispersion becomes institutionalized in forms of cultural brokerage.

Such a brokerage, up to its most specialized version taking the form of the virtuosity of the Word, functions to mediate between grass roots symbolic-communicative systems and the crystallization of special hermeneutic games. Meanings that originate from "lower" levels of communication are reshaped in their ultimate significance for the construction of the supreme order, but also, in reverse, these specialized constructs do influence everyday communication. "The secular, empirical terms are 'infused by the spirit' of the 'transcendent' term." (Burke, [1961] 1970, p. 37). The idea itself of a definite meaning isolated from the temporal sequence of linguistic elements of an utterance acquires authority with respect to everyday communication. The "politics of meaning", being rooted in a transfiguration of the mechanisms of communication, become an integral part of social reality.

Ernest Gellner's metaphors of wilderness vs. gardening (see Gellner, 1983, p. 50 and Bauman, 1987, p. 51) can visually convey the difference between "low" and "high" cultures: absence of effort, because of a spontaneous order, in the first case, and laborious endeavour, coupled with "a sense of precarious artificiality", in the second, finalized to impose an order onto a reluctant object. But the image of gardening also reflects an activity whose aim is to *show* the Order, through an increasing competence in discursive manipulation that surrogates charismatic gifts.

It should not be surprising that from a linguistical (or, in Burke's words, "logological") point of view this specialized construction of the universal order, of a sacred *cosmos*, is inherently tautological, since it relies on a cluster of concepts implying one another without any definite principle of logical priority. What redeems this circularity is transcendence (Burke, [1961] 1970, p. 182). From being a mere linguistic-technical function, transcendence is promoted to the institutional practice of "standing back and looking beyond – a kind of critical, reflective questioning of the actual and a new vision of what lies beyond" (Schwartz, 1975, p. 3). The actual is given by the experience, prior to the concept, of the order that one discovers in structured patterns of communication. It consists of both the order of the mind and the order of community as of human relations.

The individual perception of the actual, outer world is the key for conceiving a systemic order. The construction of the soul as *microcosmos* has to be sustained by the postulation of an order of "nature", a *macrocosmos* that mythologically or philosophically pinpoints the ultimate dimension of order. The representation of what lies beyond the visible world is mediated by the linguistic act of transcendence. At this level of hermeneutic specialization, the "politics of meaning" functions as "politics of beyond".

To use the words of Coleridge, the Biblical method of sacred narrative competes with Greek philosophemes in stating the order. As shown by the work of Plato, the opposition between the mythological-narrative and the philosophical practices of constructing the order should not be over-emphasized. However, the narrative style is closer to the structure of rituals, as it is premised on a temporal sequence. This style allows for specialized interpretations, but is still open to forms of reappropriation comparable to non-specialized participation in rituals. The philosophical style, instead, marks a further level of disembeddedness of meaning, the beginning of a one-way road in the specialization of discourse. In both cases, the manipulation of language according to the linguistic properties of negation and of progressive abstraction allows for the determination of a principle. A cosmological view anchors within the individual soul the principle of a natural order encompassing the community. The principle of a *moral* order takes form, where the common sense of right and wrong is solidly grounded on a conception of Right and Wrong, Good and Evil (Burke, [1961] 1970, p. 186).

As the idea of order is derived from the experience of communal relations, it is no mere attribution of logical positivity or negativity, but implies injunctions, strivings to induce dispositions, the tension between Yes and No, "thou shalt" and "thou shalt not", as condensed in the Muslim obligation of *al-amr bi-l-ma'ruf wa-l-nahi 'an al-munkar* ("commanding good and prohibiting evil"). While this sort of tension implicit in the concept of order has a stabilizing effect on the "soul", another, intractable tension is left behind the specialized act of transcendence, resulting from the enduring chasm between cosmological and communal normativity. It is, however, this gulf that legitimizes the virtuosity of the Word and its task of constructing a moral order built over the principled abyss of transcendence.

The moral order sits on this tension and is nurtured by it. Virtuosi of the Word formulate moral paths to performing the good which permit overcoming the tension and attaining salvation. The hub of the order based on transcendence is the human soul.

The historical break that gave rise to these "politics of order" based on disembedded meaning and transcendence was the emergence of so-called Axial civilizations during the first millennium BC, as theorized first, implicitly, by Max Weber and later, explicitly, by Karl Jaspers and, more recently, by authors like Benjamin Schwartz and Shmuel N. Eisenstadt. As any other theory of major historical turns, it should be treated as an heuristic notion and not as an all-encompassing explanatory model (Schwartz, 1975, p. 3). In the more recent sociologization of "Axial-age theory", that reflects the need to identify an incisive breakthrough that precedes and justifies the subsequent modern one, the focus is precisely on the emergence of groups of specialists charged with mediating between the grass roots production of communicative order and the moulding, fixation and articulation of the very *concept* of order.

This emergence has to be located in the context of structural changes in the dimensions and stratifications of communities and in the corresponding distribution of power, in turn influenced by developments in agriculture and war technology. The way the phenomenon of disembeddedness and transcendence was articulated depended on the institutional arrangements regulating the axis between the actual holders of power and the newly crystallized component of the élite, the formulators and administrators of cosmological frameworks. This scholarly class, represented by the *'ulama'* in the Islamic case, was formed out of the dissolution of the equilibrium of "pagan" cultures, where forms of ritual and magic prevailed which were not dependent on any encompassing conceptual formation resting on a disembedded idea of an order, as they were expressions of the need to regulate the due course of predominantly rural activities. The memory of this previous equilibrium split in the myth of an uncontaminated proto-order preceding a "fall" on the one hand, and the image of a subsequent unstable counter-order on the other. The pagan world is hence the world of chaos and ignorance, a *jahiliyya* in Islamic terminology. As the last Axial civilization, Islam provides the most consequent conceptualization of the counter-order.

This enhancing of the concept of "transcendence", elevating it from a technical feature of language to the key to a hermeneutic solution, is typical of Western post-Axial civilizations born of a blend of Hebrew narratives and Greek philosophemes (cf. Turner, 1994, pp. 78–81). While the emergence of

Christianity constitutes a crucial intermediate wave of consolidation of the Axial-age spirit, the rise of Islam is the last manifestation of this civilizational break in the Western world. As we will see, the related claim of the Last Prophecy contributes to making "Islam" a potentially different civilizational solution to the problem of order, different from the one that gradually took shape in the European Christian environment and happened to be called, in time, the "West" (see Chapter 3). Both are, however, solidly embedded in the Occidental mode that is based on transcendence and differs from Asian versions of Axial civilizations, which lack this ideational tool.

It is evident that the activity of defining and administering the outerly cosmological, innerly moral order was not politically neutral, as it was clearly used by certain clerics in different historical conjunctures within the context of the formation of protest movements and of the definition of ruling coalitions, in political conflict and accommodation. Crucial to this dialectic between different sections of the élite is that the formulation through the scholarly class of a cosmological order built over transcendence makes the communal/political order neither autonomous (this recognition will be typical of the "modern turn": see Chapter 2), nor dependent, through clear patterns, on the more encompassing one. The link between both is given by the concept of *accountability* of the ruler to God or, more specifically (as in Islam), to God's Law (Eisenstadt, 1986, p. 8).

The paradox of these dynamics is that as shapers of the idea of a supreme order, the scholars were in principle committed to stability (a practical corollary of order), but the imperative of the ruler's accountability was a source of permanent instability, and finally of what we call "social change". The winning versions of the order, along with the underlying ethos of rationalization that became institutionalized in each historical situation, were intrinsically fragile. Changes in social abilities, interests and needs were still part of the game, but were not manifested in a direct form. Voicing dissatisfaction at the dominant version of the order happened to become the obliged channel of social change. From the Axial break onward social conflict became inherently complicated by having to be expressed in a language which did not refer to localized and circumscribed issues, but was dependent on the invocation of communal or even universalist frameworks derived from ultimate imperatives. The emergence of specialized hermeneutics and the rise of the scholarly class acted as the source of social transformation. However, this change-inducing function was never recognized as a value in itself (this will be a primary attribute of modernity), but was always reconstructed in terms of the duty to work out the correct interpretation and practice of the moral order.

If it is a matter of faith to accept that Muhammad was the Last Prophet of the unique and personal God, it is a matter of fact that the religion grounded by him is at the origin of the last significant wave of the Axial breakthrough. In a certain sense, the outline sketched above of Axial patterns of truth-mediation through the power of the Word fits the Islamic case better than any other. The determination of the contingent historical reasons that favoured the teaching of Muhammad and the consequent, as it is called, "rise and spread of Islam" is a genuinely historiographical task (see Lapidus, 1988). This can be usefully integrated by the construction of more systematic models for defining the conditions of survival and change of Muslim societies through the interaction between material structures and hermeneutic practices (see Gellner, 1981). What follows is not intended as either a synthesis or a surrogate of both such scholarly enterprises, even less as a reproposition of the Orientalist desire of determining what Islam is in its essence.

I want only to suggest the extent to which the outcome of Muhammad's predication and the paradigmatic patterns that acquired authority thereafter fit a general pattern of "Axiality" comparable with that at the origin of European Christianity. However, Muhammad's teachings were also original for being able to capitalize on previous waves of the Axial breakthrough, and thereby prefiguring a different receptivity of Islam's "high" cultures to both endogenous and exogenous forms of intellectual modernity (see Chapter 3). The following analysis provides the necessary platform for investigating the relationship between the hermeneutics of Islam and the political discourse of modernity.

As I said that I would avoid a general definition of "religion", I should skip the exercise of defining "Islam" once and for all, as done in the particular transcultural game that made this name the label of a distinct "civilization" (see Chapters 4, 5 and 6). I have rather to move to examining the "logological" grounds of this belief system and communal-universalist framework, along with the underlying dialectic between symbolic-communicative system and specialized hermeneutics. This analysis will again meet the hurdle of the well-crystallized concept of "religion" that, as we will see better in the next chapter, is the product of developments mediated not by an Axial breakthrough but by a modern one. This difficulty is further aggravated by the fact that from the Western point of view, Islam is the "other", competing civilization, with the result that, when applying the Western concept of religion, Islam has been usually defined in terms of deficit and dissonance (see Chapters 4 and 6). In particular, the problem is whether Islam provides a peculiar version of the Axial paradigm of the accountability of the rulers to God, resulting in Islam's inherently political character, and thereby prefiguring a solution to the problem of the social and political order unredeemable by modern postulates of separation and differentiation between religion and politics.

In 1942 the leading German Orientalist Richard Hartmann introduced a lecture by saying: "Islam is rightly considered an eminently political religion. This can be easily explained by reference to its origin." (Hartmann, 1943, p. 68). About forty years later Ernest Gellner stated: "Islam is the blueprint of a social order . . . Judaism and Christianity are also blueprints of a social order, but rather less so than Islam" (Gellner, 1981, p. 1), in what seems to be a specification and an attenuation both of the political import of Islam and of its supposed peculiarity *vis-à-vis* other Western cultural-religious units. A further specification of the enhanced socio-political impetus of Islam is provided by Franz Rosenthal, when he says that Islam is a religion where from its origin "man was seen . . . as the center of action in this world" (Rosenthal, 1983, p. 36). After quoting this statement by Rosenthal, Lawrence Rosen adds: "In religious doctrine and popular view alike human beings are seen so endowed with the capacity for reason (*'aql*) that they may acquire control over their passions (*nafs*) and thus avoid the chaos (*fitna*) that their own forgetfulness and urges might otherwise engender." (Rosen, 1989, p. 102). Along this chain of subsequent specifications, Hartmann's synthetical statement is made increasingly analytical: the claim that Islam is a political religion is transformed into the thesis that as a cultural system it lays a particular stress on man's rational endowments in managing problems inherent to community life and relations.

What all these statements have in common is the mechanism of essentialist predication that has become familiar to students of Islam since the publication of *Orientalism* by Edward Said (1978). At this stage I do not intend to tackle the question of the epistemological foundations of Orientalism and the way it essentializes "Islam". Aside from the problem of defining essentialism and its function (see Chapter 4), it is useful to look at the Islamic case on the basis of the assumption that it shares with all other traditions of authorizing discourses the property of engendering unitary hermeneutic dynamics and a sense of commitment to the tradition itself, in spite of the existence of scholarly disputes and divergencies. A tradition is always constructed through history, and its shifting "fundaments" should be submitted to an analysis of keywords of texts endowed with a particular authority.

This analysis should take account of the logic of any Axial breakthrough, thereby paying attention to the articulation of the tension of transcendence, and more precisely of the position of God's transcendence *vis-à-vis* man. Here is the crux, from the viewpoint of the analyst, where the tension or paradox is located, and which can engender an interpretive short cut. We can reformulate the question as the problem of the extent to which what we call the afterworldly dimension of any religion or civilizational paradigm is indistinguishable from the innerworld, so becoming a function within the latter. It is important to stress that this is *our* question, formulated in terms that are familiar to the sociology of religion, but are extraneous to the prophetic mind in general, and in particular to Muhammad, his early followers and all Muslims of the formative era of Islam. They did not problematize such a tension in that they experienced the new faith in purely eschatological terms, within a tense expectation of the imminent Day of Judgement. All that followed in terms of community organization, legal rulings and political conflict was either subordinated to this basic experience, or influenced by extra-religious, pre-Islamic customs. This situation is quite typical of Western Axial civilizations.

The most tangible textual references incorporating the tension of transcendence are in the different meanings of the Koranic keyword *din*, which it is misleading to translate simply as "religion". We will see through the following analysis, which is largely indebted to Wilfred Cantwell Smith, that the semantic area embraced by *din* comes surprisingly close to a possible definition of "symbolic-communicative system".[4]

The first distinctive feature of the word *din* is that, beyond the sense of "personal religion", it carries the meaning of a particular "religious system" (Smith, 1962a, p. 81). "Islam, it could be argued, may well in fact be characterized by a rather unique insistence upon itself as a coherent and closed system" (p. 84), thereby being, from its inception, "the most entity-like" among all religions, "more reified than any other of the world's living faiths" (p. 85). However, the communal-systemic dimension in the meaning of *din* is well-grounded on the individual ability and receptivity consisting in the "part of a man's psychology . . . by which he perceives and responds to religious truth or to God or to moral imperatives." This is no peculiarly Koranic meaning, but rather the result of a long-term development common to the equivalents of *din* (the most important of which, for their evolution, was the Persian *daena* used by Zarathustra) in various Near Eastern languages both within the Semitic and the Indo-European linguistic families (p. 99).

The special character of the Koranic *din* lies in the fact that differently from other key prophetic voices within pre-Axial and Axial religions, such as Moses, Zarathustra, Buddha and Jesus, Muhammad was conscious that he was "founding a *din*". In doing so, he had a prominent predecessor in Mani, whose teachings, however, did not crystallize, in the long run, into a successful religious system (pp. 94–7). Mani was the first conscious founder of a religion: "Others had spoken what eventually became or was becoming scriptures. Mani began with the concept 'scripture', and wrote books to fill this role" (p. 95). Such a consciousness was even stronger in the case of Muhammad (p. 105). By the time of Koranic revelation, in virtually all Near Eastern languages the community dimension was well consolidated in the meaning of words equivalent to *din*, signifying in some cases "systematic religion: the abstract pattern of beliefs and practices characterizing a particular tradition or group" (p. 101). Arabic was no exception, and Muhammad had no difficulty in adopting this meaning for the scope of his predication. As a consequence,

> of all the major religious communities of the world today the Islamic is the only one that has come into historical existence this side chronologically of that period in human history when schematized religious systems had evolved, and in the part of the world where the process of systematizing them was developing (p. 108).

Wilfred Cantwell Smith immediately draws the important conclusion that this was "the first of the long-range processes of reification that would help to explain how it happened that Koranic *din* came to be a named entity" (p. 108) called "Islam".[5]

Besides being a successful and conscious manifestation of self-identification, Koranic *din* embodies two other layers of meaning that contribute to its distinctiveness. The first, originally Arabic, signifies "usages, customs, standard behavior", and seems to address a basically non-religious dimension of intersubjectively relevant action (p. 102). The second, conforming to an ancient Semitic root, represents the act of "judging", "passing judgement" and *consequently* "sanctioning" (Smith, 1962a, p. 102, and Khuri, 1990, p. 28). The religious dimension of this meaning is most clearly revealed in the frequent Koranic formula of *yawm al-din*, the Day of Judgement.

Disentangling the above-mentioned three basic dimensions of meaning for Koranic *din* is not easy, not even for specialists in Koranic studies. Nonetheless, conforming to the strategy of identifying a terrain of interpretive constraints for all subsequent variations in the hermeneutics of Islam, I intend to risk a definition of *din*, extracting it from the cumulation of meanings found in the Koran: the community-bound commitment to God's Will and Judgement, as transposed in the Day of Judgement. *Din* as God's ultimate Judgement is in this case reflected mirror-like in the individual Muslim's judgement, based on his "capacity for reason" (*'aql*), as well as on the "customizing" dimension of *din*, which consolidates its wider communal, intersubjective meaning. The ancient Arab proverb *kama tadin tudan* ("as you judge, so you will be judged": see Smith, 1962a, p. 291, n. 71 and Khuri, 1990, p. 28) best shows the mutual reflection between God's Judgement and man's judgement, and is coherent with the primacy of transcendence in the warning before the imminent Judgement that was central in Muhammad's teachings and in their reception by the first Community of Muslims.

It is well-known that Muhammad's *hijra* from Mecca to Medina marked a crucial passage in the growth of the Prophet's Community, and that Koranic revelation has been accordingly divided into a Meccan phase and a Medinan phase. As we have seen, *din* means not only "judging", but also "sanctioning". When reference is made to Muhammad, the act of passing judgements is expressed, in some passages of the Medinan part of the Koran, such as in the sura *al-ma'ida*, through the linguistic shift to the word *hukm*. These textual clues are often invoked for grounding claims for an Islamic state, or also for justifying the interpretation of Islam as an essentially political religion, since the triliteral root *hkm* has provided the whole set of terms pertaining to the vertical dimension of politics, including "government" (*hukuma*). To be sure, positing the *din* as calling for the *dawla*, the "state" – *islam* being indissolubly both – is a typically modern claim, as we will see in the analysis of the Islamist slogan *islam din wa dawla* (see Chapters 3, 5 and 10).

An assessment of the Islamic articulation of the Axial question regarding the accountability of political authority cannot be based on an anachronistic discussion of the problem of the state, but has to be limited to the analysis of the function of *din* within the newly grounded Community of believers, the *umma*. The crucial moment of the translation of Muhammad's prophetic charisma into forms of polity leadership is constituted by the contract between the group of Muslims emigrated from Mecca to Medina under the guidance of the Prophet and the Medinan clans: the outcome was the grounding of the *umma* as a "confederation/community". The prominent role of Muhammad within the *umma* did not originate from a formal acknowledgement of his political leadership, but resulted automatically from his prophetic charisma. The new *umma* was thereby legitimized by a kind of authority that was fully new for its Arab environment. It did not abrogate the tribal mechanisms of organization and decision, but integrated and sublimated them through an acknowledgement that the ultimate source of unity of the *umma* was the only God on whose behalf Muhammad, *rasul Allah*, was speaking (Noth, [1987] 1994, pp. 35–40).

This view "from above" should not obscure the most radical innovation at the level of the first converts or "companions" of the Prophet (*sahaba*), whose experience has a particular paradigmatic appeal for the construction of any Islamic tradition. They engaged in the new faith and Community on the basis of an individual deliberation to respond to the only God and to His Prophet alone. This act marks a passage from being only a member of the tribe to being also a member of a superior Community that has its justification in transcendence (Noth, [1987] 1994, p. 45). In its original form, the new Community, the *umma*, was constructed on the basis of equality among believers, in their double identity of subjects and objects of *din*, though this equality later crystallized into a multi-layered scale of élites, as the degree of proximity to the Prophet became the marker of a new nobility.

Purified of the most contingent aspects of community dynamics, the grounding specificity of the early success of Koranic *din* rests on a construction of individual responsibility that is even more cogent than in any other Occidental Axial path of salvation, due to the enduring absence in mainstream, Sunni Islam of a strongly institutionalized mediation of the gap of transcendence, as in the Christian Churches. On the other hand, the stronger definition in abstract terms of the communal bonds resulting from the combination between individual conversions and tribal alliances provided a conceptual constraint for conceiving the Community either in the pragmatic jurisprudential terms of approximating legal rulings to the Medinan paradigm as far as possible (a dominant practice of the doctors of the Law – the *'ulama'/fuqaha'* – and the central discipline of *fiqh*, sustained by the circular figure of the Consensus among them – *ijma'* – as the last instance of validation of truth), or in the utopian construction of a normative system (*shari'a*) directly emanating from God's legislating Will (*shar'*), the adherence to which was mediated by the faculty of the single believer to transcend his purely human nature according to the example (the *sunna*) of the Prophet (al-Azmeh, 1993, pp. 93–6). This view, which animated in particular the minoritarian, but lively Hanbali tradition having its root in the *madhhab* ("school") grounded by Ibn Hanbal (780–855), is one of the historically most coherent versions of the Axial construction of a moral order based on transcendence.

This is not the place to raise the too general question of why, in the long-term process of conversion to the Koranic faith in the regions under

Muslim rule (especially in the geopolitically and culturally most central regions from Egypt to Iran, as well as among the politically and culturally stronger social groups) the Islamic articulation of the order succeeded in giving a civilizational response to the instability of several Mediterranean and Near Eastern countries and cultures which the proliferation of Christian and non-Christian paths of salvation had not stabilized. However, there may be a factor of strength in the Islamic path more attuned to its being the last, and in a certain sense a belated, Axial civilization than in the feature, emphasized by Max Weber, of "warriors' religion" (see Chapter 6). I mean here the particular ability to express a pronounced minimalist (as in the practice of *fiqh*) and a markedly maximalist (as in the Hanbali utopia of *al-siyasa al-shar'iyya*) construction of the order, and to justify both extremes through the same logological and mythological paradigm.

This distinctiveness may well have been influenced by the geo-economic and structural setting of Muslim communities in the wake of the historically contingent diffusion of the Koranic faith and related institutions. This process engendered a type of centre-periphery relationship, on a regional scale, which favoured a higher equilibrium between the Great Tradition, as embodying the post-Axial, "orthodox" versions of the problem of order, and Little Traditions, as the heritage of pre-Axial, locally-based cultures revolving around ritual and magic. Here "scripturalism gave the townsmen and the tribesmen a common idiom, even if they used it differently, and made them into parts of what certainly was one continuous moral order." (Gellner, 1981, p. 24).

In the case of Islam, the crystallization of particular forms of cultural brokerage and the generalized reverence for the Word, the flexibility of *fiqh*, but even more the frequent cumulation of the role of *'alim* and of Sufi master might have allowed a type of cultural gardening (according to Gellner's metaphor) better modelled on the inherent harmony of wilderness (see Lapidus, 1983, pp. 421–4). Within this context, the Hanbali option alone would have proved too scholastic to engender a spirit of reform as the antithesis of an adaptationist mood. In fact, most medieval movements of maximalist-utopian "awakening", especially in North Africa, were animated by chiliastic Mahdism (messianism), closer to popular cultures than any form of specialized *'ulama'* discourse.

To encapsulate the allegedly original dynamics of Muslim societies into a kind of cyclical model inspired by the theory of Ibn Khaldun (1332–1406) – according to a vision where modernity intervenes in the process from without, and thereby relaunches the reformist option (see Gellner, 1981) – would, however, obscure the key Axial distinctiveness of Koranic religion as the one most reified from the beginning, and the following cumulative process of reification that was already well advanced, and had probably already passed a critical threshold, when European colonialism began to encroach upon Muslim lands at the end of the eighteenth century. An important stage in this process was the scholarly systematization of the couple of words into which the multi-layered meaning of *din* split, *iman* and *islam*. The deepening of the process of reification, which consists of distancing oneself from a living practice, objectifying it as a target of analysis or an instrument for social action, and finally depriving it of its original impetus, has occurred especially through the latter word, which has gradually acquired an unchallenged prominence in designating what we identify, unhesitatingly, as "Islam".

The theological-juridical disputes on the domains of reference of *iman* and *islam*, which have animated the Islamic *umma* since very early in its history, were based on scriptural figures that puzzle the contemporary observer unfamiliar with the Koran. Here *Allah*, the Arabic word for "God", is employed 2,697 times and *din* 92 (Smith, 1962a, p. 298, n. 106), while *islam* recurs only eight times in the form of a verbal noun. Much more frequent are various inflections of the corresponding verb *aslama*, which manifest a dynamic, non-reified reference to the meaning of "giving oneself in total commitment". The other term, *iman*, which differs from *islam* by pointing out a more internal act of assent close to the word "faith", is five times as frequent as *islam*, and the same relationship occurs between their participial forms, *mu'min* and *muslim* (p. 111). Thus, what Muslims as well as non-Muslims who look at "Islam" today read as "*din*, in the eyes of God, is in truth *islam*" (Koran, III, 19) originally signified something like "to behave duly before God (*din*) is to surrender to Him (*islam*)" (Smith, 1962a, p. 113).

It is not necessary to recapitulate the debate among the Islamic schools about the proper, conceptual-theological relationship between *iman* and *islam*. It is interesting, however, to mention the solution provided by Ibn Taymiyya (1263–1328), a leading medieval Hanbali *'alim*, whose reputation has been further enhanced during the last century by a warm reception of some of his writings within the wider realm of "Islamic reformism", which also includes so-called Islamist views (see Chapters 5 and 10). He stresses how *islam*, as grounded in the *shahada* – the witness of faith consisting in recognizing the unicity of God and the final Prophecy of Muhammad – constitutes the more formal, practical and intersubjective aspect of *din*, to the point that it no longer bears any direct relationship to the hereafter. Only *iman* would yield the promise of Paradise, as this is held to signify "assent (*tasdiq*), acknowledging (*iqrar*) and knowledge (*ma'rifa*)", thereby being "a kind of inner act of the heart (*'amal al-qalb*)." (Izutzu, 1965, pp. 76–9). According to this classification, *iman* would be the key to the building of the responsibility and subjectivity of the individual Muslim, whereas *islam* is the vehicle to the reification of *din* as the expression of its intersubjective dimension.

The interpretation provided by Ibn Taymiyya reveals the paradox that it has been precisely the maximalist-utopian Hanbali tradition to carry further the social reification of the concept of *islam* (see also Chapter 3). It is the long-run development of this tradition or type of option, more than "Islam as such", that provides a strong blueprint for a social order and is finally more concerned with problems of social interaction. It is evident, again, that within each Axial civilization, whether Occidental or Oriental, one can find comparable tendencies. On the other hand, the enhanced utopian character of the Islamic view of the legislating efficacy of the *shar'* provides the best immunization against both theocracy and caesaro-papism (Casanova, 1992, p. 50). If one wants to risk extrapolating a particular character of Islam as an Axial civilization, it is in the tendency to suspend the accordance of legitimation to any mundane power by confining the question of account-ability of the ruler to God either to the pure realm of principles or to a pragmatic accommodation to the existing configuration of powers (in fact very often via an appropriate blend of both attitudes).

This general assessment would seem to fit the recently established paradigm in the study of Islamic history that has been termed "strong society, weak state", coherent with Gellner's model of Muslim societies and not contradicting Weber's own synthetical evaluation of Islam (see Chapter 6). This approach, that has been defined and stigmatized as neo-Orientalist and neo-Weberian (Sadowski, 1993), characterizes Islam as "monotheism with a tribal face". It disregards, however, the methodological kernel of Weber's sociology of religion, the paradoxical way through which ideational constructs may redirect the course of structural-institutional developments. Especially neglected is the import of the process of reification of *islam*, which in the modern era has contributed to purge the utopian claim of the Hanbali tradition from its rigorous appeal to transcendence and make it suitable for reconstructing the relationship between the horizontal and the vertical dimensions of the social order. Within this background of analysis of Islam's place within Axial civilizations, we may work out a comparative framework for the analysis of the formation of models of intellectual distinction reflecting the recognition of the social autonomy of power, a process that marks a new historical turn drawing from the Axial heritage: the breakthrough of modernity.

NOTES

1   Any discussion about the nature of such experience would cross the border of a social-scientific consideration and bring us onto the terrain of theological discourse, however this may be disguised.

2   Emphasis on formal structures is tantamount to diffidence towards meaning. In this sense it is true that a genealogical perspective (see Introduction) is historically indebted to the structuralist paradigm.

3   By historical accident, or through a peculiar coincidence of factors, it may also happen that at some place in our world a science of "nature" liable to engender cumulative technological offset arises. But even in this very special case the basic tension is more or less identical.

4   Along similar lines, in Chapters 3 and 5 it will be shown that the chronologically later specification of *din* in terms of *islam* is the product of a modern essentialist view of religion.

5   By "reification" we mean the process of reduction of the dynamic properties of a concept designating a practice or an action, to a consolidated, entity-like keyword of discourse. It is a process of "objectification" of lively features of individual and social action into categories useful for specialized communication. "Objectification" neutrally points to the rationale of the operation of object-making, while "reification" adds to this meaning a sense of loss of the symbolic impulse objectified. A possibility of rescuing the loss of reification is through processes of "subjectification", which occur when the social actor constitutes itself as "subject" of action and master of reified categories. These are used by him to construct a path to truth, salvation and self-renewal which transcends the static identification with objectified categories of collective identity (see also Chapters 2 and 3).

CHAPTER 2

The power of discourse
and the discourse of power

For several reasons, I must start by referring to the historical experience that I see as constitutive of the "West": first, because this is considered unique and yet determines the criteria of normality and dissonance in any judgement on modernity within the transcultural dimension tackled in Part II of the present work; second, because there is plenty of historical and interpretive material on the emergence of the West's alleged uniqueness. Yet in the Arab–Islamic case, research on the intellectual history of the seventeenth and eighteenth centuries, crucial for assessing the type and degree of a modern breakthrough in Islamic terms, has been long hindered by the transcultural dynamics themselves and the related standards of normality. These are hostile to the hypothesis of an endogenous path to modernity in Muslim Arab lands (cf. Schulze, 1990a; see Chapters 4 and 6).

The Arab–Islamic case will be introduced at the end of this chapter through some general considerations concerning the applicability to Arab intellectual history of the rules of modern discourse. This operation has to be preceded by establishing the peculiarities of the dominant paradigm of modernity, in its concatenation between the consolidation of a modern concept of religion, the modern awareness of power relations, and the related mutation of discursive procedures. Finally we will see the emergence of the intellectuals as the self-proclaimed critical legislators of "society", the heroes and authors of the political discourse of modernity. Chapter 3 will provide a more balanced terrain for developing a comparative perspective, with reference to the more circumscribed examination of the rise and function of the public sphere within the formation of modern frameworks of communal reference. Chapter 5 will address the historical and discursive landscape within which it makes sense to hypothesize the formation of an Arab–Islamic framework of reference under the influence of transcultural dynamics. The following large excursus on the genesis of the modern intellectual distinction in the West provides the background for understanding the rules governing the discourse of virtually all the participants in the transcultural space I will examine in Parts III and IV. This includes authors both Western and Arab in origin and location who seek to deal with the relationship between Islam and the political discourse of modernity.

I refused in Chapter 1 to ground my analysis on a preliminary definition of religion. Now we must focus on the processes that historically affected the definition of the concept of religion, after this word was exhumed from its classical use and given a new and more precise meaning by the modern Christian European – later "Western" – discourses, theological, moral and philosophical. The classic, Latin concept of religion denoted the respect due to the gods and their ensuing cults (Tenbruck, 1993, p. 38). Early Christian theology was more familiar with concepts like *fides*, *pietas*, *cultus* etc., but also reappropriated religion for a use conforming to the apologetical formula of *vera religio*, i.e. for the sake of rationally justifying the truthfulness of the Christian faith. This happened when awareness grew of the potentially universal character of religion (pp. 52–3).

This property of the word *religio*, in Western Christian theology, to identify one's own religion as the only true one is, not surprisingly, comparable with the Koranic *din* (see Chapter 1). The necessary by-product of the Christian theological rationalization was also the beginning of a process of reification of "religion". The use of this keyword engendered a rationalizing, distance-taking, reifying attitude *vis-à-vis* Christianity (p. 58). The consequence was a gradual strengthening of the "blueprint" character of the order's construction which was not implicit in the originally eschatological message (p. 54).

The revival of the concept of religion after its partial eclipse during the Middle Ages coincides exactly with the conventional beginning of the modern age (p. 58). The constraint of a rational justification of faith acquired new momentum especially after the rise of modern science, following the success of nominalism that gradually eroded the rationality of scholastic schematizations (p. 61). This created a new semantic field, where reflection on questions of a general order shifted towards a reflective problematization of religion itself (p. 45). The unity and universality of religion as a field of problematization replaced the idea of a universal Church, made obsolete by the Reform (Matthes, 1993, pp. 19–20).

Another way of accounting for this shift is to hypothesize a transition from the Axial polarization between this world and the hereafter, towards the building of a new tension between two spheres: a religious and a secular. The Church had established itself at an intermediate position and as playing a mediating function within the first duality. The erosion of this function forced the previous specialized activity of shaping a cosmological order based on the gap of transcendence to constitute the autonomous field of religion, projected into the hereafter but conforming to the rules of the human mind and solidly rooted within this world (Casanova, 1994, pp. 14–15).

Religion as "the concept of a transhistorical essence" (Asad, 1993, p. 29) established itself during the seventeenth century. The scheme of reduction to fundamentals of sixteenth-century reformers was gradually abandoned, in favour of the formulation of the idea of "natural religion", solidly centred on individual "belief" and *as such* (and not primarily through the mechanism of reward and punishment) able to generate codes of conduct (pp. 40–41). In the context of a shift from God's Word to God's Work, nature became the terrain of validation of both religion and science, the one rooted in inwardness, and the other in outwardness (p. 41). And so "religion" began to act as a differential concept, first with regard to science, and later, as we will see, to "society" as well. Moreover, it permitted a comparison between different articulations of this "natural" type of interior experience, i.e. between different religions (cf. Matthes, 1993, pp. 20–21).

As a result, the modern concept of religion was born of the emancipation from the hermeneutics of the text, grounded on specific authorizing institutions and discourses. It reflected, first, the reduction to fundamentals and the dissemination of interpretive authority, and second, the shift towards postulating an essence natural to the human mind.[1] This making of "religion" expressed a despecialization of the construction of the order that was anticipated by the extent to which ancient and medieval Christianity contributed to defining a sphere of subjective inwardness as the proper realm of faith, as is evident in Augustine (354–430). Unmistakable was the claim by Martin Luther (1483–1546) pointing to an "inner" realm of freedom that manifested itself through religion, opposed to the subjection of the "outer" dimension of the individual to mundane powers (Casanova, 1994, p. 33).

The relevance of this internal mutation of the concept of religion has often been overlooked in Western narratives of the genesis of modernity and the Enlightenment. Even Max Weber, who attempted to discover a unique Western European path of rationalization by highlighting the paradoxical role that dogmatic constructs play in shaping the economic ethic and social praxis at large, moved from a static, ahistorical and highly reductionist concept of religion. Thus he largely missed the importance of the rise and evolution of "religion" as the marker of an autonomous field of problematization. Certainly dominant in cross-cultural comparisons between the "West" and "Islam" (see Chapters 3 and 4), and well reflected in Jürgen Habermas's account of the genesis of modernity as a "project" (Habermas, 1992b), is the view that the path to the Enlightenment was forged by fully secularized, privatized individuals highly motivated in discussing questions of common good within an increasingly structured public sphere. This is an idealized, distortedly Kantian version of the Enlightenment contradicted by the evidence of a lengthy historical evolution or, at a given historical moment, a large spectrum of attitudes *vis-à-vis* religion ranging from the most traditional versions of Axial equilibrium to the vanguards of atheistic thought. It was less the latter which led the whole process, but rather the intermediate positions within the spectrum, where the concept of religion and its translation into codes of life conduct were continuously metamorphosed according to a scheme which converted Divine Grace or Will into individual reason and finally Reason: in other words, transcendent into immanent ethics.

Well-grounded in Ernst Cassirer's reading of the Enlightenment but scarcely represented in historiographical works, the mutation of the problematization and practice of religion in modern Western history has recently received fresh assessments (see Maclear, 1992; Jacob, 1992; Asad, 1993; Tenbruck, 1993; Matthes, 1993). In particular, Habermas's restriction of the so-called private sphere to interests within market relationships and to the intimacy of family, and the consequent bracketing of religion, has been considered untenable (Jacob, 1992, pp. 61–5 and Calhoun, 1992, p. 43, n. 16). Between the end of the seventeenth and the beginning of the eighteenth centuries a "religiosity of the mind" became more and more visible, tendentially anti-Trinitarian, crucially concerned with virtue and animated by an acute awareness of the centrality of discourse, sometimes opposing to theology not the discourse of philosophy but the new narratives of the novel (Jacob, 1992, pp. 75–6). This idea and practice of religion cannot be reduced either to the opposition between the deism or atheism of a bunch of philosophers or to popular forms of faith, as its distinctiveness is precisely in the smooth conversion of the symbolism of the inner light into the light of Reason (p. 74). An expression of the most dynamic social strata, this transformation probably functioned as the crucial engine of change across the full spectrum of historically given attitudes to religion.

While the modern making of "religion" is the main path of immanentization of the order, the shaping of a new domain of reference, classified as "society", was needed in order to relocate the resisting tension of transcendence and legitimize a respecialization of the quest for order through the modern virtuosi of the Word, the "intellectuals". However, before the completion of the scientificization of society as the object of sociology during the nineteenth century, it was the idea of "civil society" that provided an encompassing theoretical construct for detranscedentalizing the views of the order which matured during the seventeenth and eighteenth centuries (Seligman, 1992, pp. 15–16).

The dependence of this process of maturation on a quite internal redefinition and mutation of the concept of religion is evident in Locke (1632–1704), whose theory of community was indebted to the Calvinist view that individuals are its members as creatures of God, from whom all authority derives. They are naturally free and able to act *as* agents of God and by virtue of submitting to His authority. As a consequence, they cannot be legitimately made subject to any other kind of authority. The political community is endowed with authority to the extent that its members abide by their natural endowments (first of all, reason) which are emanations of God's Will. Here Grace is transformed into a principle of action and a resource of reason. Locke reconstructs the social order through an explicitly political enhancement of the Calvinist theological discourse on the Community of Saints and of the corresponding construction of individual responsibility and morality in daily affairs. The mechanism of validation of innerworldly dynamics is still dependent on an explicit view of transcendence (pp. 22–4).

The exit from a theological discourse (whatever its metamorphosis) bound to transcendence coincides not with the suppression of one pole of the tension between this world and the hereafter, but with its relocation, through the transformation of the Axial "politics of beyond" into the modern "politics of behind". The intimate field of belief recalls what is on the surface, on display, and the related games of representation. Religion as a new field of problematization was shaped within the dualism between being and representation that established itself theoretically during the seventeenth century.

Pietistic movements turned the relationship between the believer and God into a practice of self-experience. The resulting idea of "inwardness" (see also Chapter 4) began to provide an ever more generalized ethical matrix for managing the dualism and constructing models of rational life conduct, developed along lines of the sort reconstructed by Max Weber in his sociology of religion (see Chapter 6). It is Norbert Elias, however, who has provided, through his theory of the civilizing process, an account of the function of inwardness that can be more easily generalized to the evolution of society at large. For Elias, inwardness is the dimension of subjectivity constructed for accommodating to the rules of ever wider networks of interaction and communication. It enhances the constraints resulting from this process to factors of a moral order and instruments of a subjective distinction from the regularities of outward social interaction. The constitution of autonomous subjects is thereby strictly associated with the increasing objectivation of social networking. How inwardness emerges as an eminently modern social function is evinced in Weber's account of the Protestant ethic as the matrix of modern rationalization of life conduct, the epitome of the art of turning the world rejection implemented by ascetic restraint into an ethic of world mastering which in the end produces disenchantment (Stauth, 1993, pp. 26–50).

In the final analysis, the constitution of religion as an autonomous field within this world should be assessed as a crucial passage within longer-term processes of subjectification. The origins of these processes are located in the personal-soteriological orientation of Occidental Axial civilizations, while their modern outcome is in the rationalization of social networks embodied in state formation and in the emergence of a capitalist economy and a modern science. Religion has a certain primacy in such modern processes of differentiation, given that the long wave of its constitution as an autonomous field precedes the formation of a political sphere determinantly eroding the universal claims of the Church. In turn, this process came to maturation before the differentiation of economic structures sustained by a new economic ethic, that itself preceded the constitution of modern science.

In the sequence, the formation of a sphere where the subjectification is more immediate precedes the emergence of another sphere which manifests more compelling systemic functions. These, however, react on subjectification and shape it according to their constraints. After it was intercepted by the other, subsequent processes of differentiation, the constitution of religion and its internal mutation acquired a speedier pace and new propelling functions *vis-à-vis* the other differentiating spheres. As a result, modern differentiation, according to an updated view of secularization (see Chapter 3), results from combining a dimension of cultural and intellectual essentialization with structural change. The first is the prime mover in the process, but it is the strength of the latter that permanently enables and influences the former. We will see how essentialization plays the role of reflecting on structural differentiation and creating new, reflexive social agents, or the ability itself to reflect scientifically on the constitution of society up to the grounding of modern social sciences, and, in particular, sociology.

The result of the process, i.e. the modern breakthrough, is the increasing subsumption of "beyond" into "behind", which makes obsolete the institutional mediation between the two opposing poles of this world and the afterworld, and reduces reality to a dualism between inwardness and publicness. The "behind" version of the politics of true meaning is developed in the context of an increasing awareness of the contingent, manipulative and strategic potentialities of discourse. Games of representation and mis-representation, games of power, are required to preserve the inner truth and make it win. The religious wars of the sixteenth and seventeenth centuries were the tragic epitome of this dialectic between the claim of the primacy of inwardness and its dependence on power games. While the Axial view of power was strictly dependent on meaning as its source and end, along a sequence meaning-power-meaning, the modern man becomes conscious of the chance to convert this sequence into power-meaning-power. Power is at the beginning and at the end of any hermeneutic game. A full consciousness of the strategic value of these games is at the origin of modern discourse in general and, more specifically, of the political discourse of modernity.

The manifestation of the power of discourse followed the emergence of a new field that problematized mechanisms of manipulation and power, and led to the formation of a modern discourse of power. Thomas Hobbes (1588–1679) resolved the tension between inwardness and representation, between morality and interest, by grounding social agency on the most elementary expression of the latter, i.e. survival and security, and making this the immanent source of the social and political order. There was no need to endow the agent of an additional moral aura grounding an ontology of political subjectivity. Hobbes's solution proved as attuned to the reality of the modern state as it was unpalatable to the new figure of the intellectual that would emerge during the eighteenth century, longing for an immanent order at the same time moral and social, and thereby demanding an inherent mechanism of mutual recognition within the community that could morally rescue the inevitable games of representation and power. As we will see, this new search for an immanent *cosmos* was tied to a process of respecialization of knowledge and to the necessity of its legitimation.

The first clear search for immanent reasons of the moral order is to be traced back to the Scottish Enlightenment, which postulated a moral sense of natural benevolence as the source of "civil society". The specification of the notion of "authenticity" is parallel to the emergence of the idea of civil society. It points to human morality as consisting of an "intuitive feeling of right and wrong", as opposed to the utilitarian view of calculating the effects of human action, a sort of "inner voice" (Taylor, 1992, pp. 25–9). However, the dislocation of moral order into reasons immanent in the subject does not make it less dependent on tautological schemes. The tension that lay between the visible and the invisible, now problematized as between morality and interest, is again solved by a fiat that is, by virtue of the specification of inwardness as authenticity, no longer theological but fully anthropological (Seligman, 1992, pp. 30–1). The moral sense natural to human beings is the key to the mutual recognition that allows us to validate the games of representation and power. The subsidence of theology into a fully-fledged anthropology was no antidote against the creation of ontologisms. The reason manifested through interests and instrumental rationality in the form of social agency, having its locus in the market theorized by Adam Smith (1723–90), was transfigured by the Enlightenment into Reason as the principle of moral and political subjectivity (pp. 33–4).

This solution could not yet eliminate the problems raised by another dissonant voice in the modern making of society through the new intellectuals: David Hume (1711–76). His distinction between the "is" and the "ought to be", between the factual and the normative, was structurally connected to the reflection on the genesis of the science of nature, and located at the root of the liberal-individualist tradition in Western intellectual history. This view confined virtue into a strictly private sphere and manifested diffidence towards any Reason incarnate in a realm of interpersonal relations. A tentative conciliation between the claim of "civil society" and Humes's objection as rooted in modern science was provided by Immanuel Kant (1724–1804), who is not by mere chance considered the most balanced representative of intellectual modernity. On the one hand, he produced a theory for anchoring within the knowing subject the transcendent properties of language (see Chapter 1), thereby laying the foundations for what has been called the "analytic of finitudes" (Foucault, 1966). On the other hand, he grounded morality precisely on the recognition of this finitude, since the impulse to transcend was evaluated as no mere fiction but morally effective, the very source of free will. The result of this subtle, and indeed fragile, solution was the ambiguous invention of a matrix of morality that is immanent in the subject but accords with the rules of transcendence, hence not transcendent but "transcendental" (Rosen, 1987, pp. 19–49). This rhetorical construction of transcendentality was needed to relocate a dualism that could never fully escape the tension of the "beyond".

Apart from this persisting tension, Kant discovered the specific dimension of the "political" as irreducible either to science or to morality, neither dependent on them, but resulting from a reflection on the groundless, non-transcendental unfolding of history. This discovery is epitomized by his response to the question *What is Enlightenment?* posed by a Berliner journal in 1784. There has been a large convergence between the two leading social theorists of our time, Michel Foucault and Jürgen Habermas, in interpreting Kant's position as the first reflective construction of a sort of political subjectivity by reference to the contemporary age. The Kantian version of the political discourse of modernity rests on a sense of autonomy from the contingencies of actuality and produces diagnostic thought as the quintessence of intellectual *Dasein* (Foucault, 1984c and Habermas, [1984] 1986).[2] The connection established by Kant between the morality of the subject and public engagement as a sublimation of social agency was still, intentionally, tenuous in epistemological terms. The antinomy between moral subject and social agent on the one hand and political subject on the other was solved in terms of a non-speculative, almost journalistic theorizing of the intellectual's concern for the present typical of the Enlightenment (see also Chapter 8).

In spite of the fascination exerted by Kant's solution, the basic problem it addressed persisted and was made more acute by the consolidation, during the nineteenth century, of the dislocation of social order into interfacing private and public spheres. The task consisted in justifying and locating the validity of both the moral and political aspects of subjectivity by reference to a public dimension. Although Hegel (1770–1831) and Marx (1818–83) provided different, very controversial, monistic answers (the one pointing to the existing state, the other to a will-be society without the state), the problematic they tackled remained consistent with the original idea of civil society: how to validate social order in immanent terms, thereby starting by social agents (Seligman, 1992, pp. 44–56). It was apparently difficult to justify the moral order without falling back into the tautological postulation of civil society. As we will see in Chapter 5, it is the Humean objection, and the liberal-individualist tradition grounded on it, which are extraneous to the genesis of modernity within an Arab–Islamic setting, where nonetheless the speculation on immanent reasons of social cohesion was not absent. It has been the combining of the tradition of civil society and the liberal-individualist objection, more than the discursively mediated subsidence of transcendence into immanence, which has secured in the West a scientificization of "society" on the basis of the concept of "social agency", which diminishes the importance of moral and political subjectivity in the construction of order.

The increasingly scientific definition of "society" and of its properties was allowed by the reification, reduction and finally marginalization of religion as a social phenomenon. This process was inaugurated by the intellectual fiction of a radical distinction from religion. This critical attitude of continental-European Enlightenment, encouraged by the resistance of the Catholic Church to the process of the differentiation of society into separate, autonomous fields, bypassed Newton's attempted harmonization between modern religion and science. Instead, it targeted religion as the epitome of traditional and pre-logical backwardness preventing the unfolding of the rational and systemic strength of science, along with its alleged socially liberating power (Casanova, 1994, pp. 24–31). Sociology was officially born with Auguste Comte (1798–1857), out of a sort of ultimate reckoning with the problem of religion, to which he denied any autonomy. Emile Durkheim (1858–1917) completed the task by reinterpreting religion, once purified of mythological elements, as a mere principle of cohesion among agents within a rationally ordered entity named "society" or "social system" (Tenbruck, 1993, pp. 61–4 and Casanova, 1994, p. 238).

Durkheim's neo-holistic sociology, that today still delimits the mainstream of the central discipline in modern social sciences, was a scientific restatement of the "duality of human existence" expressed by the eighteenth-century concept of "civil society" (Seligman, 1992, p. 29 and Eriksson, 1993, pp. 251–4).[3] Sociology was the end-product of a long process of universalization and objectification of "religion", that provided the foundation-stone for the inescapably reifying attitude of the new science of society (see Heller, [1988] 1990, pp. 38–9). The principal medium of this process has been the theory of secularization, which has scientificized the Enlightenment critique of religion into the scarcely proven and undifferentiated thesis of religion's resilience, occurring parallel to the consolidation of social order via processes of structural differentiation (see also Chapter 3).

The success of the construct of "(civil) society" is strictly bound to the emergence of new intellectuals as the heroes of a radical distinction, for whom religion epitomized the backward culture of those social groups from which they, the cultural vanguard of the bourgeois class, wanted to be set off: old aristocracy and popular classes, and finally – over time – the larger educated bourgeoisie itself (cf. Fraser, 1992, p. 114 and Calhoun, 1992, pp. 25–6). Since then, any definition of intellectuals has been dependent on their definition of society – and the other way round. They are those who produce abstract, universal – hence disembedded – meaning (Coser, 1970), as their Axial counterpart already did, but also – and this is the novelty – insist on the relevance of this meaning for shaping a social order grounded on Reason. "A discourse of publicity touting accessibility, rationality, and the suspension of status hierarchies is itself deployed as a strategy of distinction." (Fraser, 1992, p. 115). Therefore, to see them as just that broader "writing class" holding the monopoly of techniques of communication would make us miss their peculiarity. The fact that intellectuals all use the same tools in their search for relevance, and all participate in the same public space of communication, basically addressing other intellectuals while claiming to speak on behalf of the public interest, is not sufficient to assess them as a class or stratum in the conventional sense (as in Schelski, 1975 and Gouldner, 1979).

Between the two opposing dimensions of intellectual *Dasein*, represented by the pursuit of self-interest and the engagement for collective well-being, the husk of the intellectuals' subjectivity is expressed by their reshaping of the tension between morality and interest successfully mediated by the idea of inwardness. This construction of the intellectual function implies, however, a paradoxical reversal of the disenchantment engendered by processes of rationalization of life conduct. The radical distinction that lays the groundwork for the intellectual role can be evaluated as a strategy of deception conducted by specific social strata for their own self-promotion, a sort of self-deception, or better a "self-enchantment". While the structural conditions for the emergence of the idea of society were in the cumulative process of formation of reduced subjects of interest like producers and consumers, who grew disenchanted in the well-known Weberian sense, the intellectual breakthrough that made possible the definition of society was dependent on a process of re-enchanting social interaction beyond the iron cage of modern capitalism. This pattern of "intellectual distinction" provides a fair basis for a "minimalist" concept of modernity suitable for comparative analysis, as opposed to maximalist views of modernity as an integrated package and as a Western monopoly (see Chapter 6).

While the concept of inwardness regulates the mechanisms of rationalization of the moral order governing life conduct these mechanisms are in turn transfigured into rational instruments for establishing a just social order. It is important to acknowledge, for the sake of comparing the different developmental paths of the "West" and "Islam" (see Chapter 3), that there is a "distinctional" pattern underlying the celebration itself of Science and Reason that is in principle separated from the Western epistemological turn that established the analytics of finitude as the only possible basis of knowledge. This pattern is grounded both on the moral distinction inherent in the construction of inwardness, and on the socially functional need of reshaping the hermeneutic specialization necessary to define the resulting social order.

A classic version of this game of definition is the *Essai sur les gens de lettre* by the French *philosophe* D'Alembert, published in 1753. The intellectual is the actor; he is autonomous; he does not depend on any authority except Reason; he *makes* history through words and arguments. He "discovers" that the world changes, *is changing*, and the intellectual is firmly located at the centre of this world. The genesis and evolution of the word "ideology" is in itself not innocent *vis-à-vis* the self-definition of intellectuals. The shaping of this word well illustrates the transition from being philosophers to acting as *philosophes* (in the sense of the French

Enlightenment, close to the meaning of "intellectual"). In its eighteenth-century, pre-Marxian meaning, "ideology" hints at the function of the intellectuals as of those that have subdued and externalized the *logos* through the construction of a system of ideas employable in society. The seeming ease of an immediate externalization produced the illusion of an automatic convertibility of knowledge into power.

Karl Mannheim's formula of *Ideology and Utopia*, representing the two contrasting options for intellectuals, can be reinterpreted as pointing to the inherent spectrum of oscillation that sustains the intellectual role and its dilemma. The construction of systems of ideas aimed at legislating for society can be sustained only by utopian fictions: first of all, that games of power and representation can be administered through the power of Reason and the Word up to the vertical level of domination. If the routinization of the intellectuals' utopian impulse through their stable assumption of an organic role within state planning and through disciplinary specialization may have succeeded in some cases and for limited periods, the main rule of the intellectual existence remains a perpetual oscillation between ideology and utopia, nurtured by the illusion of convertibility (cf. Turner, 1990).

An acute, and historiographically grounded, diagnosis of this dilemma has been provided by Reinhart Koselleck, who has shown how intellectuals discount an inexorable "irrelation to politics" due to the utopianism in-built in their genesis (or "pathogenesis"). Preferably disguised in philosophies of history, this feature has systematically led "to negate historical factuality, to 'repress' political reality" (Koselleck, 1988, p. 12). Intellectuals surrogate this reality with grand visions where history is invariably on the side of the citizen, as epitomized by the free thinker (Koselleck, 1959, pp. 110–15). The reason for the intellectuals' pathology is "that the Enlightenment itself became Utopian and even hypocritical because – as far as continental Europe was concerned – it saw itself excluded from political power-sharing." (Koselleck, 1988, p. 1).[4] In other words, as the codifiers of reified entities, intellectuals are crucial to shaping the kernel of legitimation for technologies of objectification-domination, despite their exclusion from partaking in their final administration. Koselleck considers his analysis of the eighteenth century representative of modern intellectual habits overall, since the Enlightenment "produced mentalities, attitudes and behavioural patterns which have survived the special circumstances of their birth" (p. 4).

In sum, the modern paradox of the intellectual is between recognizing, differently from its Axial counterpart, the power-meaning-power world of limits, while being only able, as a free thinker, to act through the meaning-power-meaning world of freedom. Any co-optation (or other less direct forms of involvement in the political bargain, as through leadership within social movements) will allow an access to the realm of politics and sometimes to the formulation of public policy. Yet, in that very moment, the hermeneutic articulation itself, as consisting of the shaping of publicly persuasive arguments, will lose its original, indispensable autonomy. In this way, the fiction that sustains the daily strategy for diluting the tension inherent in the role and reproducing it, the fiction of authorship, is eluded: argument is accommodated to a political bargain and the intellectual betrays the promise of independence and originality.

The construction of the intellectual as author is both a socially viable solution to his search for relevance and an indispensable way to validate the meanings he produces in a world no longer governed by a given *logos*. If we consider "text as choice . . ., involving selection amongst options within what one might call the intertextual potential of an order of discourse (i.e. available repertoires of genres, discourses and narratives)" (Fairclough, 1992, p. 212), then the intellectual task of constructing publicly reliable knowledge must be fulfilled within an environment of interpretive constraints encompassing both a diachronic ("enterprise-specific": Fish, 1989, p. 99) and a synchronic (issue-led: Donati, 1991, p. 143) dimension. However, to reduce authorship to a function "by which one . . . since the eigtheenth century . . . impedes the free circulation, the free manipulation, the free composition, decomposition, and recomposition of fiction" (Foucault, [1969] 1984b, p. 104) may obscure the ambivalent rationale of this regulatory construct. This is not just a device functional to the unfolding of a discursive formation, but a figure indispensable for holding together the various tensions and layers that make out the intellectual praxis, which culminates in crafting convincing arguments. The dilemma entailed in this activity is given by the impossibility of escaping circularity while being drawn in the spiralling motion and expansion typical of argumentation, a circularity that is liable to become more and more vicious the less argument is constructed by considering its intrinsic limits.

What is peculiar to intellectual argument, against the general constraints of the form of hermeneutic activity that I have identified as "virtuosity of the Word" (see Chapter 1), is that the need to fix ideas and project them into a public sphere of communication opens up a distinctive hermeneutic game with the author at its centre. Beyond a first, general level of the "author-function", as depending on the need to secure intrinsically volatile ideational constructs, we should be aware of the phenomenon of metaphorical circularity. This is the relentless tendency of meaning to return to a given question's point of "origin" (see Chapter 1). What warrants the viability of this circularity is the property of metaphors, which carry a signifying tension able to cement otherwise isolated segments of meaning. In the context of modern intellectual activity, the domestication of this circularity raises new problems and calls for fresh solutions, as there is no longer a taken-for-granted transcendence that validates argument. The result is the impulse towards enabling the inherent intratextual fragility to seek refuge along a downloading path, by way of entering "in-circling dynamics" through the establishment of hermeneutic affiliations and the search for legitimation within the constructed boundaries of a community (or circle) of interpreters.[5] The modern construction of authorship is thus the condition for providing a text with an intertextual dimension, that surrogates the Axial homogeneity of the *logos* and constitutes the terrain for ideological contentions.

Closing a text symbolizes cutting the circularity of reflection and argument through allowing it to circulate. Thus it is exposed to a potentially infinite interpretive uncertainty, governed by the *intentio lectoris*. This would mean, however, the end of intellectual argument. Signing the text with an author's name is the antidote against this danger, the superimposition of an *intentio auctoris* to hermeneutic dispersion. Nevertheless, this construction, like the more general author-function, is in no way autonomous, but always dependent on an "enterprise-specific intention". Beyond the modern need to individualize, signing a text is the crucial act for relieving the weight of the argument's circularity in its desperate effort to refer to external, non-textual reality, through the building of another kind of external reference. This hermeneutic externalization is achieved through relating the authorial name to a concrete community or circle of authors (cf. Fish, 1980 and 1989). Such a reference is revealed in the text crafted: first by the use of a particular, and intrinsically limited, disciplinary, subdisciplinary or interdisciplinary vocabulary and language; second by the application of specific framing devices. Once argument is so validated, it can unfold its acting strength, its power to persuade.

To recapitulate: the way discourse is made can be seen as the product of the tension between an inherent tendency towards hermeneutic dispersion and the impotence of argument, due to its circularity, to overcome this dispersion autonomously. In this sense it is true, according to the approach propagated by Foucault during the 1960s (see Foucault, 1966 and 1969), that the way this tension is "processed" has to be located in a genuinely transindividual dimension (the realm of "formations"). Intratextual argument is certainly dependent, for its validation, on the construction of the author figure, but this is again a mere medium for downloading intratextual circularity in an intertextual dimension (see Fairclough, 1992, pp. 84–6).

This dimension, however, is not just an abstract one, since it can be identified and analysed inside the text itself, through implicit and explicit references to other texts and other authors. In this sense, it is an oversimplification to state that the discourse is prior to the author, and that the author is a mere function. The author, considered in his concrete intellectual dimension, and not just as a name, is, rather, a crucial medium of discursivity, representing the interface between intratextual argument and intertextual cross-validation. We see, then, how discourse is made out of a sequence *text-author-text*, corresponding to the classical sequence meaning-power-meaning, but entailing a genuinely modern novelty, an enhanced awareness of the individualization of authorship's authority. If the actual unfolding of argumentation and validation in concrete texts is not taken seriously, any analysis of discourse is condemned to be void.[6]

The view that Arab intellectuals have inherited a distinctive character with regard to the fundamental procedures for relating the known to the unknown and for validating argument has led many to stress the marked "logocentric" character of Islam as an Axial civilization (see Chapter 1). Frequently supported by the explicit or implicit application of psychologizing devices of the kind which have not surprisingly been among Edward Said's most favourite targets for critique in *Orientalism* (see Chapter 6), this kind of theorizing gained fresh momentum during the 1980s, as one of the most acute contemporary Arab thinkers, the Moroccan philosopher Muhammad 'Abid al-Jabiri, has approached the alleged structures of the "Arab reason" (al-Jabiri, 1984, 1986 and 1990).

After having raised the question of Arab thought as syndromatically circular since the Arab *nahda* ("renaissance"), whose beginning is traced back to the latter quarter of the nineteenth century (see Chapters 4 and 5), he attempts to explain this circularity by reading into Arab history a strong factor of hermeneutic continuity, the primacy of disciplines having as their object the text, or rather the Text (the Koran). These were *'ulum al-bayan*, the disciplines of "explication", applying an analogical method (*qiyas*) in submitting the unknown to the known. The most ancient among all Arab–Islamic disciplines, these sciences encompass rhetoric, philology, Koranic exegesis, sciences of *hadith* (sayings and doings of the Prophet), *fiqh* (jurisprudence) and *kalam* (speculative theology) (al-Jabiri, 1984). Since the object of *'ulum al-bayan* was not nature, but something predefined, intellectual progress was inherently limited after the "age of recording", when the Holy Scriptures were definitively laid down (see Boullata, 1990, pp. 52–3).

Al-Jabiri was evidently induced to search for the peculiarities of the "Arab reason" in order to explain the alleged recurrence, in Arab thinking, of reference of the new to a (past)-model (*namudhaj*). His view of *qiyas* as more than a juridical method, the pivot itself of the "Arab reason", is lightheartedly transformed into a proof of the "indirectness" of Arab thought as a whole, which in turn should explain the Arab attitude of practising politics indirectly. He denounces the absence of a tradition, in the Arab–Islamic civilization, of an autonomous political discourse. This is at the origin of the Islamist attitude, in modern times, of disguising an actual political problem, like the one of *nizam al-hukm* (the system, or method, of government), as one inevitably posed "within Islam" (according to the formula *nizam al-hukm fi-l-islam*). This procedure entails the suppression of an explicit concern for the present of contemporary society, so negating the basic condition for a modern political discourse to unfold its diagnostic power (al-Jabiri, 1982, pp. 59–61).

The fact that Arab intellectual discourse appears to lack an endogenous tradition providing a self-validating path to supporting the claim to a privileged access to the formulation of societal good, as in the Western case, is no argument for its indirectness in politics. The posing of a political problem "within Islam" raises in fact the question of the meaning of "Islam", that is not merely the inherited label of a civilizational unit, but the newly reshaped and further reified term of reference for a sort of intellectual distinction, as we will see better in the comparative analysis of the public sphere's genesis (see Chapter 3). Here we need remember only that the reference to models and the constraint of "indirectness" is an inherent feature of hermeneutic-intellectual activity. However, we will see (Chapters 3 and 5) that at least from the era of the Arab *nahda* the fiction of intellectual authorship, though functioning according to the rules of distinction previously specified, was further complicated by the need for a second distinction aimed at establishing the "authenticity" of the Arab–Islamic cultural heritage. This complication was an immediate result of the challenge of the discourse and disciplining practice of European colonialism, regulated by the assumption of embodying a superior civilization, the only one apt to engender modern patterns of behaviour and societal organization (cf. Mitchell, 1988).

Al-Jabiri's argument, instead, focuses on transhistorical deficits. It claims that in Arab–Islamic intellectual cultures argumentation might have been especially closed in itself, fully circular and not spiralling, due to the enduring presumption that the *logos* was fixed, textualized in the Koran. This made it impossible to acknowledge that textualization is dependent on an intertextual, ideological terrain of hermeneutic contention. In purely logical terms it might be plausible that, grounded on a revised, and socially effective form of Platonism, which made the divinized concepts subject to a continuous process of normative interpretation and adaptation (especially in the discipline of *fiqh*) on the one hand (Gellner, 1981, p. 23), and on the utopia of *al-siyasa al-shar'iyya* (see Chapter 1) on the other, the Koranic way may have functioned too well as an antidote against the hermeneutic dispersion inherent in the *logos*, thereby discouraging externalizing paths leading to the invention of "ideology".

At this point, however, the question should be raised: has such a form of Platonism, with its particular strength and coherence in Islamic cultural history, hindered the emergence of a modern intellectual distinction? To what extent is modern Arab thought still conditioned by this Platonism? I will not be able to answer these questions once and for all, as al-Jabiri does, by going back to a presumed original sin. Instead, I will try to specify the characteristics of the terrain of interdiscursive exchange as well as the genesis and the conditions of modern public discourse in Arab Muslim lands and in "Arab–Islamic" terms (Chapters 3 and 5). We may anticipate that the regulation-simplification performed by "scripturalism", which has been, in the long term, a major influence on the modalities of modern Arab–Islamic discourse, cannot be reduced to an inherited logocentrism. Scripturalism has functioned rather as the medium of a mutation-standardization and strong reification of inherited concepts entailing a distance-taking, externalizing attitude: a process that might use and domesticate references to static past-models.[7] The historical crux of the problem, that al-Jabiri leaves entirely unproblematized, is the extent to which the Arab–Islamic intellectual *Dasein* reflects long-term processes of subjectification and reification shaped by endogenous factors and transcultural constraints (see Chapters 3 and 5).

NOTES

1   The reduction to fundamentals is normally bound to the enumeration of elements, whereas the postulation of an essence reflects the impulse to define a unitary matrix that transcends any single enumerated fundament.

2   For a more analytical consideration of the Kantian text among others pointing to the same crucial phase of the late eighteenth century, see Eder, [1985] 1991.

3   A further manifestation of the transposition of "religion" into "society" is "Parson's extreme interpretation of modern industrial society as the institutionalization of Christian principles" (Casanova, 1994, p. 240).

4   These words are taken from Koselleck's new Foreword to the English translation of *Critique and Crisis*.

5   This is the mechanism underlying the formation of hermeneutic circles (see Introduction), like the ones that will be analysed in Parts III and IV.

6   A similar critique to Foucault's use of the conceptual tool of "discourse" has been levelled by Fairclough (1992, pp. 53–61). My perspective is indebted to the "post-modern" turn only to the extent that this is interpreted – from the viewpoint of a sociology of intellectuals, i.e. avoiding its most extreme and fashionable manifestations – as allowing and legitimizing a step back from the externalized reflexivity of the legislators and towards the internalized one of "new interpreters". This has, first, induced a denunciation of the fictitious character of a secondary *logos* ("ideology critique"). Finally it has helped to formulate the hypothesis that the difference between "classical" and "modern" knowledge lies in the passage from the assumption of a fixed *logos* to the engagement in "discourse", regulated by the laws of the public arena. This recognition urges one to submit the tautology of the modern intellectual distinction to the same nominalistic and sceptical scrutiny that early modern thought applied to the Axial heritage.

7   If there is any particular status of "text" in the Arab intellectual discourse, it is not due to the legacy of logocentrism as the inherent marker of an irrelation to politics, but as the consequence of an aggravation of the general power-knowledge syndrome among intellectuals. In particular, the frequent use of redundancy as a validation strategy among Arab authors can be assessed as distinctive, not primarily of the allegedly heavy heritage of *'ulum al-bayan*, but rather of a need to counterbalance the denied access to politics through a propensity to over-occupy public discursive arenas via an "over-textualization" of argument.

CHAPTER 3

Public communication and frameworks of communal reference

A proper comparative terrain for examining the Arab–Islamic path to modernity can be provided only by establishing a significative connection between the genesis of an intellectual function and the emergence of a public sphere during the last quarter of the nineteenth century. This in turn requires that we start taking into account the constraints coming from the transcultural dimension of communication between the "West" and "Islam". As historical constructions pinpointing identities and predetermining patterns of communication, these general labels merit a separate analysis, the bulk of which will be found in Part II. On the other hand, the assessment of whether the paradigm of so-called fundamentalism is inscribed in the modalities for affirming an Arab–Islamic political discourse of modernity requires a discussion of the most salient historical passage situated between the unfolding of the Islamic version of the Axial paradigm (Chapter 1), and the rise of a public sphere in Arab societies under Western colonialism.

The evaluation of this passage is the subject of a controversy over the hypothesis of an endogenous path to the maturation of a modern break-through in some Muslim regions during the eighteenth century, a turn which would be comparable with the Western "intellectual distinction" as reconstructed in Chapter 2. The dispute is of special interest in that it can help us to understand the social processes underlying both the development of models of personal responsibility and subjectivity, and the mechanisms of reduction and reification of a network of keywords inherited from Islamic traditions, where *islam* not surprisingly features increasingly centrally. Among the "revisionist" authors emphasizing endogenous factors is Peter Gran. His *Islamic Roots of Capitalism* (Gran, 1979) attempted to induce an interpretive shift from the "pathology" of Islam as a civilization not endogenously redeemable by modern patterns of social rationalization, to the "physiology" of an autochthonous, complex process of modernization taking place in central regions of the Muslim world like Egypt, in the context of thriving market relations with Europe, during the second half of the eighteenth century. Reinhard Schulze tackles even more directly the cultural-sociological side of the question, thereby challenging classic Orientalism on its own terrain. Whereas Gran was interested in the roots of *Islamic Capitalism*, Schulze aims to define the possibility and genesis of an *Islamic Enlightenment* (1990a).[1]

The crucial question is given by the extent to which there was, or was not, an endogenous shift in the hermeneutics of Islam that made it the medium of a conscious appreciation of social change and a direct critique of political authority, both of which being no longer dependent on the typically Axial mechanisms of mediation (see Chapter 1). The innovative strength or even the modern character of the Wahhabi movement in the Arabian peninsula during the eighteenth century, a movement of Hanbali affiliation named after its founder, Muhammad ibn 'Abd al-Wahhab (1703–92), was already acknowledged in the period preceding the rise of the revisionist thesis on the genesis of modernity in Arab Muslim lands.[2] We owe, however, to at least some of the revisionist historians the stress laid on the category of "neo-Sufi" movements, a notion inherited from Western colonial scholarship (O'Fahey and Radtke, 1993, pp. 61–4), but duly reshaped in order to classify Islamic "revivalist" movements of the late eighteenth and early nineteenth centuries stemming from the broader universe of Sufi practices and organizations, differently from the anti-mystical orientation of Wahhabism.[3]

The novelty of the neo-Sufi opposition movements spanning from North Africa to South-East Asia well beyond the boundaries of the Arab world, and their analogy with the Wahhabi case despite all their differences, lies in the new modalities of propagation of a model of community epitomized by the one of Muhammad's era (Schulze, 1982, pp. 108–9). These views witness a sharp acceleration in the hermeneutic variability allowed by the scripturalist setting, the ensuing emergence of a discursive axis favouring a not merely chiliastic projection into the future, a not purely esoteric stress laid on the disciplining of the subject and, much as a product of both, the emphasis laid on what represents the *essence* of Islam as a social force.

This essentialization, however, is not yet performed through a full reification of a framework of communal reference and universal projection,[4] but by way of a strong emphasis on the socially binding character of Muhammad's *sunna*, i.e. his model of life conduct. The transformation of the act of commitment signified by *islam* into a socially immanent subjectivity does not yet usher in a fully reified vision of the social order. This is a case where the horizon of salvation is still inscribed within a dimension dominated by symbolic references to transcendence, but where both the path of access to truth and the determination of life conduct acquire an autonomous and differentiated status via an implicit reference to a communal normativity.

The rationale of this immanentization of the order through a new emphasis on the subject as a social being is the denunciation of *taqlid* as the practice of imitation of traditional interpretive patterns, and the vindication of the faculty of creatively adapting reason to the requirements of the time by practicing *ijtihad* (the concept of "free reasoning" in Islamic jurisprudence). This is considered necessary to redefine norms of conduct whose validity transcends the internal hierarchical order of the *tariqa* (Sufi brotherhood), and affects every member of the community. The search for truth, as inspired by *tawhid* (traditionally indicating the "unicity" of God but also the mystical union with Him), is still considered the highest form of human activity, but the way of conceptualizing God's unicity is by now the path of access to an immanent, socialized truth. *Tawhid* is no longer a mere dogmatic principle, a formula of faith or a way to achieve a *unio mistica*, but the essential medium to the comprehension of the Prophet's *sunna* and, through it, to the redefinition of the norm guiding socially responsible selves.

It is true that in the neo-Sufi discourse there seems to be hardly a place for a disembedded, human Reason. The discourse of reason is still formulated through a vocabulary drawn from the Islamic tradition, and is finally made possible precisely through making *islam* and affiliated keywords the labels for covering the "reasoning" function of the socially responsible subject. Compared with the Western model (see Chapter 2), this can be interpreted as a less spectacular, but similarly functional affirmation of at least the subjective conditions of intellectual modernity.

The soundness of the neo-Sufi hypothesis as such has been challenged through the partly convincing argument that it does not derive from an extensive and careful reading of the sources, but is rooted in the Western colonial fear of political activism prompted by the metamorphoses of Islamic traditional doctrines and organizations. On the crucial question of *al-tariqa al-muhammadiyya* ("the path of Muhammad"), that according to the neo-Sufi model is the central vehicle of detranscendentalization, this critique asserts that the *imitatio Muhammadi* had always been a salient Sufi practice preparing the final union with God, a function that appears to persist in one major case of a North African neo-Sufi master addressed by the critics (O'Fahey and Radtke, 1993).

Without pretending to engage deeply in the dispute, it should be recalled that the emphasis on a specific practice can shift according to social and historical context. The seeming changeless record of the practice in written texts is no proof against the view of a mutation, and the study of the context beyond the text along with the application of social-scientific categories is precisely what sets revisionist historiography apart from text-bound

Orientalist scholarship.[5] On the other hand, the criticism levelled against the concept of neo-Sufism is not based merely on philological objections but is also dependent on an insistence on the uniqueness of Western historical development (typically supported by a simplified reading of Kant: see Chapter 2) and a consequent hostility towards conceiving a comparable, though certainly different, path of access to socially immanent rationalization expressed in Islamic terms (cf. Radtke, 1994). It emerges from the dispute that there is an opposition between different models of framing Islamic history in Western scholarship that depends on underlying views of modernity, Enlightenment and Western uniqueness before any philological and historiographic arguments are introduced into the discussion (see Chapters 4, 6 and 8).

It is not my task to test further or refine the neo-Sufi hypothesis or to propose a more neutral label and concept for the "revivalist"[6] movements that emerged between the end of the eighteenth century and the beginning of the following one. Rather I wish to help overcome a deficit that affects both the classic and the revisionist models of Islamic history, and is represented by the gap in accounting for the relationship between the Islamic intellectual asset endogenously produced during the eighteenth and the early nineteenth centuries, and the subsequent intellectual developments triggered by the European impact on Muslim lands. My attempt is grounded on a view of the function of public communication and of what is called the discursive "public sphere", or even the larger dimension of "publicness"[7] , as common to both the Western and the Arab–Islamic models of modernity in spite of their being premised on different historical breakthroughs. This function cannot be reduced, as we will see, to the sheer presence of the infrastructures of modern public communication or to the use of public discursive skills by the intellectuals, but is a direct emanation of the "intellectual distinction" (see Chapter 2). The rise of an independent press in Egypt between the 1870s and 1880s was the vehicle for the unfolding of modern Arab–Islamic discourse: "the introduction of the 'editorial' to express, develop and argue a single idea clearly, briefly and logically was a far cry from the tortuous and encyclopedic ramblings of earlier traditional writings." (Vatikiotis, [1969] 1991, p. 184).

One key to tackling the question of the genesis of Arab–Islamic publicness is to assess the relationship between the innovative impulse of revivalist movements that typically occurred in semi-peripheral contexts and strove to reconstruct communities in the form of states (see Keddie, 1994; however, a prominent exception was Cairo, as a major centre of Islamic scholarship: Voll, 1994 [1982] pp. 41–9), and the patterns of intellectual modernization of "reformist" *'ulama'* located in major urban centres and invoking the same tool of *ijtihad* as opposed to *taqlid*. The neo-Sufi break inadequately satisfies the requirements of the intellectual distinction as exemplified by the Western case (see Chapter 2). It might meet its preliminary, necessary conditions by virtue of its socially reflective and normative stance towards existing, "traditional" life practices. This it does by showing a clear essentializing attitude towards what the "right" Islamic path has to be.

However, the sufficient conditions for initiating a dynamics of public communication, as represented by the capacity to articulate a public discourse on the common good premised on an intellectual will of distinction and emancipation from traditional subordination or acquiescence to established hierarchies, were not mature until the European intrusion into the Arab–Islamic world passed a critical threshold and defied not only local, basically autocratic rule, but also challenged its ideological basis of legitimation. As we will see, this passage, that inaugurated the urban movement of *islah*, or Islamic reformism (see also Chapter 5), coincided with the first emergence of a pattern of transcultural communication between the "West" and "Islam", within a process through which these broad and flexible, but powerful frameworks for cultural identification constituted themselves discursively and began to influence public communication (see Chapter 4). The following considerations apply in particular to Egypt, as the centre of gravitation of intellectual life in the Arab–Islamic world, as well as of attraction of intellectual energies from especially the Syro-Lebanese cultural environment (see Hourani, [1962] 1983).

The concept of a framework of reference provides the lowest common denominator for a "minimalist" definition of modernity from the point of view of intellectual production and public communication (see Chapter 2). It highlights the success of new modalities of discourse that emancipate themselves from the compulsory reference to traditional structures of domination or to a transcendent *logos*. Socially valid meaning is produced by seeking reference and consensus towards a wider community or "nation" (in fact towards its intellectually receptive and publicly engaged components), mostly with the aim of reforging it under the banner of a "renaissance" or encompassing "reform" (see Chapter 5). Publicly accountable communication patterns represent the terrain of validation of norms propagated as universally valid, and applying to the "common good". The strength of a framework of reference lies in the formal abstraction of its referential function, that can embrace shifting interpretations and practices along a broad spectrum of possibilities delimiting a consensus within the socially immanent sphere of communication (Bourricaud, 1987, pp. 19–20).

While in the West a framework of communal reference and universal projection results from the combination of a national identity with a more encompassing "Western" affiliation, in Arab countries it has been shaped by adding Arabism (*'uruba*) to *islam*. This pairing does not make sense in purely logical terms, as these two principles are heterogeneous, the one pertaining to *qawmiyya* ("nationalism"), the other to *din* (see Chapter 1). The two terms can be freely combined in various ways according to contingent discursive needs, within a range that spans from neo-traditionalist thought to a basically areligious pan-Arabism, where all positions are compatible with the "Arab–Islamic" character of the reference sought. Only the drastic suppression of one of the two poles would imply a departure from the consensus of communication (cf. al-Jabiri, 1992, pp. 30–2).

In historical perspective, we can observe an initial division of labour between the civil and ethical character of the Islamic reference of so-called Islamic reformism at the turn of last century (revolving around the keyword *islah*, "reform": see Chapter 5) and the immediately political character of Arabism in the form of Arab nationalism. This ideology has proved to be compatible with "regionally" circumscribed forms of nationalism modelled on the existing colonial entities and its successors, or on historically and geographically well-delimited units, like Egypt. Whereas Arabism in its mature, Nasserist-like form had to accommodate Islam especially as a way of appealing to the "people", the latest fashion of Islamism in Arab countries since the 1970s has proven able gradually to adapt Arab nationalism to its discourse centred on clearly Islamic keywords. Though separate instances, Arabism and Islamism do have to reappropriate each other in order to meet the consensus of communication. Moreover, they own a "power of mutual convertibility" due to their common reference to the *umma*, that is at the same time the community grounded by the Prophet on the basis of Koranic *din* and the "nation" in a fully-fledged nationalist sense. As a consequence, in Arab political discourse the idea of the community of reference or nation is never fully mundanized and scientificized by implicit or explicit reference to a concept like "society" (see Chapter 2; cf. al-Azmeh, 1993, p. 61 and Schulze, 1994, p. 23). In a similar way, the dominant paradigm of "reformism", originally animated by an impetus of ethical renewal but increasingly affected by nationalist imperatives, has prevented the consolidation of sociology as an autonomous science of society (Roussillon, 1991).

Within this historical background, it is correct to observe that Islamic references have undergone a gradual "politicization". However, this is true in the sense that *islam* has first succeeded as the keyword for a universal reference, a pivotal category within public communication, and has later

unfolded its force of mobilization as its public agitation has been reappropriated, especially during the last two decades, by a class of "new Islamic
intellectuals" or *Lumpenintelligentsia*, distinct from both the professional,
however modernized, *'ulama'*, and the "secularist" intellectuals, and who
represent the most original social product of an increasingly generalized
access to secondary and higher education and public communication
(Eickelman, 1992 and Roy, 1990). The expansion of the public sphere
beyond the limits of a restricted intellectual élite of double (traditional
and European-like) education has deepened the normative import of public
discourse, which has increasingly to cope with the interest and values of a
large spectrum of individuals and autonomous social groups.

As in the case of the trajectory of demise of the Nasserist consensus in
Egypt that came to full maturation during the 1970s (Gilsenan [1982] 1990,
pp. 222–29), the growth of "Islamic publicness" is reflected in the structuring
of consumption models (Starrett, 1995) and in the promotion of development
and welfare through private voluntary organizations (Ben Néfissa-Paris,
1992 and Sullivan, 1994). Last but not least, the ordering and rationalizing
functions expressed in Islamic terms cohere into a new consensualist
normative claim: the resulting, ambiguous call for the implementation of
the *shari'a* (as the assertion of a principle of lawfulness for or beyond the
existing, post-Nasserist state) is discursively reformulated in order to match,
influence, redirect and "normalize" the plurifunctional Islamic references at
different levels of individual and social life (Salvatore, 1995a).

As a consequence, the scope of *islam* and related key categories
has been reshaped, after their previous reification, through a new turn of
subjectification that is comparable to that of eighteenth-century "revivalist"
movements. The main difference is that in the more recent breakthrough of
the 1970s a newly subjectified Islam can thrive only if strategically invested
into public disputes. Its communicability is subordinated to the rules of the
public sphere, which again requires processes of reduction and reification.
The developments of the last three decades show a high coherence between
the discourses produced and their normative impact on forms of life
conduct.[8] At a mature stage, reification is not merely the product of
constraints of public communication, but reflects the reifying effects of
social networking within human relationships (see Chapter 2). In this sense,
reification is "functional" to social integration – as are the reification
processes within Islamic publicness.

The first crucial passage in the reification of *islam* (whose transcultural
dimension will be better highlighted in Chapter 4) was achieved towards the
end of last century. At that time, in titles of books published in Arabic, *islam*

as the more "systematized and externalized" term for the Koranic *din* outnumbered the "personalist and activist" term *iman* (see Chapter 1) by a ratio of over thirteen to one. Since then, *iman* has virtually disappeared from the headlines of public discourse, which has been solidly hegemonized by *islam* (Smith, 1962a, pp. 114–17), as the most suitable term for constructing a framework of reference. Though in some cases the meaning of personal commitment might still be present or even dominant in *islam*, its swift reification and systematization follow the subjection to the rules of public communication.

While the *islam* of Wahhabism was still centred on the dimension of commitment, as reflected by the formula of *fadl al-islam* ("the merit of Islam" as a personal surrender to God's Will), that is the title of a book written by the movement's founder, the similar heading built on the plural of *fadl*, *fada'il al-islam* ("the virtues of Islam" as a system), an expression not uncommon in turn-of-the-century literature, witnesses a leap from the subjectifying impulse of revivalist Islamic movements to the reifying rationale of Islamic publicness. The use of *islam* as the subject of sentences (thereby representing an autonomous social force), as well as the formula *fi-l-islam* ("in Islam") – that has a remarkable precedent in the title of a work by the Hanbali scholar Ibn Taymiyya (see Chapter 1) – as well as the spread of the adjective *islami* (= Islamic), are basic proofs of the turn achieved (Smith, 1962b, p. 493).

It is well known that a crucial keyword of the reified Islam propagated by Islamists, and therefore one central to the Arab–Islamic framework of communal reference (for its being a source of mobilization and a subject of contentions) is represented by *shari'a*, the normative system projected by God's legislating Will (*shar'*) onto the Community of believers. Authoritative precedents of a similar meaning of *shari'a* are not absent in pre-modern times, as in the work of al-Ghazali (1058–1111). It was, however, not until the rise of a public sphere (see Smith, 1962a, p. 276, n. 23) that the word *shari'a* began to consolidate as an abstract medium of social normativity, distinct from the concrete laws applied by the courts, and also from the science of jurisprudence (*fiqh*).

It might seem paradoxical that this meaning emerged in the context of a process of introduction of positive law in the legal systems of Arab Muslim countries. It would be a simplification to argue that the shaping of *shari'a* as a notion of systemic-normative order was a reaction to positive law, according to the "reactivist" model that reads every manifestation of an Islamist ethos as a reaction to the modernization induced by Western penetration. *Shari'a* rather became a popular keyword in public discussions at a time when the imperative of reform encompassed all levels of social action and organization, and thereby acquired a systemic connotation that replaced the holistic one of pre-nationalist times. Since then, the invocation of *shari'a* has always been a tool for shaping an autochthonous rationale of hierarchization and centralization of the legal system, and in fact also of its secularization, to the extent that it implied a transfer of functions and powers from largely autonomous religious institutions to a non-religiously legitimated state and its judiciary. It represented a plea for predictability versus discretion, exactly the opposite of the "Kadi-justice" theorized by Max Weber as the antithesis to the rule of law (see Chapter 6).

The modern idea of *shari'a* is irreducible to a corpus of positive law, and this is why it is a simplification to translate it as "Islamic law". One can even say that *shari'a*'s ambiguity is peculiar to its function. What is prominent is its socially functional degree of abstraction, as in the Islamist call for its implementation, that amounts to a restoration of the proper function of the legal system, through the invocation of a truthful, abstract lawfulness being capable of infusing societal institutions. While this use entails a privileged axis between idea and institution unmediated by practice, it is also true that the modern understanding of *shari'a* might convey a sense of orthopraxis. Here the main emphasis is not always on correctness, but on praxis itself, also to be understood in its fully-fledged social dimension, not far from its Marxist meaning (cf. Schulze, 1994, p. 21).

The reference to the normative system embodied by the *shari'a* well represents the logic of the process through which Islam has become the umbrella category for a discourse able to convert a more encompassing transcendent order into a set of socially immanent norms. Nonetheless, the ambiguity, as well as the appeal, of the term *islam* as agitated in public communication, in addition to most of the other keywords strictly associated with this use, lies in the fact that despite being mainly a reified reference to an immanent system, it persistently signifies an act of personal commitment to a transcendent God. It is clearly not the case of a drastic suppression of transcendence and of a full autonomization of social subject and social system, as in the Western model of intellectual distinction, but rather of the making of a permanent mechanism for translating transcendent normativity into social. This process provides the latter with an autonomous rationale even without a theoretical justification for this autonomy, or even, paradoxically, via a conscious, ideological rejection of this autonomy, as in the Islamist claim of God's absolute sovereignty (*hakimiyya*) upon the Community.

Aside from being a paradox of intellectual *Dasein* in an Arab–Islamic context (if judged from the point of view of the Western path), this ambiguity has turned into an element of strength in public communication and political mobilization. It has helped to capture the consensus of ever wider social strata, parallel to their access to public education and also in its absence, to the extent that the written word has kept its impact even on illiterates, both by virtue of its recognized authority, and through the practice of the spontaneous formation of groups for reading a book, a pamphlet, a newspaper, where the illiterate has access to texts through listening. This helps to explain the increasing centrality of *islam* and Islamist discourse in the public sphere of most Arab countries during the last century.

From the civic Islam of Muhammad 'Abduh (1849–1905) to that of Rashid Rida (1865–1935) and the Muslim Brotherhood (grounded in 1928), more directly concerned with the political community, it is evident that the first phase of the public venture of reified *islam* was supported by a fraction of the *'ulama'* class, which asserted an intellectual distinction without having to reject tradition, but instead invoked the strong thread of *islah* ("reform") within that tradition (see Chapter 5). In so doing, they did not need to overemphasize the legislating pretension of a new historical subject, as in the case of "secular" intellectuals, but found it both easier and necessary, in order to preserve their centrality in the "high" fields of cultural brokerage, to construct the *shari'a* as a given, divinely ordained, legislating system. This operation identifies the Islamic way to intellectual modernity as a "soft" distinction, as opposed to the "sharp" distinction of the Western model.

The major obstacle to seeing the making of an Arab–Islamic framework of reference as an original, though less spectacular token of modernity is precisely in the reconstruction of the Western model of Enlightenment modernity as a rather brusque passage, a clear break with "tradition". According to this heroized and simplified, but still solidly dominant view of the modern intellectual breakthrough (see Chapter 2), Arab–Islamic modernity could be at best assessed as being blocked at a proto-modern stage still waiting for an "enlightening" turn, at the threshold of a Lockian formulation of a community of free individuals as an actualization of Divine Will. Increasingly questioned as to its neutrality and validity with reference to the evolution of religion in Western history (see Chapter 2), the Enlightenment critique of religion and its sociological reformulation claim a residual explanatory value for assessing the religion of the Other, first and foremost Islam.

What hinders at the outset a comprehension of the Arab–Islamic way to intellectual distinction and to the building of a public sphere is the inherent theoretical partiality of the theory of "secularization" as the unnegotiable kernel of modernity. According to the original version of this theory, grounded on the classical sociology of Weber and Durkheim, the successive stages in the differentiation of an autonomous field represented by "religion" as operating according to innerworldly rules, and as such a part of a more encompassing process of functional differentiation (see Chapter 2), has been unduly interpreted as correlated to an inexorable resilience of religion in general and its confinement to a private sphere in particular (Casanova, 1994, pp. 11–39).

The first serious attempts to test the taken-for-granted package of the secularization theory go back less than thirty years. By then the thesis of the inevitable decline of religion began to be unveiled as a corollary of the most radical versions of the modern intellectual distinction (see Chapter 2). Even more significant is that the idea itself of an encompassing secularization began to be seen as reflexively embedded in the sociology's own ideology as a tool of self-legitimation (see Robertson, 1971). Correspondingly, the historical variation of religion was recognized in a movement towards some sort of adaptive change, but not towards its outright disappearance (see Berger, 1969). Yet the immediate output of the revision was a theoretical reduction, with Luckmann's *Invisible Religion*, of the theory of secularization to the thesis of the privatization of religion (Luckmann, 1967).

We should recognize the importance of rescuing the theory of secularization as a broader theory of social differentiation in which the mutation of religion plays a crucial role (see Chapter 2). At the same time one should reject the claim of a generalized historical necessity of a decline of religion in modern societies, as this simply conflicts with the empirical evidence from recent trends from all over the world (Casanova 1994, p. 213). In this context, the privatization of religion thesis is still useful for comparing the Western and the Arab–Islamic paths in terms of the place of religion in the public sphere, or rather of the phenomenon of religion "going public". In fact, the specific influence of modern concepts of religion on the shaping of the "grand dichotomy" between a private sphere and a public one has remained largely unexplored (see Casanova, 1994 and Weintraub, 1996; see also Chapter 2).

What we can say with regard to Koranic hermeneutics is that a significant alteration in the meaning of all keywords directly or indirectly related to *din*, as in the relationship between *iman* and *islam* (see Chapter 1), has also produced a separation between two spheres of action based on a religious commitment. This transformation of *din* has impinged upon the traditional repertoire of keywords through a process of reduction and reification of their signification. It is clearly not the case of a drastic rupture or sharp distinction via a propagation of a fully "secularized" intellectual culture and science of nature. We have seen, however, how also in the Western case the sharp distinction is to a large extent an intellectual fiction resting on a marginalization of religion that does not do justice to its role in the modern breakthrough.

The sociological thesis of the privatization of religion acknowledges this as a process embedded in social differentiation, but does not formulate a normative standard for privatized religion to be converted into patterns of social action and public communication. The question to be raised in comparative perspective concerns the extent to which any conversion of a personalized or privatized religion into a tool of publicness or even into the symbolic axis of a framework of reference is compatible with a process of modern differentiation and intellectual distinction or instead betrays the premises of such processes. The first consideration concerns the claim of the basic inadmissibility of such a conversion which the liberal version of the private–public distinction propagates. This, in fact, is the view which has provided the classic, "mythological" version of the theory of secularization, spanning from the Enlightenment critique of religion to the grounding paradigm of sociology. If we recognize in the liberal objection one possible normative version of Western modernity among others, it can no longer aspire to the status of an unobjectionable social-scientific truth. Thus, the virtual absence of a liberal-individualist version in the endogenous trajectory of the Arab–Islamic path is no obstacle to a comparative assessment (see Chapter 2).

It is important, however, to take seriously the liberal position to the extent that it is still part of the self-understanding of many (though not necessarily all) Western modern states, most notably those determinantly shaped by the Enlightenment critique of religion. In this form, the scientific claims of the older theory of secularization are duly reduced to ideological tools serving a public religion of "secularism", as – in a Durkheimian mood – a functional religion of the community or the nation on its own, securing the necessary cohesion in the organization of modern societies (see Robertson, 1989, p. 14). This religion of secularism has been kept distinct – and developed by way of an intellectual distinction – from the religion based on God's transcendence, after the latter had been essentialized and confined to a private sphere. An important variant of public secular religion is the civil religion of American shape – as reconstructed by Robert Bellah (1970) – compounding a secularist liberal view of the separation of function with a Calvinist vision of a political community built on the covenant between God and believers (Casanova, 1994, p. 58).

More than a separation between politics and religion, this process reflects a distinction between different types of religion as well as between private and public spheres, a distinction functional to a normative blueprint of organization of a modern polity that envisages a smooth conversion of the believer into a loyal subject and later citizen, endowed with obligations and rights towards a state separated from any church, and holding the monopoly of political power. The view of an almost symmetrical division of functions in this liberal version of the private–public dichotomy obscures, however, the tense and dynamic, never completely normalized relationship between the dislocation of the sources of the moral order into a sphere of inwardness that is the source of a free reconstitution of religious communities, and the emergence of a public or civil religion as a modern form of community cult that helps to legitimize the modern state (cf. Casanova, 1994, pp. 45–8).

Little attention has been paid to the way a reformed, puritan or pietistic appropriation of religion has itself influenced public religion. While the contribution of the "Protestant ethic" to the privatization of religion has been carefully highlighted, its formative influence on the legitimation of a "secular" public space of social action has been mainly recognized as unfolding through oblique ways, by virtue of the interest of Protestant minorities in having an extra-confessional public religion. There is some historical evidence that the public religion has not always emerged through a mere spiritualization of community in the form of the state, but also through an upgrading of the potentialities of private ethic into a public ethos, a passage promoted by men of religion more than men of state (Maclear, 1992). On the other hand, the conversion of private religion into public politics was also performed through the critique of nonconformist sects towards a state considered unjust because it did not fulfil the duties inherent in its public function. As a result, the "deprivatization" of religion is a possible, legitimate option resulting directly from the dynamic tension between religious communities and community cults. This tension reflects the interaction, in modern societies, between the differentiated, changing field of religion based on the unfolding of models of subjectivities, and the systemic dimension of the polity's constitution along an axis linking society and state (Casanova, 1994, pp. 40–66).

The main difference between the Western and the Arab–Islamic historical paths is the less binding presence, in the second case, of a force-monopolizing entity demanding a special legitimation for itself (the modern state) in competition with a centralized instance of articulation of the Axial, cosmological and moral order (the Church), as happened in Christian Europe. Therefore, the discursive patterns of subjectification and reification have marked a landscape of civility and publicness not (or less) influenced by the need to shape a modern community cult suitable for the legitimation of the state. As a result, the constraint to formulate explicitly a dislocation of the tension between individual and society into two distinct but not fully dichotomic regions of experience like privateness and publicness, that imply one another, has been less compelling. It would be a mistake, however, to refuse to read through the mutation of signification and function of Koranic keywords in Islamic history a similar tension and a comparable development, characterized by a process of dualization, reduction, reification and functionalization of the terms used. At the present state of historical research, nobody can argue that processes of individualization of the sort constituting the civilizing process reconstructed by Norbert Elias (see Chapter 2) are completely alien to modern Islamic history (see Hofheinz, 1993).

It is true, nonetheless, that a full differentiation of an autonomous public sphere in Arab-Islamic societies was achieved only through the belated consolidation of the state under the indirect or direct influence of colonialism, in particular during the last two decades of the nineteenth century. The establishment of *islam* as the banner of the public function of religion, on the one hand, and as a major key to the definition of a consensus of communication on the other, was a direct offshoot of the recomposition of the indigenous intellectual field in response to colonialism and in the name of reformism (see Chapter 5). However, the articulation of the public side of the self, and the conceptualization itself that sustains the private–public dichotomy, have been in the Islamic case different from the Western model and largely impervious to the liberal paradigm.

We will see how it is possible to see many more affinities on the basis of the "republican" model and its view of privateness and publicness. More in general, in a comparative perspective, it is fairer and more fruitful to look at the public sphere and its dynamics pertaining to what has also been called "political society" (Weintraub, 1992), more than at any configuration of "civil society". This concept, which has become fashionable during recent years, is less suitable for a comparison since it has been too deeply influenced by the Western liberal-individualist tradition and conceived as the emanation of private relationships. The question will be, accordingly, not whether and to what extent a civil society has developed in Arab Muslim countries (for a standard negative answer, see Hall, 1995), but which categories of public communication might have fulfilled a role (similar to the concept of "civil society" as used in Western discourses, both liberal and communitarian) to account for the tension between individualization and social cohesion.

The only way to make a comparative view effective is by relativizing any concept of the polarization between private and public, and between individual and collective or the like. Any such concept should be considered as a socially immanent, normative view of the social order, or as a critique of the dominant one (Weintraub, 1996). This normative dialectic revolving around the "proper" view of the private–public dichotomy as the genetic code of social self and social system unfolds according to rules allowing a fluid passage from respecialization to despecialization of public intellectual functions. In other words, views of the public sphere are genuine products of an intellectual distinction but act as vehicles for conceptions of generalized citizenship: they fix the entitlement to act as a publicly engaged intellectual at least as part of the (reading) "public". In this way a normative concept of the public sphere, by virtue of its being a product of the social process, turns into an objectively functional condition of public communication and as such into a principle of structuration of modern polities. Citizenship is transformed from a normative claim into a principle of organization of political society. "Public sphere" is a necessary complement to "political society", in that it provides the latter with the indispensable infrastructure of discourse and deliberation.

Thus, a public sphere can function only on the basis of the assumption of a generalized specialization, that is in turn grounded on the consolidated metanarrative according to which *there is* a public space for discussion accessible to every citizen and that public communication is likely to influence the decisions of the political authority. The passage from "civil society" as characterized by a general sociability between atomized individuals, to a "political society" sustained by a diffuse sense of legitimate publicness is warranted by the modern intellectual concern for the present and for the welfare of the community (see Chapter 2). The public engagement in the name of religion, along with the sometimes implicit, sometimes explicit complement of an integrated, normative concept of the configuration of the private–public dichotomy and of its boundaries, is thoroughly functional to modern rules of public communication exercised in the name of an intellectual distinction, to the extent that it incorporates this metanarrative and helps to generalize citizenship and legitimize public discussion and deliberation.

In several cases within Arab–Islamic public spheres, Islamist positions come close to historic Western notions centred on so-called "republican virtue" as the engine of publicness. These views are often animated by religiously experienced forms of subjectivity and participation, and are critical of the reduction of public life to the interaction between the interests of atomized unities, as well as of the banishment of any moral criteria from the public sphere (cf. Casanova, 1994, p. 43). The historically fragile moral legitimation of Arab–Islamic nation-states, as well as of the corresponding public articulation of questions of common good, adds to the impetus of Islamist normative critiques of dominant institutionalizations of the private–public dichotomy. The long-term imperative of national liberation demanding of intellectuals an engagement without partisanship aggravates the general "irrelation to politics" of intellectuals at particularly critical historical junctures (cf. Roussillon, 1991, pp. 132–4). This trend places a comparative advantage on those views of publicness and social order which can dispense with "autonomous" political discourses, instead insisting on moral imperatives demanded by religion.

There is, however, a limitation to the presumption of a generalized specialization resulting from the construct of authorship and its rules. This limitation lies in the changing influence of an evolving media landscape. The author-function reproduces a respecialization constraint within the public sphere. Provided with adequate resources, both financial and in the form of "intellectual technology", receptivity can be converted into authorship, and hence new forms of specialization can emerge. The above-mentioned case of the new Islamic intellectuals is paradigmatic. Any emergence and major restructuration of a public sphere governed by a newly defined consensus of communication is dependent on the work of "professional" intellectuals who fulfil the "sufficient" conditions for that emergence, namely the skilled manipulation of reified concepts and their convenient reduction and combination into public discourses. Also an Islamic publicness can include a thriving multimedial mass-culture industry that is as alien to critical discussion and deliberation as any other such industry may be (Gonzales-Quijano, 1991).

In sum, even if we accept that the Arab–Islamic framework of reference has its endogenous roots in the eighteenth century, nobody would deny that it was definitively shaped, and provided a functioning public sphere, in the course of the following century as a "reaction" to the challenge of the colonial penetration. The 1860s witnessed massive European inroads into Egypt, and the emergence of critical journalism dates back to the following decade. It was further boosted by the British occupation in 1882. In this sense, it is true that in an Arab–Islamic context publicness has emerged through oblique ways. The still largely insufficient legitimation of the existing states, even after they have been taken over by indigenous élites, has reproduced this obliquity and has added to the Arab intellectuals' irrelation to politics.

The differentiation between necessary and sufficient conditions as between the rise of modern normativity and the emergence of modern discursivity, permits us to transcend the ahistorical question of whether Arab Muslim societies would have attained intellectual modernity along a basically endogenous path, without the West's encroachment upon their countries. On this basis, the opposition between the basically endogenous vs. exogenous character of the modern turn in the constitution of an Arab–Islamic framework of reference, as reflected by the controversy on the assessment of revivalist movements that were not merely induced by a Western challenge, becomes obsolete. What it is important to bear in mind is that the very public activation of an Arab–Islamic framework of reference automatically implied its embeddedness in the new transcultural space characterized by partly colliding, partly converging, certainly imbalanced essentializing processes between the "West" and "Islam" (see Chapter 4).

The result of the hybridization of exogenous impulses and endogenous dynamics has been that in Arab–Islamic countries the public sphere has never definitively coincided with the form of the nation-state, because the latter has been incapable of polarizing the ultimate loyalties (though its apparatus holds the strongest means of reward and punishment). The public sphere tends instead to expand well beyond its boundaries towards the flexible but identifiable borders of an Arab–Islamic framework of reference. To condense this situation into a formula, we can say that this framework reflects a combination of a strong public sphere transcending state-national boundaries, and weak nation-states.

To recapitulate, by keeping the conceptualization of the modern turn within these "minimalist" terms, it is not difficult to conceive of an Arab–Islamic version of such a breakthrough which differs from the Western one: first, for the weaker impact (though not absence) of processes of modern state formation, due to the too lengthy erosion of the power balance between centres and peripheries; second, and probably subordinately, for the "belatedly" Axial (hence from the beginning more self-reified) character of Islam; third, for the lower level of hierarchization of cultural brokerage; and last, for the dynamics of colonialism and neocolonialism. As a result, the intellectual distinction in Arab–Islamic modernity discounts at the outset, compared with the Western model, the lack of a sharp and spectacular break. This is due to the fact that "in Islam, and only in Islam, purification/modernization on the one hand, and the reaffirmation of a putative old *local* identity on the other, can be done in one and the same language and set of symbols." (Gellner, 1981, p. 5). Whereas in the Arab–Islamic case the postulation and validation of social order *can* be grounded on a reified view of *islam*, the Western model is characterized by the need to shape a fully new and entirely mundanized domain of reference called "society" (see Chapter 2).

The specificity of the Arab–Islamic case and of its historical conditions has to be checked against the "paradigm of fundamentalism". This has been increasingly employed over the last two decades not only in order to classify contemporary Islamist movements and thinkers, but also to explain the evolution of certain forms of public discourse within an Arab–Islamic framework of reference. The reactivist constraint embedded in the emergence of the framework might have produced a sort of "fundamentalist trap", by giving a boon to fundamentalist articulations of the framework. This success is reflected in the popularity of forms of reification and specification of *islam* such as in the formula *islam din wa-dawla* (roughly translated as "Islam is religion and state": but see also below). Its first documented presence in the Arab Middle East goes back to the formative phase of a space of public communication during the end of last century. Even before, the similar expression *din-ü-devlet* (where *islam* was implicitly present as the object to predicate) has been used in the Ottoman literature of "political advice" at least since the end of the seventeenth century (Aksan, 1993). It expressed the idea of the concrete manifestation of the order based on the *shari'a* and the actual laws. The passage from such a use of the concept in the centre of the Ottoman empire – where the existing power configuration was taken for granted and the stake was given by the perceived need of administrative, and later constitutional reforms – to a use, in some Arab regions of the empire, that increasingly exalted a normative-utopian impulse through an explicit, and markedly reified reference to *islam* as *din wa-dawla*, has not yet been elucidated.[9] It is clear only that the slogan acquired a particular prominence after the demise of the Caliphate in Istanbul between 1922 and 1924, and in particular from the 1930s, especially through the socio-political activism of new, organized Islamist groups like the Egyptian Muslim Brotherhood (see Ayubi, 1991, p. 123).

There is more than one possible reading of this formula, and the major difficulty lies in establishing in which phase it is legitimate to situate the genesis of one particular interpretation. The basic structure of the slogan reflects a reification of Islam followed by its predication, consisting in stating, almost programmatically, what Islam ought to consist of in social reality. In order to interpret the formula properly, we should recall the problem of the historical differentiation of the meaning of *din* (see Chapter 1).

If *dawla* remains rather stable, from the end of last century, in representing the "state" as the vertical dimension of social organization, the shifting meaning of *din* is the variable responsible for the changing meaning of the entire formula. Careful investigations into the transformation of the meaning of both the slogan as a whole and of *din* in it should help to illustrate the relationship between the shaping of the formula and the turn-of-the-century discourse of *islah* performed by the first generation of intellectualized *'ulama'* (see Chapter 5). Pending such studies, we can dare an interpretation of the formula according to which *din* ("religion") seeks, by projecting itself into the public sphere, to appropriate the denied level of the *dawla*. This projection is sought from a dimension where *din* has been "fundamentalized", i.e. individually appropriated through personal engagement in the interpretation of Scriptures and the shaping of an ethic of life conduct. If there is any analytically useful meaning in the much used and abused term "fundamentalism", and any sense in relating the main Islamist slogan to it, it is in its positing the *din* – as the grounding horizon for the attribution of sense and value that is private to the individual believer and social actor (cf. Asad, 1993, p. 216) – as the sacred standard for redeeming the social and public spaces of human interaction, through controlling the discursive sources of legitimation of the vertical dimension of community organization.

Thus, the agitation of *islam din wa-dawla* has affirmed a capacity to invest the public arena with a category loaded with mobilization power, and reflecting feelings of alienation from the existing, colonial or post-colonial, state, which it is no longer possible to settle through mechanisms of social integration and intellectuals' co-optation. In this sense, what one calls Islamism is the result of a combination between a "fundamentalist" private ethic and a "republican" public ethos. The fragility of the "liberal age" (Hourani, [1962] 1983), and related socio-political arrangements and intel-lectual trends, in Arab societies encouraged a radical-republican contestation of its order through merging a fundamentalist reading of tradition and utopian calls appealing to the republican virtue of Muhammad's Medina. Is this a vision of citizenship writ Islamic, of authority without domination, a stateless grace for the *umma*? Existing states are often overstepped and publicness is reconstructed at a sub-state as well as at an interstate level.

It is therefore necessary to dilute the most extreme reactivist inter-pretation of the slogan. This is grounded on the view that since "secular" intellectuals began to invoke a separation of temporal and spiritual powers, thereby reflecting the standard Western political discourse of modernity (whose undue translation in Arabic and in terms of the Arab–Islamic historical experience almost automatically, but quite incorrectly, condenses into the claim to keep distinct *dawla* and *din*: see al-Jabiri, 1982, pp. 59–76), Islamically-oriented thinkers responded by claiming their unity. Beyond this mechanistic reading, it is possible to read *din* as a keyword able, at the modern turn, to enhance all the potential signification incorporated in the Koranic word in terms of a cumulation of the systemic and the personal dimensions of faith (see Chapter 1), and to see this meaning as finally transposed onto a level of social action, by way of the upgrading of a "private" ethical commitment to a tool for moralizing public life and restructuring social order.

In this way *din* begins to adumbrate the idea of "people", of "we" (Schulze, 1992a, p. 115), thereby substantiating the anti-establishment, social self that seeks unity with the *dawla*, the state, in order to become rule.[10] The most interesting aspect is that the preliminary reification of Islam has been fertilized by its subjectification, thus combining the two basic generating axes of modern political discourse, and producing a sort of Islamic justification of citizenship (Schulze, 1993, p. 89). It is difficult to state with precision at which stage this process of fertilization might have become theoretically mature, but it is certain that with the late writings of the Islamist thinker Sayyid Qutb (1906–66) the element of subjectification acquired a marked prominence (see Chapter 10). It is through this process that the invocation of *shari'a*, whilst keeping its abstract character, becomes a formidable tool in the public discursive arena for asserting *din*'s primacy in society along with God's sovereignty, *hakimiyyat Allah* (or, significatively, simply *hakimiyya*).

In this sense, Islamism should be grasped in more subtle terms than as a mere politicization of religion. Its political relevance is not in the purpose to take over the state, but in the redefinition of the sources themselves of political legitimation within society as well as of the model of citizenship within it. Islamism reflects a synthesis between the patterns of constitution of a new socially engaged subjectivity that was typical of the revivalist movements mentioned earlier in this chapter, and the competence to act in the public sphere through the agitation of reified categories, that is the heritage of the "reformist" turn at the end of last century. Central to Islamism are the understanding and use of *islam* and related keywords within the modern, long-term formation of an Islamic metanarrative of public communication, where references to *sunna* often stand for the subjective, and to *shari'a* for the systemic dimension of civil life and normative discourse.

It is clear, however, that the Islamist invocation of an "Islamic state" through the symbolically powerful medium of the call for the implementation of *shari'a* entails an element of radical utopianism and of irrelation to the immanent rules of the political system: within this impulse, the concept of *shari'a* surrogates the lack of constitutional guarantees in the legitimation of political community in existing Arab Muslim states. There is no inherent contradiction between the calls for enforcing *shari'a* and the constitutional process, but rather an irreducible historical tension that is due more to the authoritarian shell of the existing states (and the Islamist alienation from them) than to their allegedly secularist outlooks. This tension is at odds with the Habermasian view of a necessary convergence between dynamics of public discussion and deliberation and constitutional guarantees (Habermas, 1992a), and makes "Islamic publicness" a problematic tool for the political democratization of Arab societies (cf. Büttner, 1991). However, this mismatch does not necessarily suppress the deliberative rationality of public communication in Islamic terms, but rather places a higher stake on it as a source of legitimation of new types of public discourse and their paths of institutionalization into autonomous spheres of social action and civil associationism, *ergo* independently of the existing states (Ben Néfissa-Paris, 1992 and Sullivan, 1994). These processes do not necessarily result in the consolidation of the relationship between "state" and "civil society", but often encourage dynamics of social secession (Schulze, 1994, pp. 245–61) or of self-encapsulation of traditional and new community aggregations. In a certain sense, authoritarian and arbitrary rule is in itself a hindrance to the chance of analysing such processes through the application of the category of civil society (Zubaida, 1992 and Krämer, 1992).

Ultimately, the Islamist slogan *islam din wa-dawla* displays presuppositions quite different from the Western concept of civil society. Yet this slogan is grounded on a comparable tension between individually appropriated authenticity and the impulse to justify or reconstruct the community. It is indeed incompatible with the liberal-individualist tradition, but can be compared with the tentative reconciliations performed in either the *étatiste* Hegelian or in the utopian Marxian terms (see Chapter 2). More generally, dynamics of social differentiation and intellectual distinction are common in both the "Western" and the "Arab–Islamic" paths of access to modernity, though the spectrum of their reflexive, theoretical and discursive outcomes is obviously different. As a result, the negation of a dimension of civility in Islam and in particular in the modern and contemporary history of Arab Muslim societies is analytically untenable. Rather, the transcultural dynamics between the "West" and "Islam" must be examined. This negation is the product of the unequal game of opposing essentialisms between these two constructed entities.

NOTES

1   The number of historians basing their work on such hypotheses has been growing since the late 1970s. Without attempting to be exhaustive, one can mention Rudolf Peters, who embodies a moderate position with regard to the possibility of a sharp modern intellectual breakthrough (Peters, 1984), thereby contesting the radical, intentionally provocative stance of Schulze (Peters, 1990), and Edmund Burke III, who has been working on the history of Middle Eastern protest movements since 1750 (see Burke, 1988, p. 26). According to Judith Tucker, if not (or not yet) of a current, we should speak of a "generation of historians" who, though belonging to different schools or traditions, are all motivated by "the criticism of the Orientalist version of the region – particularly of its essentialist and ahistorical aspects" (Tucker, 1990, p. 210).

2   The leading Muslim thinker Muhammad Iqbal used to consider Wahhabism as the first pulsation of life in modern Islam (Roff, 1987, p. 34), whereas the French Orientalist Massignon saw in the Wahhabis "the first of those who worked together towards the Arab renaissance" (Merad, 1978, p. 143).

3   It might appear contradictory to juxtapose the neo-Sufi phenomenon to the Hanbali Wahhabi movement, on the grounds of the presumed radical anti-Sufi hostility of Hanbalism. George Makdisi (1979) has shown the extent to which this is in no way a general rule, since the two currents have in common a strong emphasis on a personal and direct approach to the Koran. Moreover, he has pointed out that the rejection of Sufism by the Hanbali scholar Ibn Taymiyya (see Chapter 1) is a myth: not only is it impossible to find any attack by him against Sufism as such, but he "was himself a Sufi" (p. 121).

4   The tension between the communal and the universal element is given by the fact that the values and norms defining membership in the community entail a vision of the "world" and a constraint to define it. This is the main reason why a modern framework of reference differs deeply from a traditional self-understanding of a virtually closed community. Moreover, the vision of solidarity between the members of a community according to a modern framework has to be based, at least partly, on a universally valid definition of values and norms.

5   A recent, excellent example of the application of this revisionist perspective to the universe of neo-Sufism is in a Sudanese case-study (Hofheinz, 1993).

6   This label is used by Nikki Keddie (1994) and John Voll ([1982] 1994), stressing the impulse of these movements to revive the virtues of Muhammad's *umma*.

7   The unusual term "publicness" is here adopted as the least free translation of the German *Öffentlichkeit*, otherwise translated as "public sphere" or "public space". In using "publicness", my intention is to preserve a sense of abstraction that is central in both the normative-Habermasian and the

functional meanings of *Öffentlichkeit*, and that is incorrect, or at least hasty, to endow immediately with a sense of social spatialness as in the common translations. In one authoritative essay both "public sphere" and "publicness" are used as virtual synonyms for *Öffentlichkeit*, even in alternation with "publicity" (Calhoun, 1992). However, I prefer to exploit the manifoldness of English public-related words and refer to "public sphere" as a particular, discursively mediated, deliberative dimension of publicness at large (for a similar, if implicit, differentiation, see Warner, 1992).

8 This thorough sociocultural transformation, dating back to the 1960s, is currently the subject of a new research project on "Islamic publicness in Egypt" conducted by this author. This project dwells on the interaction between subjectification and reification in the genesis of new Islamic forms of public discourse and public display more deeply than the present work – concerned as it is with the transcultural dimension of communication along with its inexorably reifying dynamics – is able to do (see Salvatore, 1995a).

9 It is evident that the formula *islam din wa-dawla* is forged on the same matrix of the older formula *islam din wa-dunya* or *dunya wa-din*, whose origin is not less difficult to determine. Sometimes the two slogans are merged, as in the formula of the three "D"s: *islam din, dunya wa-dawla*.

10 One could even observe a linguistic similarity with the intellectually shaped concept of *Volksstaat* in early nineteenth-century Germany, which marked the making of a German framework of communal reference (also a "belated" one).

PART II

THE EMERGENCE OF TRANSCULTURAL DYNAMICS

CHAPTER 4

The "West" and "Islam": opposing essentialisms in an imbalanced game

We should now look at the constants and variables in the operation itself of defining and predicating "Islam" in the era following the consolidation of a colonial situation in Arab Muslim lands. This analysis must be placed in a historical perspective and must take account of the particular transcultural constraints emanating from the uneven game of opposing essentialisms between the "West" and "Islam". It is necessary to approach the problem through a preliminary unearthing of the basic terrain for any effort to interpret and reconstruct Islam. In this sense, my attempt to distance myself from the interpretive and definitional game does not result in a sceptical or deconstructionist evaluation of Islam as a purely pretended unitary entity, that does not do justice to the high variability of practices and inter-pretations within Muslim cultural settings. I will rather try to explain why a plurality of grass-roots, practical, "sub-intellectual" cultures lead to the intellectually mediated emergence of "Islam" as a powerful medium of collective identity.

The specific problem in the analysis of the formation of such a "generic Islam" is that it is the product of a transcultural game between different variants of both the Western and the Islamic path to intellectual modernity, comparatively examined in Part I. The genesis and the evolution of such a dimension of interaction, and how it acquired "transcultural"[1] properties, has to be approached directly in Part II of this work, since its concrete shape and evolution through history is crucial for understanding what kind of influence it had on the formation of an Arab–Islamic collective identity taking the form of a framework of communal reference and universal projection (see Chapter 3).

In order to construct such a framework, the intellectual distinction always needs an external Other. In the Western case, the view of the Islamic "Orient", and the process itself of its "orientalization", has been crucial for defining the Western path of modernity. The uniqueness of Western modernity can be properly assessed only by reference to another uniqueness, represented by Islamic history, and this not merely because of affinities or "neighbourship", but on the basis of the transcultural dynamics emanating from these. The origin of a transcultural dimension goes back to the second half of the last century, when defining "Islam" as a reified ideological system, or as a framework of communal reference, became a major concern for both Western (Orientalist) *and* Islamic authors.

Beyond the oversimple distortion of the "reactivist" model of reconstruction of modern Arab–Islamic history (see Chapter 3), it is evident that the overall scenario of Arab intellectual endeavours is the "encounter" with the West. The distinctive properties of the transcultural space between the "West" and "Islam" at a mature stage of evolution are phenomena of meaning's merging between the two sides of the space, up to the point when the location of the original source of a certain signification is either no longer possible, or has become irrelevant. I consider the emergence of the transcultural properties of the communicative space between the "West" and "Islam" as the consequence of a long process that reached its crucial phase after the zenith of classic European Orientalism, first with Weber's study of Islam in the context of his comparative sociology, and later with the crisis of the resulting "Weberism" (see Chapter 6).[2]

The making of a generic "Islam" is therefore strictly dependent on the making of the "West". The joint construction of the West and Islam through transcultural dynamics is the result of the imbalanced interaction between two differents paths of essentialization, the one more offensive, the other constrained to a quite defensive stance, yet both grounded on the same kind of intellectual distinction comparatively analysed in Part I. There is a proto-essentialist dimension of "otherization" between Axial religions/ civilizations and in particular between Abrahamic faiths that is performed according to criteria that are typical of Occidental Axiality, as they result in strategies to exclude the rival faith from the universal consensus. It is an otherization that directly derives from what I have called the "politics of beyond" (see Chapter 1; see also Turner, 1994, p. 105). Essentialism proper, however, emerges with the staging of the "politics of behind", based on a dualist horizon inscribed in this world and sustained by the construction of "inwardness" (see Chapter 2). Western and Arab–Islamic essentializing models differ in power and modalities to the extent they have displayed diverse patterns of secularization-distinction both before and (even more profoundly) after their physical encounter inaugurated by the European colonial encroachment on the Arab world.

In the Western path of essentializing Islam, it is not by chance, remembering Montesquieu, that the question "How can one be a Persian?", reflecting a sense of amazement towards the inexplicable otherness of non-Westerners, was first posed in the context of the Enlightenment (see Bourricaud, 1987, pp. 14–15). Here we can see how what is called essentialism is indispensable to the making of a modern distinction that cannot exhaust itself in its reference to an *ancien régime* or to a backward culture or class structure, but requires a game of exclusion in universal terms, of confrontation with an ultimate type of otherness. The making of one's own communal reference and universal projection has to be made through a negative reference to *another* universe. The transcultural dimension has its roots in this paradox of two opposing "universes". The focus on this game of opposing essentialisms finalized to construct and legitimate patterns of uniqueness risks obscuring the local variety and mobility of identity references, as well as the diversity of intellectual traditions. It is interesting, however, to analyse how, when and why such reductions are formalized, and how they became powerful discursive constraints. The relevance of the frameworks at stake is of a markedly formal nature, as they claim validity precisely through a game of reciprocal reference by virtue of distinction.

The label essentialism is used here to designate the cognitive modalities generated during the emergence of the intellectual distinction and of one of its main products, the ability to shape frameworks of communal reference and universal projection. The term essentialism as applied to cross-cultural knowledge normally stresses the (over)simplifying aspect of a cognitive process. My perspective, instead, focuses on the opposite dimension, on its being a product of social differentiation and intellectual distinction. I consider essentializing procedures as starting at a level of sophistication where the need for distinction enters a dimension of hermeneutic dispersion of the kind illustrated in Chapter 2. The role played by an "essence" in the modern intellectual mode of thinking is, in a first approximation, that of delimiting the field and the scope of the domestication of the Other. This enterprise entails selecting and collecting proof in the form of "sources" which, being disparate, have to be reduced to a common denominator. On the contrary, "defensive" ethnocentrism does not depend on these constraints, and does not need to play with essences, as the substance of the problem of defining identity is virtually given along lines dictated by an "inside–outside" polarization, not subject to frequent change and hermeneutic dispersion. Of course, the beginning of the game of essentializing Islam goes back to the European Middle Ages, as that epoch saw the beginnings of the creation of a Christian-European self-understanding. But as long as communication across the two cultural-religious universes was not institutionalized, the task of defining the Other was almost automatically given by the "primordial" impulse of drawing boundaries, and did not need to engage in any truly essentializing game.

If an ethnocentric view is quite common, as part of the game of stabilizing identities, the intellectual practice of essentializing should be assessed as typical of a modern self-understanding. Essentialism is a tool for exerting control that develops in parallel to both a process of "subjectification" and of emergence of "reifying" attitudes (on this link, see Chapters 2 and 3). The resulting intellectual version of ethnocentric imagery is always expressed by a mixture of strivings of domestication and fears of contamination, whose final product is the elaboration of a specific, and mostly ambiguously "technical" vocabulary essentializing the Other. What Said has called "imaginative geography" (Said, 1978, p. 49) was in fact a sophisticated practice of control: the product of the new essentialist attitude was the orientalization of that "world" where another Abrahamic religion informed or at least legitimized models of life conduct and social norms, a world situated south and east of Christian Europe, previously a target of attention and study within the limits of doctrinal and dogmatic polemics. "Orient", "Near Orient" (later "Near" and/or "Middle East") are constructs incorporating a much higher level of abstraction than the fragmentary, distance-taking, and strictly instrumental knowledge produced on Islam by medieval Europe.

Essentialism proper cannot be reduced to an outright instrumentalization of the Other: it is rooted in the specific construction of "inwardness" (German: *Innerlichkeit*)[3] as the outcome of processes of subjectification ushering in, first, the differentiation of a field of religion and, then, a modern intellectual breakthrough (see Chapter 2). Georg Stauth has showed that at least in the case of German Orientalism, that is significant for its influence on Max Weber (see Chapter 6), the process of defining inwardness as an autonomous source was complete only with Romanticism. This movement reacted to the too straightforward identification of the intellectual distinction with public engagement performed via the Enlightenment, and to the sense of lack of relevance generated by the accompanying "irrelation to politics" (see Chapter 2). From then on, the weakness of the intellectual affirmation of the rationality of public discussion and deliberation was matched and balanced by an appeal to inwardness much more compatible with the rules of *realpolitik*.

It is within the tension between the claim to publicness and the appeal to inwardness that a new sense of order integrating the intellectual distinction in the modernity of bureaucracy and science came into being. In the course of the nineteenth century inwardness became professionalized through the institutionalization of the academy: in this way, a socialized inwardness produced a new ethic of public responsibility, through which the professional intellectual succeeded in easing the frustration generated by the utopian burden of the claim to publicness. A crucial medium of this rescue process was the blueprint of a "universalization of Europe", harmonizing the two tasks of understanding the world and dominating it (cf. Stauth, 1993, pp. 28–31). Colonialism was the apt world-political context that provided the institutionalized inwardness of intellectual work with the figurative objectivation necessary to its relevance-seeking.

The essentialization of the culturally Other is thereby a function of the stabilization and systematization of inwardness: the idea of a world that has to be made sense of through the universal application of the European sense of inwardness (both as a tool and as a standard of evaluation) helps to keep alive the modern fiction of an unfolding subjectivity. Inwardness becomes a systemic function, the crucial link between subject and system. The institutionalization of intercultural studies as most prominently in the case of Orientalism (the study of a civilization of the text, i.e. Islam, performed by another civilization of the text, i.e. European, later Western Christianity, or simply the West) designs a field of transcultural exchange, regulated by the European adoption of inwardness as the criterion for judging the path of inwardness of another *Kulturreligion* (pp. 42–3).

Essentialism is not limited to the cases where the essence is externalized, but is also at work when the search for an essence is kept within the implicit claim to the universal validity of the method chosen, as in a social-scientific perspective. In other words: an interpretive approach, like the classic Orientalist one, places the essence ("Islam" as the antithesis of the "West") very visibly in the middle of the argumentation, while patterns of explanation focusing on structural factors conceal the essence in the definition of the variables, and particularly of the independent ones, which emanate from the Western self-understanding via historically successful conceptual patterns. In both cases, the essence is constituted by how the Self (the "West") is constructed. The critique of Orientalism has regularly produced indictments of the first, classic case of interpretive essentialism (see already Abdel-Malek, 1963) as explicitly revolving around the ahistorical essence of "Islam". The completion of this criticism through the recognition that "Islam" merely derives from the construction of the "West" (Said, 1978), has not yet led to a recognition of the degree to which this construction is also determinant in the second, more sociologically-oriented model of essentialism. Essentialism always reflects a primacy of the essence as an emanation of processes of subjectification bound to procedures of intellectual distinction. The inconclusive character of the Orientalism debate that followed the publication of

Said's book (1978) is probably due to the tendential equation between Orientalism and essentialism, as well as to the desperate effort to go beyond Orientalism by suppressing essentialism.

One can of course object that this second kind of essentialism, which we might classify as "explanatory", is no real essentialism, but only a methodological perspective influenced by a fair degree of ethnocentrism. My definition of essentialism, however, depends on conceiving the essence not necessarily as an entity with a given name, but as the product of a cognitive mechanism for the reductive constitution of a discipline's object on the basis of subjective concerns (see Foucault, 1966). It is a "maximalist" definition of essentialism that fits well a minimalist definition of intellectual modernity as consisting of the construction of frameworks of reference (see Chapters 2 and 3): modernity as the "act" or "process", essentialism as its cognitive "tool". Essentialism is the result of the reciprocal knowledge, definition and cognitive domestication which take place between cultural universes capable of producing, at some time in history, and by virtue of inner impulses or external stimulation (or a combination of both), frameworks of universal reference. A prominent example of this phenomenon is the game of opposing essentialisms which has constituted such entities as the "West" and "Islam".

Let us look more directly at how essentialism works. Essentializing Islam from a Western perspective is not to damn it (as in the medieval attitude) but to state the extent to which it came close to the Western path of rationalization and universalization but was finally excluded from it. This evaluation may result either in a positive or a negative attitude to Islam (it was positive indeed, or at least ambivalent, in the case of such different thinkers as Hume, Voltaire, Goethe, Herder and Nietzsche). However, what is mostly relevant is that in both cases the essentializing procedures conform to the same logic: that any potential discourse of sameness in the comparison between Islam and Western Christianity almost invariably turns into a discourse of difference, though for variable ends (Turner, 1994, p. 46). This is most visible in the case of Carl H. Becker, the Heidelberger islamologist who had probably the strongest impact on Weber's view of Islam. It is remarkable how he transformed the most outspoken recognition of the commonalities between European Christianity and Islam, as well as of their comparability as civilizations, into a discourse of opposition between Oriental despotism, that was allegedly crucial to Islam's consolidation even in doctrinal terms, and Western civility (Stauth, 1993, pp. 177–8).

However, if we want to trace the roots of this discourse of difference back to a time that precedes the academic consolidation of Orientalism, most significative is the case of Friedrich Hegel, who first constructed Islam in general historical terms as a unitary cultural force (thereby determinantly preparing its reification by way of nineteenth-century Orientalism), and then denied it the capability of engaging in a process of subjectivity-formation, that remained thereby a Western Christian monopoly. Remarkable is how Hegel justifies his vision of Islam on the basis of the concept of the absolute unity of God affirmed by the Koran: a procedure that was to have a major impact on Max Weber and, through him, on the late-classic Orientalism of Gustave von Grunebaum (see Chapter 7) that represents the first ring of the hermeneutic chain of "political Islam" that I will examine (Stauth, 1993, pp. 112–13). As a result, the transcultural space was opened up, from the stronger, Western viewpoint, via an arc stretching from Hegel, through the zenith of classic Orientalism represented by Ignaz Goldziher and Carl H. Becker, to the comparative sociology of religion of Max Weber. The Heidelberger sociologist operated an upgrading of the strategies of essentialization through a formal recognition of the prism of identity-alterity, of similarities and divergencies between different world religions. The result was a definition of the deficits of the Other in terms of subjectivity, civility and modern rationality (see Chapter 6).

The basic Orientalist argument, which had an immediate impact on Weber's view of Islam, was that the rise of this cultural-religious unit rested on tribalism (an element which posed severe limits to universalist potentialities), and that its consolidation succeeded by virtue of a reappropriation of historically available patterns of "Oriental despotism" (thereby jeopardizing the development of civil society). What has been called the neo-Orientalist paradigm (see Chapter 1) accepts (and indeed refines) the first thesis but reverses the second. Thus, it opens up the possibility of seeing elements of civility in Islamic history, but finally tends to negate them as the question of the relationship between society and state in Islamic history is solved by asserting that there could not be a civil society where there was no modern state. This assessment did not pay enough attention to subjectivity-formation and self-control as the sources of civility, subsumed by Norber Elias under the label of "civilizing process". This can be variably associated with different paths of state formation that have not necessarily to correspond to their "strong", exemplary version represented by few Western European cases. The main line of continuity of Orientalism is precisely in the refusal to problematize the relationship between individualization, society and state formation following Eliasian canons. This makes it possible to deny Islam a search for a hidden truth, the "politics of behind", that only grounds subjectivity, and that in Western European cases is strictly connected to processes of state formation (see Chapter 2). As Stauth has pregnantly pointed out, the continuity of any form of, however sociologized, Orientalism or also sociology of Islam is given by the view that in the Islamic case "the truth consists precisely in the acceptance of ritual and not in its essentialization". Truth is no more than simulation: there is no hidden essence to be searched for (Stauth, 1993, pp. 196–7).

In sum, one should recognize that the instrumental character of Orientalism is not so immediate and crude as the mid-1960s' critique of Orientalism began to adumbrate, by seeing its crisis as deriving almost automatically from the dawn of colonialism (Abdel-Malek, 1963, p. 109; see also Chapter 7). It is true that the academic consolidation of Orientalism at the beginning of the nineteenth century, paralleled by European colonial enterprises in Muslim lands (epitomized by Napoleon's occupation of Egypt and the pervasive scholarly undertaking of the *Description de l'Egypte*), appeared to reflect a symbiotic exchange between political–economic interests and academic scholarship, one major theme of Said's *Orientalism*.[4] But the long phase of what we can call "proto-Orientalism", spanning from the sixteenth to the eighteenth centuries (to which too little attention has been devoted by scholars interested in the history of Orientalism), would seem to demonstrate that the paths of instrumentalization are much less direct, and probably situated within the broader process of the emergence of intellectual modernity as sustained by a "will of distinction" (see Chapter 2). As we have seen, this is particularly evident in the analysis of the genesis and development of German Orientalism (Stauth, 1987 and 1993), that Said consciously neglected (Said, 1978, p. 18).[5]

For these reasons, we cannot accept that the game of distinction towards the Orient became ineluctably monodirectional in the wake of the institutionalization of its study during the nineteenth century, thereby engendering a stable representation of Islam as the contrastive image to a Western identity in the making. The use of the Islamic Orient by non-Orientalist thinkers of the century became even more open to the contingencies of actual political agenda or, more generally, of the sense of a civilizational crisis. It has been suggested that from Montesquieu to J.S. Mill and Toqueville, the Orient, through the analytically odd concept of "Oriental despotism", was used as a foil to produce a discourse on the difficult process of transition, in Western Europe, from Enlightened despotism to mass democracy, a discourse concerned with protecting liberal values and political leadership. On the other hand, Nietzsche constructed Islam as the countertype to the long-term Christian dialectic of resentment culminating in ascetic Protestantism, the embodiment of an active, masculine principle opposed to the allegedly reactive, resentful and life-repressing impetus of Christianity (Turner, 1994, pp. 96–9).

It cannot be denied that Orientalism consists of a set of essentializing practices and institutions with very distinctive features. Western uniqueness is in this case supported by the material power that Europe has acquired and exercised upon Arab Muslim territories since the beginning of last century. The absence of an Occidentalist equivalent of Western academic Orientalism is, however, no proof against the existence of more or less standardized intellectual practices of essentialization on the Islamic side, obviously taking no neatly mirror-like attitude to the "West", due to the power asymmetry between both sides: an imbalance due to their diverging capacities to select and control the "sources" for making sense of the Other, as well as to elaborate appropriate techniques for their scrutiny.

It is debatable whether, when and how in the Arab–Islamic world an interest in knowing, delimiting, cognitively domesticating Christian Europe arose that was modern to the extent that it was characterized by the kind of projectuality and sense of involvement that is typical of intellectual procedures of essentialization. A direct consideration of these practices cannot be an objective of the present work. It is clear, nonetheless, that after the turn in the power balance that took place between the end of the eighteenth and the beginning of the nineteenth centuries, the modalities of relational essentialism were destined to differ deeply in rationale and format among the two "universes".[6] The Arab–Islamic model of essentialism has consequently been made defensive, and the corresponding consensus of communication restricted, because of the consolidation of a colonial situation and the active intervention of Orientalists in defining the limits of this consensus. Both developments were responsible for a radical breakdown in the lines of tradition of Muslim thought that must be located between the 1870s and 1880s (see Schulze, 1994, pp. 31–2).

The delegitimation of indigenous Muslim intellectual traditions jeopardized their capacity to appropriate modernity selectively but reflexively, as in the work of the Egyptian al-Tahtawi (1801–71), matured in the positivist climate of the first two-thirds of the nineteenth century. The breakdown became tangible in the crude way the surplus in the technologization of order and meaning vehicled by the encroaching Europe engendered a view of "Oriental" disorder and lack of institutions in societies where the spirit of social and intellectual reform was not absent, but feeble if compared to the sharp patterns of modern distinction of the West (cf. Mitchell, 1988, pp. 58–9). Since then, any attempt at rejuvenating Muslim thought had to be related either to European modernity through the agitation of the keyword of *nahda* ("renaissance"), or to the formative period of Islam, on the basis of the concept of *islah* ("reform"), or to a blend of both (see Chapter 5). In either case, any attempt to state an Arab–Islamic position towards modernity as represented by Enlightenment, Romanticism and Positivism was forced to make use of European categories and accordingly hindered from retrieving innovative developments in Islamic traditions that had unfolded during the immediately previous centuries, and in particular the seventeenth and the eighteenth.

The transcultural dimension has a virtually foundational value in the process of construction of an Arab–Islamic consensus of communication, as it intervenes on an endogenous process of reification of Islamic categories at a still immature stage of evolution of the underlying patterns of intellectual distinction (see Chapters 3 and 5). In Egypt the emergence of a constitutional movement relying on an increasingly autonomous public sphere during the 1870s was no truly endogenous development but one embedded in the critical relationship between autocratic modernizing rule and increasing financial and political vulnerability to the influence of European powers. These were much more keen to reduce and control the power of the Khedive than any Egyptian social group. On the other hand, the first boost in the political press was supported by the Khedive himself and addressed against European control and, after 1882, British domination. Only gradually "resentment against strong foreign influence was transformed into resentment of the ruler" (Vatikiotis, 1991, p. 165), and the press began "to concern itself with the public debate of social, economic and political issues" (p. 180).

As a result, the timing and modalities of the reification of Islamic key-words in public communication could no longer accord with endogenous dynamiçs, but had to bow to the transcultural constraints dictated by the stronger Western essentialization. It is symptomatic that *islam* appears only in titles of books written by the most famous Arab Muslim intellectual of reformist leaning of that time, Muhammad 'Abduh, in two responses to outside attacks on Muslim civilization (Smith, 1962b, p. 499). More in general, in the period from the 1880s to the First World War, approximately half of the books with *islam* in their titles are either translations of French works, or written by non-Muslim Arab authors, or written in response to external challenges against "Islam" (pp. 500–1). The conclusion can be drawn that through the consolidation of transcultural dynamics between the "West" and "Islam" the originally endogenous process of reification of the latter (see Chapter 1) became ineluctably heteronomous and no longer in pace with its subjectification. As a side-effect, Western Orientalists gained increasing legitimation for their view according to which Islam *as such* is the vehicle of a communal ethos and a collective identity that are, nonetheless, virtually devoid of any subjective labour comparable to the modern Western one.

To recapitulate: the transcultural dynamics between the two universes of the "West" and "Islam" is a unique phenomenon. It consists of the way in which a strongly internalized (Western) idea of religion, additionally refined through the paradigm of sociology (see Chapter 6), becomes the standard of evaluation of a less internalized and still quite diffuse, yet not undifferentiated (Muslim) idea of religion. At a mature stage of development, reached after the spread of a "Weberist" paradigm (see Chapter 6), this transcultural dynamic will be governed by an even more restricted reference to "rationality" as the quintessence of inwardness (Stauth, 1993, p. 51). It is through these processes that the Western concept of "religion", in conjunction with the idea of nation, has been imposed on the Arab–Islamic reflection, thereby prompting answers in terms of what Islam is behind *din*. This keyword has been translated simply as "religion", instead of being analysed as a comparable, but different concept, that has been subject to an analogous process of reification and subjectification (see Part 1).

The activation of a transcultural space of communication is what speeded up the formation of a public sphere grounded on an Arab–Islamic consensus of communication; at the same time it restricted the range of possible discourses on other aspects. It is this embeddedness that on the one hand has warranted the conditions sufficient for setting the Arab–Islamic framework of communal reference into operation (see Chapter 3), but on the other has narrowed its potentialities of expression because the framework has been constrained to operate reactively. This is mostly evident in the discourse of *nahda* that emerged in Arab societies during the last three decades of the nineteenth century. Apart from its translation as "renaissance", *nahda* means "to stand up", with a connotation of "being fit", or "ready for". Its most likely field of denotation points to "the rebirth of Arabic literature and thought under Western influence since the second half of the nineteenth century" (Tomiche, 1993, p. 900). To be sure, the actual use of the term *nahda* during this period was not as widespread as in more recent times, after Arab intellectuals have begun to reflect retrospectively on the alleged formative phase of their "renaissance". A foremost exception to this belated elaboration on the meaning of *nahda* is constituted by Jorji Zaydan, an eminent journalist and popularizer of the Arab–Islamic heritage, who used the term to stress the interaction between the West and the East inaugurated by Napoleon's occupation of Egypt.

Both in its actual and belated use, the declaration or invocation of *nahda* was grounded on a general political-civilizational level, prompted by the consciousness of a historical break towards a decadent past. The external European challenge was considered the propulsive force of the "rebirth". In this sense, the *nahda* was the expression of the construction of an Arab–Islamic framework of reference in the immediate context of the transcultural dynamics initiated by the European colonial impact. At the same time, the Arab renaissance bracketed the innovative import of the Islamic revivalist movements, many of which preceded the colonial impact (see Chapter 3). It is true, however, that while most of these movements emerged in contexts that were semi-peripheral in both cultural and economic terms (most notably, in the Arab world, the Wahhabites of the Arabic peninsula), the Arab "renaissance" was the creation of urban intellectual élites.

As these groups were the most sensitive to the new embeddedness of Arab economies and intellectual cultures within markets and communicative spaces dominated by Europe, the *nahda* revealed the inherent fragility of the undertaking of shaping an Arab–Islamic framework of reference: a distinction in basically internal and ethical terms, appealing only to an allegedly autochthonous Islamic tradition – as the one attempted by the supporters of *islah* (see Chapter 5) – was not sufficient; a second distinction of a markedly identitarian shape was needed in order to take into account the "external challenge" and counter and emulate its exemplary model of modern intellectual distinction. The dilemmas of the Arab *nahda* were due to the constraint of having to perform a double intellectual distinction, and to the difficulties of performing both distinctions at the same time.

NOTES

1   This term refers to a dimension of communication across cultures, where it is not merely exchange of meaning to link both sides of a space of interaction, but their concern for the Other as functional to the definition of the Self.

2   For the purposes of the present work, this question is central with reference to the crucial passage of the early 1970s, when a thorough metamorphosis of the transcultural space set new conditions of subordination of the Arab–Islamic framework of reference to these dynamics, through the medium of the emergence of what I will call the hermeneutic field of "political Islam" (see Introduction, Part III and Part IV).

3   Stauth warns against the risk of translating *Innerlichkeit* into any other European language, since he refers (as I also do) to a specifically German concept. This notion, however, ended up influencing mainstream Western views of Islam by way of Weber's own elaboration of the concept (see Chapters 6 and 7).

4   Pending more careful studies on the process of institutionalization of Orientalism at the crucial passage between the eighteenth and nineteenth centuries, we have to accept Said's claim that "After Napoleon . . . the very language of Orientalism changed radically." (Said, 1978, p. 87).

5   Said does not deny the ambivalent character of Orientalism, but tends to play it down especially in the case of its strictly academic branch, whose perverse rigidity of outcomes he is mostly eager to denounce.

6   Only studies on the working of these modalities during the seventeenth and eighteenth centuries could prove the existence of rather "inherent" differences.

CHAPTER 5

The genesis and development of "Arab–Islamic" discourse

Each framework of reference has its own specificities, facilitating certain types of public discourse and excluding others, according to the symbolic power irradiating from its central keywords and images. An "Islamic" framework of communal reference (here considered in its central "Arab" version, where the value of *'uruba* defines and delimits *islam*: see Chapter 3) depends on an exercise of defining "Islam" which takes place within a hermeneutic spectrum representing a continuum. Within this, however, some critical threshold can be identified which marks the separation of two different interpretive schemes which we can term "conflationism" and "deconflationism". These correspond to the opposing attitudes towards the tense relationship, common to all Axial religions, between the dimensions of the worldly and the afterworldly, the visible and the invisible, *al-manzur wa-ghayr-al-manzur*, the *civitas mundi* and the *civitas Dei*: the opposition is between conflating or deconflating the two poles, between affirming or denying the necessity of a correspondence between their normative orders (see Chapter 1).

The first definition of an "Arab–Islamic" framework of reference occurred through the transcultural interaction between two discursive formations, Orientalism and Islamic reformism. These shared some crucial keywords (first of all an increasingly reified reference to an ever more dominant *islam*) through a language that, by virtue of direct exchanges or translations, was largely common and similarly subject to the rules of what could be called the "iron cage" of essentialism (Asad, 1993, p. 13). However, the meaning of the notions shared was specific to each discursive formation, and the relationship between the use of these terms and other categories more original to the single formation has also undergone continuous change. Aside from shared references, since the emergence of a transcultural space Orientalism and Islamic reformism have showed a similar propensity to provide solutions to the definition of Islam which oscillate between conflationism and deconflationism. Both such interpretive paths depend on the same view of Koranic religion (*din*), in a highly reified form, as "Islam". After the general introduction into the working of transcultural dynamics provided in Chapter 4, I will examine in this chapter the trajectory of Islamic reformism, while Chapter 6 will focus on some crucial displacements in Western Orientalist and post-Orientalist views of Islam. Both the present and the following chapters cover the formative phase – stretching until the period between the two World Wars – of the definition of an Arab–Islamic framework of reference.

The type of social action and intellectual procedure that delimits the contention between "conflationism" and "deconflationism" (see Introduction) is that pertaining to the construction of Islam as a framework of communal reference and universal projection, i.e. as a medium of collective identity as well as of visions of world history. By the time that defining "Islam" as a reified ideological system, or as a framework of reference, had become a major concern for both Western (Orientalist) *and* Islamic authors within a transcultural hermeneutic game, the Axial polarization between the worldly and the afterworldly became modernized according to the dualism examined in Chapter 2, as between the necessity and the contingency of the relation between "faith" and "politics" in Islam. This is a more general formula of dualization than the one that distinguishes between private and public spheres (see Chapter 3). It provides, however, a conceptual terrain better attuned to the vocabulary used by the two discursive formations during the period examined here.

In order to show where the difference between a class of conflationist and deconflationist statements lies, one should point to two opposite attitudes and hermeneutic procedures, by comparing different statements, or analysing the internal dynamics of a textual clue in its basic dependence on one type of procedure, or also in its oscillation between both. Deconflationism sees Islam as limited to *din* or also encompassing the *dunya*, the "world" (according to the formula *islam dunya wa-din*), and sometimes as still strictly depending on the *iman* (the inner commitment of faith). Meanwhile, the opposing scheme tends to conflate two poles that can be called Islam and politics, or Islam and the state, or Islam as *din* and Islam as *dawla* (*islam din wa-dawla*: see Chapter 3), and the like. In spite of the appeal of the latter slogan, we will see in this chapter that the deconflationist matrix was strong enough in Islamic reformism and even coherent with a basically neo-Hanbali setting (see Chapter 3). Chapter 6 will address the grounding primacy of conflationism in Western views of Islam. From Chapter 7 on, Parts III and IV will follow up with an analysis of texts showing how during the last three (and especially the last two) decades the two matrixes have evolved through a sort of hermeneutic chain stretching through both sides of the transcultural space.

The examination of the idea of *nahda* in Chapter 4 has showed one major constraint of the Arab–Islamic perspective, the need for a double distinction. A further major distinctional category at the time of emergence of a transcultural publicness, and specific to the current that has been called "Islamic reformism", was *islah* (see Chapter 3). A possible reading of the relationship between *islah* and *nahda* is: "the one, endogenous, sought an internal revision of the Islamic phenomenon . . . The other, exogenous, was born out of East–West contact . . . a liberation and rejection of the shackles of the past, as well as an advance towards modernism as represented by foreign models" (Tomiche, 1993, p. 901). *Islah* pointed to both internal and external reform, within a wide spectrum ranging from *islah al-nufus* ("the reform of individual selves") to *islah dakhiliyyat al-mamlaka* ("the reform of the internal affairs of the reign"), thereby manifesting both the principle of reform and the concrete strategies for its implementation (Merad, 1978, p. 144).

Differently from *nahda*, grounded on a general level of civilizational rebirth (see Chapter 4), *islah* reflects a concern for the historical development of a responsible subject. Though it has some rooting in the Koran, the first conscious self-identification of some thinkers as committed to *islah* is contemporary to, and complementary with, the process of reification of *islam* in public discourse that has taken place since the end of the nineteenth century (see Chapter 3). *Islah* represents a blueprint for reconstructing an original tradition in Islamic terms. The propagators of *islah* liked to feel in a line with the chain of cyclical reformers initiated by Muhammad and anticipated by him in a famous saying (*hadith*). The feeling of intellectual distinction is given here by the conviction that reformers of Islam since Muhammad have always been "alone (*ghuraba'*) in the world" (pp. 141–2).

In this sense, the reformist striving as "concentrated on the need to improve, correct, reorganize, renovate and restore" (p. 144) embodies a will to legislate for a reluctant Community through the restoration of the allegedly pristine model of discipline of the subject and of regulation of intersubjective relations. This is no contradiction, since the word *islah* signifies performing the good in the assumption that the good is known, as incorporated in the idealized Islamic community. In the final analysis, the legitimation of *islah* results from its reflecting the fulfilment of the canonical obligation of "commanding good and prohibiting evil" (p. 141). The actual content of "reform", however, depends on working out the societal needs of the hour.

As a result, in spite of the fact that Muhammad's community functioned as a model, the novelty of *islah* is that it replaced an arbitrarily sacralized

Consensus of the Community (*ijma'*) with another kind of consensus, based on the immanent rules of public communication (see Chapter 3). In the intellectual production of the leading figure of *islah*, Muhammad 'Abduh, and more generally in the whole of the *islah* movement, the de-evaluation of the traditionally conceived Consensus (Hourani, [1962] 1983, p. 147) as an actual source for the determination of binding doctrine is as much invoked and practised in public discourse as little justified in coherent doctrinal terms (Merad, 1978, p. 154).

I will examine the point in the trajectory of *islah* when its impulse is carried to the extreme consequence through the adoption of a perspective close to one of social theory. The goal of Islamic reformism is here the final dismantling of *ijma'* and the revitalization of *ijtihad* ("free reasoning" in the determination of binding truth) as an instrument for working out solutions for the life of the *umma* and its welfare. This was no mere theoretical stance, since the practice itself of reformers was to perform *ijtihad* in such a way as to capitalize best on its public impact. The dynamics of success of the most famous work by Muhammad 'Abduh, *risalat al-tawhid* (1897), arise not so much from the degree of doctrinal innovation as from its actual modalities of publicly conveying a highly compact and easily readable reformist message in a virtually journalistic style (see Merad, 1978, p. 159). As a result of this public enterprise, the *islah* defined the basic "fundamentalist" path within the Arab–Islamic framework of reference, as it tried to reduce the fundamentals of the truth to the Koran (p. 148) and to enhance the public relevance of individual access to them via *ijtihad*, which Islamic "revivalist" movements of the late eighteenth and ninteenth centuries had first promoted (see Chapter 3).

The range of *islah*'s impact reached well beyond its original field of irradiation, that pertained to standard Islamic science (*'ilm*) or sciences (*'ulum*).[1] It influenced wide intellectual circles (p. 144), thereby becoming the category of reference for several "systems of interest". The capacity of *islah* to become not merely the leading intellectual current at the turn of the century but the very epitome of a modern intellectual distinction that functions as the source of critical-normative public discourse is given by its reshaping of the original hermeneutic range of *'aqida* ("dogma", "doctrine") into a sort of "intellectual theory", through a direct projection of an idealized model of society into the public discursive arena (Schulze, 1990b, pp. 45–6). The crucial passage in the construction of an Arab–Islamic framework of reference was thereby carried out by a group of intellectualized *'ulama'* who practised a reflexive and publicly-projected *'ilm* in the context of the vision of an all-encompassing *islah*. The crystallization of a distinct category of *mufakkirun*, "those who think reflexively", "intellectuals", is a later development. It is clear that at some point in the evolution of reflexive *'ilm* the type of public discourse produced loses any significant analogy with those characteristic of traditional *'ilm*, except in terms of genre and style.

Nonetheless, the scope of *islah* can be understood only in the context of transcultural dynamics. The reformist view is the result of the tension between a construction of Islam in terms of what this ought to be beyond the act of commitment to God, thereby affecting a systematic organization of this commitment within the community (a construction that has endogenous roots in the Hanbali tradition, going back at least to Ibn Taymiyya: see Chapter 1), and a definition of Islam as a tangible historical entity, a "civilization", that is of Western Orientalist origin. The *salafi* (i.e. "traditionalist-classicist") dimension of *islah*, and its underlying task of balancing the reifying dimension of *islam* with its subjectification, is the product of this tension: the solution it provides is a way to legitimize the project of reforming Islam from within, and conforming to an impulse allegedly immanent in Islam, preserved through a discontinuous tradition of reformers even through epochs of decadence.

The three key authors in the autochthonous making of a "generic Islam" of reform, al-Afghani, 'Abduh and Rida, were all active in restating motifs of the Enlightenment, Romanticism and Positivism. As a whole, the trajectory of *islah* represented by these three authors reflects different concerns with the need of balancing the process of reification through the promotion of subjectification, and an increasing eagerness to stress the centrality of Arab language, culture and finally nation in the historical and contemporary definition of "true Islam".

Al-Afghani (1839–97) was the leading personality during the phase of agitation for such a true Islam of reform and reason that began during the crucial turn in the impact of European colonialism on Arab lands reached during the 1870s. Al-Afghani's discourse attempted to stir up a sense of solidarity and an activist stance among all Muslims, to be based on renewed efforts at performing *ijtihad*. Islam was constructed as a force that can unfold its high civilizational potential and challenge the encroaching West, if cleansed of the forces of backwardness. The immediate political reference of thus conceived Islam was still considered the Ottoman state (in the context of so-called "Ottomanism").

Muhammad 'Abduh (1849–1905) was the undisputed leader of a reformed Islam understood as a non-immediately-political, civil force of orderly social change to be grounded on education and a pervasive use of reasoning unbound by *ijma'*, and mainly attending to the domain of social interactions (*mu'amalat*). His thought represents the culmination of a process of reconceiving Islam as "true sociology" (cf. Chapter 2; see Hourani, [1962] 1983, p. 149). In 'Abduh's vision we observe an increased emphasis on the Arab's centrality in the *umma* to the detriment of the Turk (whom he tended to make responsible for the crystallization of *taqlid*, "imitative tradition"), also through the recognition of the merits of the Wahhabi movement for its reforming impetus and its stress on fundamentals (p. 155). The most conscious formulation of this position coincided with the turn-of-the-century consciousness that a pan-Islamic nationalism identified with the Ottoman state and taking the form of Ottomanism was no longer feasible, and that no valid alternative political reference expressed in purely Islamic terms could replace it. 'Abduh attempted to transform this lack of political opportunities into a vision of Islam as a universal force intervening in the formation of modern subjects and loyal citizens. Such a bid was able at least partially to balance the overcharge of reification in the first phase of construction of an Arab–Islamic framework of reference, and most coherently condensed in the keyword *islah* as the propelling force of *islam*.

Muhammad Rashid Rida (1865–1935) followed up with an attempt to balance reification and subjectification, system and subject, in the definition of Islam, according to a sort of late-positivist design comparable with the trajectory of European sociology. Moreover, writing and being active at a time of growing efficacy of nationalist agitation in Egypt (the 1920s and 1930s), he spelled out definitively the national and potentially nationalist (here Arab) dimension of the construction of Islam. In particular, the combination between what he and 'Ali 'Abd al-Raziq (see below) wrote between the early and mid-1920s in the context of the inner-Islamic controversy about the Caliphate (after its formal dismissal in Istanbul between 1922 and 1924) and in a largely reciprocal polemical attitude, determinantly contributed to sketch the field of oscillation between "conflationism" and "deconflationism" as expressed from within an Arab–Islamic consensus of communication (see Chapter 4). Through this dispute, the consensus was definitively emancipated from the traditional juridical fiction of the *ijma'* and the related taken-for-granted justification of the Community.

The determination of the terrain of contention and of the terms of discourse of these two authors took account of the Western legacy of discussing the relationship between modern religion and the problem of the social order, as articulated mainly through the options and solutions provided by Hobbes and Locke (see Chapter 2). However, the rules and key categories of the sort of public discourse emerging from their writings are specifically

Arab–Islamic to the extent that they reflect an attempt to restore a line of intellectual tradition brusquely interrupted by the hard political and cultural impact of European colonialism since the last quarter of the nineteenth century. As a result of such developments, the modern road to the public reification of Islam appears to be a combination of transcultural constraints and selective (often ahistorical) resort to a Hanbali tradition. This goal was achieved through a double reappropriation of Ibn Taymiyya's doctrine and of the revivalist impulse of the Wahhabi movement (see Chapters 1 and 3), as well as via their adaptation to the rules of production and diffusion of discourse within a modern public sphere. As we will see, both the conflationist and the deconflationist paths are well-rooted in the same mode of discourse.

Rida consciously constructed Islam as a principle of societal and political cohesion. This is, however, clearly to be anchored in the conscience and action of the individual Muslim, that have to manifest the capacity to harmonize spiritual motivation and social concern (Rida, [1922] 1988, p. 74). He claims, accordingly, that the efforts of *islah* must condense in the conscious formulation of a solution to the problem of the *imama*, i.e. of the leadership within the *umma*, through constituting the latter as *jama'a*. This is a sort of willed community and sovereign society, that functions on the basis of a new consensus worked out by the *'ulama'* according to the principles of justice and equality among all believers-citizens, principles that are essential to *islah* and to the injunction of "commanding good and prohibiting evil" (*al-amr bi-l-ma'ruf wa-l-nahi 'an al-munkar*: pp. 75–7). Rida is very explicit in asserting that there cannot be any *nahda* but through *islam*, and in particular through the Arab people that constitutes Islam's source of origin (p. 74).

The Caliphate is reinterpreted as the supreme instance of legitimation of the interpretive centrality of reformist, intellectualized *'ilm* within the Islamic community. This centrality is nonetheless conceived as perfectly compatible with the reality of the nation-state. The result is a utopian vision of the political import of public communication governed by Arab-speaking scholars exercising *ijtihad*, as fitting the political structures and technologies of domination of the existing states, and envisaging the institutionalization of *islam* as *din siyada wa-sultan* (i.e. as *din* of sovereignty and domination: pp. 93–4). This takes the form of an Islamic public sphere within consolidating Arab Muslim nation-states, and provides the terrain of legitimation and self-representation of reformist *'ulama'* irradiating their legislating authority directly upon the consciences of Muslims within the *jama'a*, and thereby enhancing each of them to a free, self-conscious *mujtahid* ("practitioner of *ijtihad*") of God's Will (*shar'*: pp. 115–16).

According to this view, any Muslim citizen is entitled to withdraw his obedience to the *imam* whenever the latter misinterprets the *shar'* (pp. 133–4). The guarantee of this duty-right essential to the functioning of the Caliphate is seen in a modern constitutional framework (p. 148). The utopian neo-Hanbali vision of the fulfilment of the truth on earth by keeping alive the Prophet's charismatic leadership is fertilized through a constitutionalist approach that takes account of the reality of the nation-states, but also attempts to transcend it through the invocation of a supreme instance for reconstituting a principled community that incarnates the perfecting and universalizing impulse of *islam*. This vision operates along an axis that anchors the subject within the system through the primacy of public and inclusivist ethics, a task that existing states are considered unable to perform, as they are inevitably bound to an exclusivist *'asabiyya* ("particularistic cohesion").

The shaping of this version of a new Arab–Islamic consensus coincided in Egypt with a period, the 1920s, when the public sphere was dominated by the agitation of Egyptian-national and European-like "secularist" views of collective identity. However, this was also a decade when the construction of viable public discourses within the consensus of communication allowed by an Arab–Islamic framework was freed from the previous, almost compulsory, reference to Ottomanist patterns of allegiance. The exchange between Rida and 'Abd al-Raziq in the first half of that decade owns therefore a significance that transcends the contingency of the Egyptian public agenda and articulates the flexible asset that the *islah* movement contributed to the construction of an Arab–Islamic framework of reference according to the new requirements of the post-Ottoman era, when Islamic public discourses had to accommodate the reality of Arab nation-states.

Published shortly before a strong conflationist position began to take root in a "social movement" dimension with the foundation of *al-ikhwan al-muslimun* (the Muslim Brotherhood), the book of the Egyptian *'alim* 'Ali 'Abd al-Raziq (1888–1966), *al-islam wa-usul al-hukm* ("Islam and the fundaments of rule"), is not prominent for countering the development of a conflationist formula through the adoption of a rival framework transplanted and adapted from European history, as in the case of other authors in Egypt and the Arab world during the same period. The historical importance of 'Abd al-Raziq's essay is in its capacity to bring to the surface the potentialities and limits of the discursive formation of intellectualized *'ilm*, defined in the four previous decades under the umbrella of *islah*. The author is conscious of arguing from within the *'ilm*, both institutionally and discursively. His work represents the culmination of a trajectory of "reformist" endeavour that had touched, with Rida, a point where in spite of the basic admission of the contingent character of power in the Islamic community the reformist logic was invested in a cogent conflationist formula.

'Abd al-Raziq performed instead a sort of deconflationist *tabula rasa*, thereby redefining the terms of future discourse both for deconflationism and for conflationism. At the same time as Rida was consolidating the argument of *islah* apologetically and doctrinally, 'Abd al-Raziq swiftly reappropriated the reformist method in order to disencumber the making of an Arab–Islamic framework of reference from the *salafi* incongruence of tendentially reading the whole of Islamic history as carrying a potential unity of "faith" and "politics". This interpretation overemphasized, as previous proto-modern political movements like Wahhabism also did, the importance of Islam's formative era. 'Abd al-Raziq's strategy was simple and straightforward: he claimed that we cannot say that Islam *is* a blueprint for government: in this way he made the set free for a discussion of what the relationship between Islam and the political domain *should be*.

'Abd al-Raziq is coherent with the general inclination of *islah* not to radically challenge the Consensus of the Community (*ijma'*) on a doctrinal level, in spite of its actual tension with the reinvigoration of *ijtihad* ('Abd al-Raziq, 1925, p. 22). His goal is rather to render its applicability questionable over the issue around which the stake of consensus was politically the highest: the invocation of *ijma'* for establishing that Islam prescribes the organization of political authority as a religious obligation. With regard to this issue, he does not hesitate to denounce the hypocrisy of the juridical argument that, suppressing any effort to analyse rationally the fundaments of political power, constructs the fiction of the investiture of the caliph (*bay'a*) as legitimated by the Consensus, whereas historical reality tells us that with rare exceptions the Caliphate was founded on the basis of brutal force (pp. 23 and 31). Following this argumentative logic, 'Abd al-Raziq straightforwardly makes *tabula rasa* of those arguments within the Islamic *'ilm* that obstruct a critical consideration of the reality of power and of its relation to Islam as *din*: he performed this task with a deconstructionist vehemence completely absent in Rida's argument, in spite of the latter's similarly innovative approach to the Consensus.

'Abd al-Raziq is certainly very eager to stress that Koranic *din* is a religion not limited to teaching the principles of fraternity and equality, but one that aims at actively educating its followers to practise these precepts and, above all, that has forged norms inspired by them (p. 27). Here he clearly establishes that Islam constitutes, besides *din*, and as a consequence of its special character as *din*, a principle of civic life, thereby affecting the *dunya*, the worldly environment with its social obligations. This position comes quite close to the postulation of Islam as a "civil religion" (see Chapter 3). Prominent in his argument is that precisely because of being this special sort of socially expanded *din*, grounded on values of equality and fraternity, Islam cannot grant to any established power the necessary legitimation.[2] As a result, Islam is *din la dawla*, religion but not state (p. 64).

In this way 'Abd al-Raziq symmetrically countered the slogan of *islam din wa-dawla* (see Chapter 3). This formula was certainly no direct product of *islah*, but matured in an intellectual climate characterized by its influence. Seeing beyond this slogan appeared to be crucial in order to eradicate the ambiguities of *islah* towards the problem of the religious legitimation of power, and to consolidate the process of modernizing the basis of the consensus, through making it dependent on communication and the strength of public discourse. According to the same logic, 'Abd al-Raziq provocatively argued that if the *fuqaha'* (Islamic jurists) mean by Caliphate or Imamate nothing other than what the political scientists mean by "government", they are completely right in claiming that the welfare of the governed people depends on such an institution. In this case, however, they are stating the obvious, and any addition to this simple truth, that would lead towards establishing the Imamate as a special, since religiously grounded, sort of government, would be unjustified (p. 45). This passage seems almost to state that the *'ulama'* are entitled to speak about government only if they subscribe to the new "consensus of communication", thereby acting as *'ulama'* of politics. But in this case they have to abandon their juristic devices, and acknowledge the rules of civic life as well as the societal function of power.

To see 'Abd al-Raziq's argument as the mere reflection of a "liberal", Westernized view of Islam[3] is accordingly misled. We have seen that the phase of activation of the Arab–Islamic framework of reference coincides with its becoming embedded in the transcultural space. This is very different, however, from seeing in manifestations of thought like those of 'Abd al-Raziq nothing other than an imitative reflex towards Western models, or their mere translation into Islamic terms. What makes 'Abd al-Raziq's claim largely innovative is that the attack he moved against the traditional consensus (pp. 14–15) is complemented by a rigorous checking of the "logical" version of the conflationist argument, which considers the Imamate or Caliphate as coessential with the religious obligation of commanding good and prohibiting evil (p. 13). This sort of argument was gaining ground in public contentions, and it is not surprising that 'Abd al-Raziq felt obliged to target Rida as the foremost contemporary supporter of the Caliphate-Imamate making use of this non-juridical argument.

It is symptomatic, however, that the only explicit reference to Rida is where 'Abd al-Raziq hints at the difficulty of sanctioning the binding character of the Caliphate by reference to the *sunna*, the source that Rida invoked after agreeing, coherently with the orientation of *islah*, to marginalize the importance of the Consensus. With regard to this issue, 'Abd al-Raziq is eager to remember how Rida himself was incapable of underpinning the religious legitimation of the Caliphate on the basis of *hadith*s recognized as authentic (p. 16), thus impoverishing the credibility of his privileged invocation of the *sunna*. The impossibility of tackling Rida's thesis directly, by challenging its logical structure, should be explained by looking at the way the arguments at stake were crafted. Rida's plea for the Caliphate was virtually unchallengeable by 'Abd al-Raziq, as it largely presupposed and appropriated the type of objections that the latter raised against any form of religious legitimation of mundane power. In this sense, it is true that the work of Rashid Rida also epitomized the passage from the Consensus of the Community to a "consensus of communication", notwithstanding his opposing conclusions on the problem of the Caliphate.

Rida's argument is similar to that of 'Abd al-Raziq only up to the point when it is forced into a justification of the Caliphate, following the claim that, in spite of the fact that authority belongs only to God and His Prophet, the *shari'a* cannot be implemented without a supervising authority that institutionalizes and keeps alive – so being faithful to the tradition of *islah* – the charismatic gift of Prophecy on *mujtahid*s of any epoch. As the supreme *imam*, the Caliph would not be a replication of temporal power, but the highest *'alim* practising *ijtihad* and exerting influence, by this indirect, moral way, on existing governments of Muslim countries (Hourani, [1962] 1983, p. 240). One can add that Rida's ultimate stress is not even on the political influence of such authority on the individual and social life of Muslims, but on the necessity of making publicly visible and constitutionally accountable an institutional representation of *shari'a*'s centrality as the manifestation of God's Will.

The opposite direction taken by 'Abd al-Raziq's argument is, however, more favourable to the elimination of the residual ambiguities in the re-definition of the place of *din* in the organization of civic coexistence in modern society. 'Abd al-Raziq is critical of the fact that the discussion of the problem of "Islam and government" lacks any awareness of the hermeneutic shifts that historically affected its key terminology, including words like "Imamate" and "Community" (p. 18). This is considered even more dangerous, since it is almost impossible to carry out a reconstruction of the terms for the problem at stake at the time of the Prophet, the crucial

era of reference for reformist thought. There is no autonomous, historiographically crafted statement on this formative period of Islam, since
Muslim authors tend to mix up several *hadith*s without adopting the critical
perspective that guides the study of other epochs (p. 46). As a consequence,
'Abd al-Raziq sees as his task the initiation, "within Islam" (p. 49), of
the necessary critical study of the relationship between *risala* ("prophetic
mission") and *hukm* ("exercise of power", "the praxis of government", or
simply "rule": pp. 48–9).[4]

His endeavour is, nonetheless, conducted not so much with the weapons
of critical historiography, but with those of critical social theorizing trying
to oppose the convergence between the contemporary doctrines of the
'ulama' and the widespread belief within the Community that the Prophet
founded a state (*dawla*) within Islam (p. 50). The result was an acritical
acceptance of the slogan *islam din wa-dawla*, that at the time 'Abd al-Raziq
wrote had not yet been subject to a fair degree of intellectual elaboration.

He maintains that when the Prophet made use of brutal force, it was not
for the sake of religious proselytism (*fi-sabil al-da'wa ila al-din*), but in order
to erect an "Islamic government" (*hukuma islamiyya*) (p. 53); similarly, the
true sense of *jihad* [5] is its being one of the by-products of the Islamic
state (*dawla islamiyya*: p. 54). It is clear that he rejects the conflationist,
deductionist argument of *islam din* hence *dawla*, which points to the necessity
of the Islamic state as a consequence of the need to create the mundane
conditions for the fulfilment of *din*, as well as, consequently, of the prescribed
acts of worship (p. 56). He accepts, on the other hand, a juxtaposition, or
rather an opposition, of *din* and *dawla* in Islam, in the sense that Islam is
doctrinally *din* and just *din*. Yet, as a consequence of historical contingencies,
it can also become *dawla*.

He warns, however, that even if this contingency was effective at the
time of the Prophet, this does not legitimize extracting a rule valid for every
epoch. First of all, we know little or nothing of how and to what extent the
Islamic state of the Prophet's time really functioned as a state, so that it is
impossible to accept this as a model in the same way as a Muslim must look
at the Prophet's time for adopting examples of ethical conduct. Second, this
contingency is bound to the prophetic mission, so that we can speak of
power in the case of the Prophet only "in a certain sense" (p. 65), since
"*risala la hukm*" ("the prophetic mission is not exercise of power, practice
of government": p. 64).

'Abd al-Raziq is aware that one can argue in favour of a contemporary
Islamic state in a different way from pointing to the "Islamic state" of the
time of the Prophet (pp. 57–8). Rida was clear in his argument – thereby

laying the foundations of all subsequent conflationist voices within the Arab–Islamic framework of reference – that the Caliphate should not be inspired by the practice of former centuries, but conform to the future-oriented necessity of making Islam compatible with the requirements of the time through the exercise of *ijtihad*. ʿAbd al-Raziq's argumentation does not offer an ultimate objection to any such conflationist discourse. In this sense, the work of ʿAbd al-Raziq ends up legitimizing *both* a future-projected conflationist track and a deconflationist option of constructing a relationship between Islam and the political, although coming very close to being a prototype of the latter option.

The reconstruction of the incommensurability of the Prophet's power with current forms of worldly power is an additional way of rhetorically underpinning, in the final part of his work, the validity of Islam – originating in the Prophet's message – as a framework of communal reference and universal projection for the modern Muslim citizen. The power of the Prophet is much wider than that normally exercised by rulers over the ruled, since it pertains both to this world (*dunya*) and to the hereafter (pp. 66–7). Since he was the Last Prophet, Muhammad's authority in this respect was complete (p. 68). ʿAbd al-Raziq recognizes that this authority is still at the basis of the Muslims being a *jamaʿa* (p. 70),[6] but this irradiation of the force of Islamic *din* on the *dunya* at the level of civic life does not demand any kind of "religiously legitimized government". The picture is simple for ʿAbd al-Raziq: as long as he lived, the Prophet exercised a kind of authority that can be defined as *riyasa diniyya* ("religious leadership", p. 71). After the Prophet, any rule legitimized by Islam, that ʿAbd al-Raziq agrees on calling "Islamic government", is clearly of another sort; it is *la-dini*, "non-religious" (p. 90). This is the culmination of ʿAbd al-Raziq's argument.

At this point, the affirmation that there is no basis in the Koran for the thesis that the Prophet exercised temporal power seems to be a mere tribute to the hierarchy of proofs admitted by *ʿilm*, but is no longer central to the logic of argumentation (p. 71). ʿAbd al-Raziq is very explicit in saying that to appeal to the Koran or the *sunna* of the Prophet to provide elements of proof is a desperate undertaking; it is legitimate to refer to them for constructing conjectures, but one cannot attain the truth through conjectures alone. This truth can be experienced only through the evolutionary impulse incorporated by Islam as a "*madhhab* ("path", "teaching", but also "movement") of *islah* for all mankind (p. 76).

ʿAbd al-Raziq was certainly capable of formulating, in terms that were obviously vulnerable to counter-arguments, the claim that there was no religious legitimacy for the Caliphate, while it remains undemonstrated that, *as a consequence*, he was denying any legitimation to the "Islamic *political* community" (as claimed in Binder, 1988, p. 138). All that we can say is that he tried to neutralize any political implication of the traditional, *'ulama'*-mediated, Consensus of the Community, at the same time as he did not deny, but reinforced, the legitimation of the Islamic community as a unity of *din* (p. 83). This community is still considered as given by, and bound to, *kullu ma shara'ahu al-islam* ("all that Islam prescribes"), from which only *al-hukm al-siyasi*, the vertical dimension of organization of the community, is excluded (p. 84).

As a result, 'Abd al-Raziq can be seen as a major reshaper of discursivity within the Arab–Islamic framework of reference, since he was able to recondense in vivid, if ambiguous, formulas what had *already* been thought since the framework had commenced in the construction of public discourses by Arab Muslim authors during earlier decades. It is clear in 'Abd al-Raziq's own formulations that the legislating subject, the source of the *shar'*, is not God, but "Islam": this is a sharp reifying shift towards established doctrine. But even more significant is that among the seven imputations that the judging college of the mosque-university of al-Azhar in Cairo raised against his book after its publication (see Binder, 1988, p. 144), there is none referring to this claim's incorrectness. By that time this ideologization of Islam, the preliminary step in the shaping of an Arab–Islamic framework of reference, was already widely accepted. Indeed it would not be difficult to demonstrate that the wording used by 'Abd al-Raziq was not completely original. The objections raised against him concerned the content of what *shara'a al-islam*, what Islam has legislated.

Not only the actual text of 'Abd al-Raziq's book, but also the patterns of reaction to it through the most authoritative instance of *'ilm* in the Muslim world testify to what, by the mid-1920s, was unquestioned in this reformed, intellectualized construction of Islam (cf. Hourani, [1962] 1983, pp. 189–92). More than that, the whole story helped to consolidate this least common, and new, consensus of communication, from which every intellectualized *'alim* – or purer intellectual – who accepted the centrality of *'ilm* in its reformed (or better reforming) version could start in taking a position within the largely new hermeneutic contention on what "true Islam" is or should be. The exercise of discursively defining Islam was by then placed firmly in the context of thriving nation-states, but it also indicated the wider realm of publicness that Islam, even if circumscribed by Arabicity, was able to attain in an intra-Islamic, trans-state projection.

NOTES

1   I use the term *'ilm*, in the singular form, to refer to the domain of traditional sciences which derive from Koranic *din*, and whose legitimate carriers are the *'ulama'* (sing. *'alim*). This domain has been subject to a historical differentiation into several sciences, or *'ulum*. When we refer to *'ilm*, it is to point out the unitary hermeneutic and discursive terrain for the *'ulama'*, who have received a basic education in many such sciences. The most relevant among these, from the point of view of the present work, i.e. from the point of view of public engagement, is certainly *fiqh* (close to "jurisprudence"), whose specialists are called *fuqaha'* (sing. *faqih*).

2   This argument bears a close resemblance to the thesis of the new strand of scholarship which, by adopting a neo-Weberian approach, reverses the classic Orientalist view of Islam as producing a "strong state" and a "weak society" (see Chapter 1), and posits instead that it constitutes a "strong society" and a "weak state" (see a critical account of this allegedly neo-Orientalist model in Sadowski, 1993). In this sense, this new paradigm is also complementary to the claim, propagated by Western scholars in recent years (see Binder, 1988 and Carré, 1993), of a potentially strong tradition of civility in Islamic history. This view allows Islam to be seen as a civil religion building the living impulse of a civil society. In Chapter 2 I warned against confusing a tradition of civil society with liberal-individualist approaches, while in Chapter 3 I expressed reservations towards the analytic value of categories like civil society and civil religion if applied comparatively to Western and Islamic history.

3   This is the logic of Hourani's evaluation, although he tried to relativize this assessment by pointing to the fact that 'Abd al-Raziq was arguing according to the terms of discourse laid down by 'Abduh (Hourani, [1962] 1983, p. 163). In spite of his effort to revise the assessment of Hourani, Binder even accentuates this perspective, coherently with the scope of his work, in search of "Islamic liberalism" (Binder, 1988).

4   'Abd al-Raziq's argument is itself built on a misunderstanding, or at least a simplification: that *hukm* is coterminous with "government" in the modern sense (see Chapter 1).

5   The mistranslation of this term as "holy war" is well-known. The word points to the act of striving for the sake of God, that can result in warfare in particular cases. The determination of such cases has been the object of an interpretive contention in which theorists of *islah* also participated (Merad, 1978).

6   One may assimilate the use of the term *jama'a* by 'Abd al-Raziq to the new meaning, not yet completely clear in all its implications, that this term acquired through the reformulation of Rida. Here the word pointed to the willed, self-constituted aggregation of Muslims taking up a role of vanguard within the wider community (Schulze, 1990b, pp. 89–90) and thereby constituting the basis for the conflationist neo-*salafiyya* of the Muslim Brotherhood and similar organizations that have occupied the political stage

of several Arab countries since the 1930s (see Chapter 3). Common to the use of *jama'a* in both cases is a redefinition of the conditions for legitimate community and consensus beyond the *umma* as taken for granted, i.e. as the locus of irradiation for the traditional Consensus.

CHAPTER 6

The sociologization of the Western construction of Islam

In the crucial phase of the 1920s the transcultural dynamics between the "West" and "Islam" began to be determinantly shaped by the culmination of a process of sociologizing Orientalism in the framework of the comparative sociology of religion developed by Max Weber. It has been observed (Turner, 1974, p. 175) that,

> Islamic reformers in the modern world have adhered to a strikingly Weberian view of social development. This results from the fact that many of the intellectual élite of reformist Islam received their training in Europe or accepted a European view of world development . . . Weber's view of motivation came to fit the Islamic case as the result of cultural diffusion.

This remark is relevant for the purpose of the analysis in so far as it affects one side of the process. However, the formation of a "Weberist" paradigm functioning as the hub of transcultural dynamics until the early 1970s has a more ambivalent dimension resulting from a refinement and consolidation of the tension between sameness and difference that has animated Western views of Islam from the beginning of their academic institutionalization.

Weber epitomizes the centrality of Western essentialism as the methodological counterpart of the academic, increasingly social-scientific institutionalization of inwardness (see Chapter 4) in the form of an "internally grounded attitude to the world" (Stauth, 1993, p. 27). Here the axis linking subjective inwardness and the world, i.e. the dynamics of universalization of innerworldliness, is definitely translated into a typological and evolutionist account of the relationship between "the West and the rest". We will see how Weberian sociology restates in a methodologically refined and highly influential way the epistemological embarrassment that has always affected thinkers in Western Christendom (Hourani, [1967] 1980, pp. 71–2):

> that peculiar difficulty . . . in finding a category in terms of which Islam can be understood, being neither "East" nor "West", neither

Christian nor unequivocally non-Christian and, wherever one places it, being linked with Europe by a long and intimate, an ambiguous and usually a painful relationship.

In particular, Weber is the author who has given a social-scientific status to the game of construction of Islam as a cumulation of deficits, through its assimilation to Oriental despotism and patrimonialism, ending in the formulation of the essentially political character of Islam as a belated manifestation of the Axial breakthrough (see Chapter 1). This construction neglects the specific Arab–Islamic articulation of the modern "irrelation to politics" (see Chapter 2).

The following brief reconstruction of the trajectory of German Orientalism is only finalized to illustrate the academic background of Weber's sociology of Islam. A recent work has supported the thesis that the pre-Weberian *Islamwissenschaft* determinantly contributed, through its cross-cultural approach and transcultural potentialities, to the justification in universal terms of the uniqueness of Western modernity, as well as, more specifically, to Weber's comparative sociology of religion. German Orientalism in its "high-classic" phase – reached between the turn of the century and the 1920s – already addressed the relationship, that will become central to Weber's sociology, between religion and social-institutional development (Stauth, 1993, pp. 53, 75 and 132). The impact of German Orientalism on Weber was not limited to his view of Islam but encompassed the method itself of essentializing other cultural-religious universes. In turn, Weber's own refinement and application of the method experienced a significatively critical impasse when he approached Islam.

Weber's achievements in general are to be read in the context of specifically German conditions of production of academic knowledge and engagement in politics. What, however, makes this reconstruction of the crucial passages in the academic division of labour in Germany relevant for the fate of Western knowledge and the Western attitude towards the Islamic Other in general, is the fact that the subsequent making of "Weberism" as a trivialization of the Weberian heritage is in no way an exclusively German phenomenon. One of the well-known reasons for the transformation of questions primarily affecting a German social and intellectual environment into a broader Western concern was the wave of emigration of German-speaking scholars to the United States in the 1930s, which catalysed the implantation of parts of the Weberian heritage, however vaguely formulated and weakly digested, within a cultural climate favourable to fix more quickly than in continental Europe perspectives of knowledge considered to be of immediate usefulness.[1]

There is an even longer line of continuity that links German thinkers of Romanticism and Idealism to the progression of German Orientalism through the nineteenth century up to Weber's time (see also Chapter 4). It is the impulse (in fact common to the Enlightenment and Romanticism) to embrace, in terms of "understanding", the entire "world" in its inherent tension between the unity of historical becoming and the distinction of civilizational units. This attitude merged with the influence of an epistemologically dominant positivist environment in the work of Orientalists representing a mature stage of development of this discipline (reached during the second half of the nineteenth century), like Ignaz Goldziher and Julius Wellhausen. The result was that procedures of "cultural classification" shaped their quest for understanding "the essence of Arabism and Islamic religiosity" by way of "categorizing, classifying and selecting the 'positive' and 'thriving' factors" (Stauth, 1987, p. 9). It is certain that in tackling Islam Max Weber was strictly dependent on the German *Islamwissenschaft* of the time (Hourani, [1967] 1980, p. 71; Schluchter, 1987, p. 18; Stauth, 1987, p. 2). Such a dependence was also due to the fact that Weber used – for understandable reasons, due to the wide scope of his work – almost exclusively secondary sources.

In the work of Wellhausen in particular, the desire to account for Western uniqueness (as epitomized by the European nation-state) in a comparative perspective was already quite transparent. Accordingly, the main deficit of Islam as a religion was detected in its overtly instrumental subservience to state formation (Stauth, 1993, p. 134), thereby laying the foundation for the view of the essentially political character of Islam. It was Carl H. Becker, however, a member of the "Weber circle" at Heidelberg, who began to sociologize the tradition of German Orientalism and made it immediately suitable to Weber's programme for a comparative sociology of religion as the investigation of (potential) paths of rationalization of life conduct and universalization of value. The interest of Becker's elaboration is in the extent to which he was able to fertilize through a new social-scientific approach the legacy of the traditional, pre-Orientalist model of constructing an opposition between Islam and Christianity, in order to derive the deficits of the former in facing a process of modern differentiation. Noteworthy in Becker is that he already inscribed those alleged deficits of Islam within a horizon of examination of models of rationalities (Stauth, 1987, pp. 13–14), thus articulating the concern for coping with a neighbour who was different enough by not being "Western", but not enough for being "Oriental" (Hourani, [1967] 1980, pp. 19–46).

Islam was planned to be dealt with in both the major projects that Weber conducted in parallel (drawing on the same sources) between 1911 and the beginning of the First World War:[2] the first (*Die Wirtschaftsethik der Weltreligionen*,[3] included in the first volume of the *Gesammelte Aufsätze zur Religionssoziologie*,[4] hereafter referred to as RS) devoted to the inner motivations, the second (*Die Wirtschaft und die Gesellschaftlichen Ordnungen der Mächte*,[5] which was posthumously included in the second part of *Wirtschaft und Gesellschaft*,[6] hereafter referred to as WG) to the "external" conditions of the evolution of *Kulturreligionen*. It is interesting to note that in the first work Islam is absent, along with Christianity, from the published version. From Weber we know directly that the essay should have ended with the cultural-religious units that he took as the closest to modern Western Christianity, i.e., in order: ancient Christianity; Talmudic Judaism; Islam and Oriental Christianity (Schluchter, 1987, pp. 20–2). It seems that among all non-Christian units Islam was considered of immediate relevance for the comparison, probably even more than Judaism (p. 14). Weber deemed Islam important for the central concern of his work (reconstructing the reasons for the uniqueness of Western development) both at the level of historical preconditions for the Western path and of contrastive specificity to it. We will see how the latter dimension happened to prevail in Weber's analysis.[7]

It is a bit of a mystery why, despite Weber's allusion to this project, no manuscript explicitly dedicated to Islam was found in his unpublished notes. Whatever the solution to this enigma,[8] it is certain that aside from some short, but very significant hints in RS, the bulk of Weber's treatment of Islam is found in the corpus of texts devoted to external conditions rather than to internal motivations. Of course the partition is in no way rigid, due to the interplay of both sets of factors within Weber's own original theoretical stance, an interplay reflected not only in the *Wirtschaftsethik*, but also in the revised version of the famous essay *Die protestantische Ethik und der Geist des Kapitalismus*[9] (hereafter referred to as PE). Furthermore, the position of Islam in comparative perspective is not, in the available texts of WG, of the kind suggested by Weber's statement. On the other hand, the fact that Weber still considered Islam crucial for his comparative project well after he ceased to study Islam around 1914 (Schluchter, 1987, pp. 23–4) is proved by clear allusions in the Foreword to RS, written after the end of the First World War and incorporating his last legacy.

Clearly in attempting to transcend the still philologically-oriented study of Islam, and inscribe it within an explicitly comparative framework focusing on the development of models of rationality, Weber could not avoid relying on Orientalist interpretive patterns. First of all, at the time he decided to expand his sociological study of religion towards "the Orient" (p. 18), he adopted "world religions" as units of analysis, a category of cultural classification inherited from Orientalism. But there is a special reason, in the case of Islam, why Weber surpassed the normal Orientalist tendency to overaggregate cultural-religious traditions, thereby contributing to the reification of Islam more powerfully than nineteenth-century Orientalism had done: this reason is the special typological interest in the seeming similarity between Islam and Calvinism, that was interesting for Weber in so far as it concerned only some aspects of the "surface" within both units (Schluchter, 1987, p. 24).

In other words, Weber's Islam played the role of the villain in the narratives of his well-known Protestantism-thesis, according to which the uniqueness of Western rationalization culminates in the innerwordly elaboration of the Calvinist idea of the "double decree" that cements the doctrine of predestination (Stauth, 1993, p. 100). He was interested in showing, by way of a contrastive comparison that becomes extraordinarily stringent in some points of the revised edition of PE, how some distinctive features that at first sight were common to Islam and Calvinism, could *not* be seen as the keys to the particular performance of the latter in terms of rational life conduct, as manifested especially at the level of "economic ethic". The extent to which Weber's handling of Islam was predetermined by his own concern for reconstructing the reasons for Western uniqueness (Turner, [1983] 1991, p. 43) was beyond the limits set by the Orientalist paradigm. The lack of a minimum of isomorphism between the two units of comparison, as between a reformed version of early-modern Christianity and a whole Axial civilization, led to an unprecedented reification (in a social-scientific form) of "Islam".

What Calvinism and Islam *seem* to have in common is the absolute character of the faith in God's transcendence (Schluchter, 1987, p. 36). This kind of faith, also common to old Judaism, distinguishes itself, according to Weber, for the absence of a solution to the question of theodicy, the problem of the justification of God especially with regard to the existence of evil in this world. Weber first provides a general definition of each ethical prophecy as a step towards the rationalization of the idea of God, and then stresses the tension between the path towards ever more cogent forms of transcendent monotheism and the reality of the world's imperfection (WG, p. 315). The tension reflected by such a religious rationalization carried to the extreme limits of monotheistic assertion (something in which Islam is probably unequalled, thereby surpassing Calvinism itself) is finally assessed as the crucial living feature of such advanced forms of Axial religion. But what is interesting is how in Weber this analytic view shifts, for the sake of the comparative task, into shaping a conflationist assessment of Islam, whose internal coherence is much higher than in earlier Orientalist formulations.

It is not my intention to discuss this operation as a possible mistake, as it would be if seen from the perspective of specialized students of Weber's work. My interest here is to reassess the novelty of Weber's view of Islam from a perspective concerned with checking how the motivational and epistemological disposition of the Western student of Islam finally influences the hermeneutic output, thereby giving the transcultural space the particular imprint it has carried until the major crisis of the 1970s (see Chapter 8). Weber constructed the difference between Islam and Calvinism beyond their superficial similarities by attributing to the first, as a solution to the problem of theodicy, a plain predeterminism endowed with a generic cosmological dimension devoid of any forceful stress on salvation, mediated by formal legalism and therefore not suitable to develop a rational economic ethic (see Turner, 1994, p. 39), while the specificity of the latter was seen in its production of a coherent doctrine of predestination suitable to promote mundane engagement (Schluchter, 1987, pp. 39–40). Most crucially, the Islamic doctrine of predestination was deemed unsusceptible of generating a "double decree" that, in the case of Calvinism, makes inwardness govern exteriority and therefore enhances the dualism of modernity (see Chapter 2) to a force of world mastery (Stauth, 1993, pp. 161 and 166).

Parts of the analysis in Chapters 1, 3 and 5 highlighted how through the double Axial and modern breakthroughs, a Hanbali-fundamentalist path of salvation, sometimes fertilized by innerworldly-oriented Sufism, may have yielded, within Islamic history, an activist, rational and essentialist solution to the dualism's tension. Nonetheless, in Weber's view overt directness in the definition of the God–man relationship, instead of subjective labour, is Islam's key peculiarity, according to the contention that the concept of salvation in its ethical dimension is alien to it. Islam's alleged imperviousness to the notion of salvation is highlighted in strict relation to the postulation of the inherent political character of Islam. This is again to be explained by its overly material character of "war religion" (WG, p. 375). Here, as elsewere, the central Weberian question of the axis of relationship between religious ethic and *Lebensführung* ("life conduct") remains largely unproblematized. The Meccan, eschatological component in the rise of Koranic *din* was assessed as merely a provisional, volatile "phase", soon and for ever overwhelmed by the militant Medinan paradigm.[10] Even more important is Weber's oversimplification in interpreting the act of "surrender" signified by *islam* by neglecting its contractual dimension and its being a historically contingent formula of specification of *din*, that reflects the quite balanced solution provided by the Koran to the God–man relationship (see Chapter 1). That the outcome of the analysis is the theorizing of the "essentially political character" of Islam as a set of regulations for this world's life (a genuinely conflationist position) is not surprising (WG, p. 375).

In his construction of Islam as a counter-type to Calvinism, Weber had to account for the undeniable success of its early history of world conquest coupled with its alleged historical failure to develop world mastery in the form of rational capitalism.[11] The medium of explanation was the emphasis laid on the centrality of *jihad* in the possibility of existence of that "belated manifestation of Near Eastern monotheism" (WG, p. 375). As a consequence, the motivational strength of Islamic doctrine was found only in extraordinary situations, typically in wars (by virtue of the alternative between booty and "a sensual soldier's paradise": WG, p. 376). In postulating an enduring primacy of military conquests in Islam, Weber disregarded that this component is devoid of any solid, direct reference to the Koran and its *din*.[12]

One could object that Weber was basically interested in the genesis of innerworldly rational work asceticism, so that his position does not directly prejudice an assessment of intellectual modernity. In fact, the very attitude to cyclical reform in Islamic history, that Weber is very close to admitting, has been precisely the basis of one famous claim that Islam has a particular predisposition to modernity (Gellner, 1981, p. 5). Gellner maintains that the cyclical movement of reform and renewal in Islam, a phenomenon indispensable for its very reproduction, culminated, in the modern era, in a more encompassing and enduring Reform (or era of Reform), imbued with a spirit of universal reference in modern terms (to this point see also the even more stringent reformulation in Gellner, 1992; for *islah* as the keyword for reform see Chapter 5). It is interesting to note that this stress on the cyclical attitude to reform was already present in Weber, but formulated in purely negative terms, in relation to its allegedly deleterious influence on rational daily life conduct, the crucial medium between religious ethics and economic ethic.

Weber's characterization of Islam in the form of an ethic of "world domination as world conquest and accommodation to it" (Schluchter, 1987) was a direct consequence of the lack of focus on its historical evolution with regard to processes of subjectification and reification. In Weber the cyclical motion is evaluated as the negation itself of the systematic and rational shaping of life conduct, which is the epitome of Western modernity brought about by Protestant self-denial (RS, I, p. 125). Weber maintains that even when a rational-ascetic element seems to play a role in Islamic history, it

ISLAM AND POLITICAL DISCOURSE OF MODERNITY

immediately turns the ethos of life conduct into a political game (Schluchter, 1987, p. 44). Thus, the syndromatically political character of Islam was firmly established, with enduring consequences – as I shall try to show – on the reshaping of the transcultural space for the rest of our century.

We should not forget, however, that Weber clearly aspired to go beyond the explanation of the genesis of rational capitalism, and to account for the whole of the uniqueness of Western culture, including "Western science" in its largest sense, as rooted in academic institutions. This is revealed by the statement: "only in the West there is 'science' in the developmental stage, to which we nowadays attribute 'validity'" (RS, I, p. 1). This contention is placed at the very beginning of the RS, and thereby reflects the position of the last Weber.[13] The problem is that he did not deal with this last topic comparatively in the context of what I have called the modern turn of intellectual distinction (see Chapter 2). There is in Weber no explicit analysis of "rationalization" through an examination of the relationship between intellectual modernity and the modernity of economic ethic as mediated by "valid science". This incongruence has not been without consequences, since the general impression of comprehensiveness of Western uniqueness conveyed by Weber has helped shape the claim of the West's exclusive credit for rational science and the Enlightenment, where both are equated with intellectual modernity at large.

Gellner has tried to show (1992) how it is possible to conceive of Western science as unique without at the same time denying Islam the ability to produce a modern framework of universal reference. More in general, in his essays on Islam framed according to the Weberian problematic, Gellner seems to take for granted that there was no inherent cultural obstacle in Islam and its economic ethic against rational capitalism. His thesis is that upon a more attentive, less pre-oriented look into the historical unfolding of Islam's conceptual system Weber should have seen in it – all obvious differences notwithstanding – substantial (and not just merely exterior) affinities with Calvinism as to the presence of rationalizing impulses. "The difference [in Islam] would seem to be less in the absence of ideological elements than in the particular balance of power which existed between the various institutions in that society" (Gellner, 1981, p. 6). More recently Gellner has stated,

given the congruence between what Weberian sociology would lead one to expect, and what is offered by High and Reformist Islam, there is a bit of a puzzle concerning why Muslim economic performance is not rather more distinguished than it actually is . . .

> But whatever the state of the economy, there cannot be much doubt about the present situation in the ideological sphere (Gellner, 1992, p. 21).

This argumentation should be interpreted in the following way: that the Weberian method of analysing conditions of modernity is substantially fine; that Weber's application of this method to Islam was basically wrong, but that as a result, one still feels uneasy with this non-integrated modernity of Muslim societies.[14]

The focus of Weber's comparative sociology was, however, on the "cultural carriers", and the combination of approach and *Fragestellung* ("problematic") concerning the links between economic and religious ethic provided a potentially powerful key to constructing fresh hypotheses about patterns of intellectual modernity in "Oriental" cultural-religious units (in our case "Islam"). Max Weber lacked, however, the appropriate sources and focus, as he disregarded those social and intellectual processes taking place during the eighteenth and nineteenth centuries which have become the object of the attention of some revisionist historians of the Middle East during the last twenty years (see Chapter 3). This deficit of Weber's sociology was directly inherited from nineteenth- and turn-of-the-century Orientalism, that was only marginally able or willing to approach contemporary intellectual innovations in Muslim lands. The exchange that few Orientalists of that time (like Ernest Renan and Ignaz Goldziher) initiated with contemporary Islamic reformers like al-Afghani and 'Abduh lacked the necessary focus on the social conditions of modern intellectual thought and did not affect the relevant core of their scholarship.[15] A clear answer to the crucial question of Orientalism's relationship to the contemporary Orient has yet to be found.[16]

In synthesis, there seems to be an increasing tendency in Weber, through the years of his comparative work, to attempt to fit Islam into a contrastive role with Calvinism as the quintessence of Western *Geist* and achievement, even more so since Islam *seemed* to be grounded on very similar doctrinal settings. It is probably of great significance that this tendency reaches its apex in Weber's additional statements on Islam in the revised edition of PE (cf. RS, I, p. 102, n. 2). These passages, due to the particular popularity of PE in the Weberian heritage, have probably been determinant in turning the "Protestant ethic" thesis into a trivialized, general epitome of Western self-understanding. In attempting to demonstrate, in the case of Calvinism, how far predestination was from producing fatalism, Weber needed to refer to a cultural-religious "type" with concrete historical rooting that could be considered liable to fatalism in routine times, due to a kind of alleged pseudo-predestination doctrine that was simply a form of predeterminism devoid of substantial anchoring in the subjective strive towards salvation.[17]

Weber's sociology combined a sociological explicitation of a "global" approach in comparative perspective with the more parochial concern for Western (or even German) developmental paths (see Turner, 1990, p. 353). Compared with classic Orientalism, Weber's grounding motivation was much more consciously formulated in terms of a Western, or more specifically German, national concern. The outcome was a dynamic essentialism, combining understanding and explanation, internal (subjective) and external (objective) variables, *Geist* and *Form*, with an undeniable primacy of the first component: a method suitable to the study of how discontinuities can arise from continuities, and that in so doing reflected the crux of social sciences at large, their combination of compelling essentialism and analytic vocation.

The methodological dimension of this process of sociologizing what we might call "the Western question of Islam" is clearly made explicit by Weber himself, where he recognizes, in the opening sentence of the Foreword to the RS (RS, p.1; see Schluchter, 1987, pp. 96 and 121 for the interpretation of this statement), the heuristic Eurocentrism underlying his comparative undertaking, whose key concept was "inwardness". In Weber's sociology this takes the form of a social-scientifically unquestionable (in spite of being admittedly Eurocentred) tool of classification and inquiry. Other cultural-religious units, and most prominently Islam, are judged in terms of their degree of dissonance from the Western path of turning inwardness into an instrument of world mastery. We have seen, however, the extent to which the concept of inwardness was the reflex – most evident in the German case – of the academic institutionalization and neutralization of the intellectuals' own "irrelation to politics" (see Chapter 4). The result is a closed circularity between the idea that legitimates the vocation of the social scientist, the method of inquiry and the mechanism of social change imputed to the processes analysed (cf. Stauth, 1993, pp. 48, 54 and 67).

This social-scientific upgrading of the essentialist method of the *Islamwissenschaft* performed by Weber was paralleled by a loss of analytic depth in defining the tensions inherent in the genesis and unfolding of the Arab–Islàmic "historical personality". Goldziher's thematization of the relation between *muru'a* ("Bedouin virtue") and *din* produced insights into the tensions between pre-Islamic Arab customs, the ethical character of Muhammad's prophecy and the allegedly resulting dimension of Islam's warrior ethos along lines of explanation whose analytic strength is incommensurably deeper than in Weber's study of Islam, even if evaluated from a perspective of historical socio-anthropology. Moreover, Goldziher pointed to the centrality of Sufism for processes of rationalization in Islam, while Weber reduced the Muslim mystic to irrational "derwish-religiosity" (Stauth, 1987, pp. 12–13 and Stauth, 1993, pp. 134–5).

Although Schluchter has claimed that Weber's analysis of Islam has not produced any major impact on any subsequent study (Schluchter, 1987, p. 84), this is true only at the level of direct and conscious influence. It is worth remembering that Said himself, at the same time as he renounced focusing analytically on Weber, explicitly recognized his importance.[18] A revisionist historian of the Middle East has been even more outspoken: "Until the last few decades, the great majority of studies of social movements in Islamic societies tended (either implicitly or explicitly) to be situated within the Weberian tradition, though often without much methodological self-awareness." (Burke, 1988, p. 20). Schluchter's evaluation is therefore correct only in the sense that for decades hardly any student of the Islamic Middle East has accurately elaborated Weber's fragmentary – but cogent enough – references to Islam, even less so in the context of his more general *Fragestellung*. For precisely this reason, Weber's influence on Islamic studies has taken a form that we can call "Weberism", which is a phenomenon of broader cultural range. It consists in a trivialized version of the Weberian heritage that operates, through the authoritative cover provided by Weber's work, on most – not only academic – Western cognitive undertakings which define patterns of distinction towards the non-Western world, and first of all towards the part of it that is most relevant for the shaping of the Western self-image, the Islamic Orient.

It is no mere speculation that different schools tried to "use" Weber, without really grasping the original features of his approach. Most prominent in the making of Weberism is Talcott Parsons' reading of Weber. As revealed by distortions and even omissions in his own translation (Gordon, 1987, p. 313), the American sociologist made an adaptive misuse of Weber moved by the urge of securing a rapid and stable consolidation of sociological theory in the post-Second World War United States. From the point of view of the study of Islam, Weberism helped to reshape the Orientalist tradition in conformity with the requirements of the new-style American hegemony (Salvatore, 1991, pp. 37–53). This process led to the establishment of "Middle East Studies" as the most prominent branch among "Area Studies" (Binder, 1976), at least *vis-à-vis* the urgencies of foreign policy.

This division of the social sciences in a mainstream sector studying differentiation and complexity in modern society and an "Area Studies" section devoted to the study of would-be societies trying to move from undifferentiated traditionalism to modern complexity, and also engaged in the task of providing the theoretical tools to help them in modernizing, reflects Weberism as operating in Parsons. In this way, within the academic setting of social sciences in the post-Second World War United States, a new division of labour was achieved in the representation of Self and Other, resulting in a further loss of analytic vigour. Very roughly, but without distorting the self-understanding of the division of labour, we can say that the reflection on the Western "prototype" provided a theory of "structural modernization" and of "political development", whereas the focus on the Other was finalized to define the field of tension between traditional cultures and strivings for modernization, up to the definition of a strategy for a concrete application of modernization theory. As in the opinion of one of the leading figures belonging to the first generation within American Middle East Studies, the result of Weberism at work in the study of modern and contemporary Islam was that "the criticisms were not based on any scientific findings regarding the prerequisites of development. They rather reflected the self-image of Western society and those values to which the dominant classes were inclined to attribute the success of the systems they dominated" (Binder, 1988, p. 210).

If we remember Weber's introductory sentence in RS (along with Schluchter's interpretation), the stated, unavoidable character of "heuristic Eurocentrism" is associated with the awareness of the danger of slipping into a "normative Eurocentrism". The occultation of heuristic Eurocentrism behind the screen of objectivist social sciences implies in the case of postwar American Middle East Studies a smooth passage to a normative Eurocentrism.[19] Weber's sentence can be evaluated as foreseeing (and fearing) the subsequent success of Weberism and its influence: this is in fact characterized by *not* making explicit the epistemological constraints visibly highlighted by Weber.[20] But Weberism was allowed by disregarding other clear and insistent warnings in Weber's Foreword to RS, concerning the status of his own comparative studies. Besides being inescapably constrained on a heuristic level (with the already-mentioned consequence that his handling of Islam was more than "oriented": RS, I, p. 13), Weber stresses, precisely towards the end of his life, that his comparative research has a markedly pioneering character (pp. 13–14) and should be assessed as such. It almost seems that Weber, conscious of the representative strength, for Western concerns, of his remarkably innovative approach, appeals to future social scientists to draw creatively from his heritage and not stiffen it into a doctrine. He seems to warn against Weberism.

We cannot, however, ascribe to Weberism alone the responsibility for a "maximalist" concept of modernity, for viewing this as an integrated package.

While on the one hand Western uniqueness does not necessarily imply, for Weber, that the way to rational capitalism cannot be found under different conditions and stages in other cultures, he tends, nonetheless, to see this uniqueness in the shaping of an anthropological type that cumulates paths of rationalization along lines that cannot be reduced to simple, different manifestations of modernity. In this sense he reshapes the moral claim to distinction inherited from the Enlightenment according to criteria compatible with – although not reducible to – the positivistic method of inquiry (see Hennis, 1987 and Gordon, 1987, p. 295). This is probably the reason why Weber failed to make clear that rational disenchantment (as assimilated to "structural" modernity, i.e. the modernity of capitalism and bureaucracies) was able to keep momentum only through an intellectual game of rationalist *re-enchantment*, consisting of intellectual modernity and the ensuing construction of frameworks of communal reference and universal projection, made possible by a game of distinction (see Chapter 2).

The making of Weberism out of Weber's variegated corpus of investigations does not seem to have been analysed as a distinct phenomenon. Specialists of Weber are engaged in reconstructing the correct interpretation of his work, so that Weberism is touched upon only in its negative side, as a mistaken interpretation of Weber's *Fragestellung*. The position taken here is that the reasons for Weberism matter in themselves, and I believe that these reasons can be grasped only within the context of Orientalism's development, through its different phases, during the last two centuries. A suggestion of something very close to, but not identical with, what I have called Weberism is provided by Colin Gordon when he affirms that "Weber is . . . innocent . . . of the so-called Weberianism that adopts a uniform, monolithic conception of historical phenomena of rationalization." (Gordon, 1987, p. 294). He situates this claim within the broader discussion, initiated by Hennis, of how Weber's real *Fragestellung* would be the study of discontinuities in subject-bound patterns of life conduct (intended also, or mainly, in an ethical sense), and not systemic disenchantment, as maintained by Weberism, so that the "maximalist" separation between a traditional and a modern universe of meaning would *not* be part of the proper Weberian heritage (p. 312).

However, Weber's treatment of Islam produces a paradoxical maximalist view of modernity that becomes unavoidable when adopting the kind of "oriented" comparative perspective characterizing the work of the German sociologist. Albert Hourani has acutely observed that the fact "that Islam is seen as virtually a pure type of warrior religion runs counter not only to what is now known and thought about it, but also to Weber's own sense of the complexity of the particular existent being . . . [H]is typology was never modified to take account of the specific features of Islam." (Hourani, [1967] 1980, p. 71.) We should probably revise Gordon's evaluation by saying that Weberism arises out of *the extent* to which Weber *failed* to fulfil his project of a "comparativist approach to different rationalization phenomena" (Gordon, 1987, p. 294) that aimed at finding out "that different societies arrive at [the] threshold [of modernity] . . . endowed with very variable levels of capability for negotiating it successfully" (pp. 312–13).

One famous controversy in 1922, only two years after the publication of Weber's RS, within the Heidelberger Weber circle, best highlights the modalities of the passage from Weber to Weberism. Carl H. Becker summed up his comparison between the paths of the "West" and "Islam" by assigning to the latter at least the world-historical function of relating the Hellenist heritage to Christian European dynamics of rationalization. This assessment was based on an appropriate blend of classic Orientalist analysis of civilizations in terms of their "rise-and-fall" and a focus on patterns of rationalization. The theologian Ernest Troeltsch, one of Weber's main partners in the academic debates of the time, responded instead by making Weber's self-declared Eurocentrism more and more a matter of selectively restricting the application of its heuristic value, through an exclusive focus on Western (European and American, basically Protestant) Christianity as the proper and exclusive source of modern rationality. The consequence of Troeltsch's position was that any future comparative study was bound to presuppose, and no longer problematize, the uniqueness of Western modernity epitomized by the innerworldly asceticism of Protestantism (Stauth, 1993, pp. 155–8).

NOTES

1   This was also the trajectory of the Orientalist Gustave von Grunebaum, who best incorporates the passage from classic European Orientalism to American postwar Middle East Studies (see Chapter 7).

2   From now on I will always quote Weber from the original German versions of his works. I prefer to proceed in this way and propose my own translations of the quoted passages, since many of their English translations (even of the titles) leave much to be desired.

3   "The economic ethic of world religions".

4   "Collected essays in the sociology of religion".

5   "The economy and the structures of social powers".

6   "Economy and society".

7   For an earlier consideration of the topic of this chapter, see Salvatore, 1996.

8   Did he allude to it programmatically? Was this manuscript nothing but the pages devoted to Islam present in WG?

9   "The Protestant ethic and the spirit of capitalism".

10 The distinction between the two phases was already well consolidated in the works of Goldziher and Wellhausen, from which Weber probably drew (Schluchter, 1987, p. 51).

11 This is a claim that in no way has the status of an ascertained fact. The first major challenge to it has come from Peter Gran (1979) in the context of the revisionist shift in the historiography of Islam (see Chapter 3).

12 It has been ironically observed (Schulze, 1992b, p. 106) that the "text" which legitimized and recorded the very concrete goal of Islamic conquest was not the Koran, but the *diwan* (register of pays and stipends). Weber's incongruous shift in attributing the pursuit of prebends to Islam is recognized by Schluchter (1987, p. 64).

13 The Foreword to the RS is among Weber's last writings.

14 Within a genuine neo-Weberian perspective very close to the Gellnerian approach, a sort of division of labour has been reproposed between the mainstream social theorist and the historical sociologist of Islam, as in the case of John Hall and Patricia Crone (see Sadowski, 1993, p.18). In this case, more than in Gellner's one, the recognition of the fact that the differences between the "West" and "Islam" are more institutional than cultural (i.e. not due to a different, or lacking, unfolding of subjectification and rationalization, but to the absence of a modern state) is still at the origin of a discourse of difference, encouraging easy generalizations more than fresh problematizations (see also Chapters 1 and 4).

15 John Lewis Burckhardt (1784–1817), who lived in the Middle East at the beginning of last century, at the same time as Orientalism began to take a solid institutional form in the European academic landscape, represents probably the most prominent exception to the Orientalists' lack of insight into contemporary politics in the region. And it is certainly symptomatic that he studied in particular, through fieldwork (since he was not an Orientalist in the conventional sense), the Wahhabi movement (see Chapter 3). A later

"proto-ethnographer", William Robertson Smith (1846–94), further enhanced the scholarly, systematic profile of fieldwork, while keeping a more solid rooting within the Orientalist establishment (Eickelman, 1981, pp. 31–5).

16 Only a systematic historiography of Orientalism could help to solve the problem. The recent Orientalism critique and debate has helped to justify the opportunity of this type of enterprise, but seems to have blocked it at the same time, because of its propensity to generalize on the basis of restricted sets of historical and textual data. The best works in this direction are already "classics" (see Schwab, 1950; Fück, 1955; and Waardenburg, 1963).

17 See also WG, pp. 346–7, where the argumentation on the status of Calvinism's predestination also shifts almost automatically into an explicit reference to Islam.

18 "Although he never thoroughly studied Islam, Weber nevertheless influenced the field considerably." (Said, 1978, p. 259).

19 This is exactly the kind of shift we will find from the first hermeneutic circle ("late-classic Orientalism") to the second ("modernization theory"): see Chapter 7.

20 This occurs in probably the most visible place in his entire work, since those who want to read the famous PE inevitably run into the Foreword to RS (within which PE figures as the first essay), whose opening sentence tackles the question of Eurocentrism.

PART III

THE WESTERN MAKING OF "POLITICAL ISLAM"

The linear hermeneutics of Islam "as such"

In this and the next chapter, I shall analyse the first crucial passage in the genesis of what I have called the interpretive field of political Islam (see Introduction): the transition from linear, monodimensional hermeneutics primarily centred on an essentialized view of Islam "as such", where the political is considered derivative of religion, to the opening of a bidimensional hermeneutic field, where the political acquires the status of an additional and autonomous dimension grounded on a concern of the observer (see Chapter 8).

The crucial unity of analysis will be constituted by an approximation of so-called communities of interpreters, that I prefer to see as "hermeneutic circles" (see Introduction and Chapter 2 for their definition and theoretical justification). These should not, as is obvious, be intended as authors' clubs meeting on Friday evenings to discuss political Islam, nor, probably, as clear-cut communities, however informal. The task of identifying circles will thus consist of a work of typification, aiming at selecting not so much ideal but concrete types, i.e. grounded on empirically accessible models of argumentation.

From the first to the fourth circles we will observe an historical-genealogical derivation along the same hermeneutic chain in the context of Western academic production of knowledge, whose main lines of development and displacement relevant for the genesis of the interpretive field of political Islam have been outlined in Chapters 4 and 6. There we saw how at the historical juncture that witnessed the emergence of Weber's comparative sociology of religion, the essentialization of Islam reached a crucial transcultural relevance through a clear-cut operation of conflation, consisting of postulating the necessity of a link between the domains of faith and politics in Islam. As a response to this conflation, some interpreters deconflate the relationship by laying a stress on its variable and contingent character. The first pair of circles that I am going to examine reflects a pendular movement between conflation and deconflation, which provides a significant platform to the formation of the hermeneutic field of political Islam. These circles are not yet subject to the constraint of building argument by taking into account the vision of "Islam" as active on the "political" scene, but their dynamics provide the immediate terrain of origin for such a vision.

The first circle, represented by the framing model of "late-classic" Orientalism, is here analysed through textual material written by Gustave von Grunebaum. This choice (to the disadvantage of other likely candidates such as Sir Hamilton Gibb, W. Montgomery Watt or Marshall Hodgson) is easily justified by reference to the genealogical principle of identifying a strong "line of descent" that best explains the emergence of the hermeneutic field of political Islam, after having chosen Weber's intervention as the salient breakthrough in the formation of the relevant transcultural scenario (see Introduction and Chapter 6).

These criteria should be regarded as sufficiently distinct from the rationale of the anti-Orientalist campaign (which I will also try to situate historically in the genealogy of the hermeneutic chain: see Chapter 8), that also made von Grunebaum a favourite object of critique. His work became a privileged target of denunciations of Orientalism's essentialism even before Edward Said started his campaign and depicted the scholar of Austrian origin as a major epitome of the Orientalists' vice of producing "essentially reductive, negative generalizations" on Islam (Said, 1978, p. 296).[1] For Orientalism's critics, the choice of concentrating on influential scholars as suitable targets serves the need for legitimizing their enterprise; from the perspective of the present work, instead, the influence of an author *within the identified hermeneutic chain* is an intrinsic methodological condition for the analysis (see Introduction).

Von Grunebaum's positions do not differ radically from those of Carl H. Becker, so that the former can be considered as representative of classic Orientalism in general. His reformulation of the basic ideas of his predecessors accords, however, with a clearly Weberist perspective. In appropriating the universal-comparative approach of Western human sciences epitomized by Weber, von Grunebaum celebrates this as "an end confined to the most modern West" (von Grunebaum, [1961] 1964a, p. 43). It has been remarked that "he was convinced that it was his duty to interpret Islam from the point of view of the Westerner deeply steeped in his own civilization at its best." (Rosenthal, 1973, p. 356.) One can argue that von Grunebaum's prominence lies in his success in giving a methodological foundation to an explicitly Weberist (hence not simply "Orientalist", as denounced by his critics) interpretation of Islam. His definition of his own work as affiliated to "cultural anthropology" warrants the scientific justification of a reflexively conscious Weberist discourse in that it legitimizes the method chosen by appealing to the Western Weberist ethos. In this way cultural anthropology becomes the crux of any intellectual undertaking resting on a comparative-sociological understanding (von Grunebaum, [1961] 1964a, p. 50): " . . . it enables us to classify and evaluate cultural analyses in Islamic (as well as other) fields in terms of their serviceableness to our primary aspirations and to the rationality of our methodological requirements" (p. 53).

Within a methodological framework of this type, von Grunebaum reappropriates to the Orientalist camp the task of reinterpreting the ranking of "inner" factors in the unfolding of Islam, which had been turned by Weber into a sociologized view of inwardness (see Chapter 6). "The purpose-directedness of human existence . . . pervades every sphere of man's activity, the technological or the economic as well as the political or the interpretative. The *why* is secondary to the *what for.*" This typically Weberist reduction of the factors of human and social development to the *Geist* component, inevitably slides towards the study of man's "progressive . . . self-revelation . . . in history" (p. 41), a formula that shows the Hegelist regression which can hide behind those forms of Weberism that are not well grounded on a social-scientific terrain. Through this operation, the author restores a much higher degree of hermeneutic freedom in interpreting Islam than allowed by Weber's adoption of a strictly comparative perspective (see Chapter 6).

In approaching von Grunebaum, it is inevitable to mention an essay of the Moroccan scholar Abdallah Laroui. This contribution is assigned the merit, in particular, of having shown how von Grunebaum's interpretation of Islam is indebted to A. L. Kroeber's culturalist theory (see Said, 1978, pp. 297–8). This observation, however perceptive, cannot provide the basis for an adequate reconstruction of the genesis of von Grunebaum's interpretation of Islam. Laroui did not ask which kind of scholarly orientation Kroeber himself embodied and transferred to von Grunebaum.

It cannot be overlooked that Kroeber acted as a vehicle for Weberism, that von Grunebaum in turn re-elaborated on his own by applying his direct knowledge of what the Heidelberger scholar had written on Islam (see Turner, 1984, p. 194), as well as of the foundations of Weber's comparative task in the sociology of religion. As von Grunebaum approvingly remarks, "A. L. Kroeber has characterized the Islamic message as a reduction and a simplification of the religious concepts of the contemporary faiths, particu-larly of Christianity." (von Grunebaum, [1960] 1964b, p. 7). This profile clearly recalls Weber's portrait of Islam as a belated manifestation of Near Eastern monotheism, a banalized version of forms of religious spirituality that were already consolidated at the time of Muhammad, who tailored the new prophetic message on the ethos and interests of a warriors' aristocracy (see Chapter 6). It is clear that in order to fit Kroeber's formula depicting Islam as a religion of reduction, von Grunebaum resorts to the *leitmotiv* of Weber's characterization: he stresses Islam's "more optimistic outlook on human nature as needful of guidance rather than of redemption and hence the discouragement of the more extreme forms of asceticism . . . in short, Islam's more realistic but also more vulgar adjustment to the world as it is" (p. 8).

Some biographical elements can help to highlight the particular trajectory that made von Grunebaum the foremost guardian of the Weberist heritage in the international scholarly landscape of Islamic studies after the Second World War. He was a typical embodiment of the German-speaking European scholar who had migrated to the United States in the Nazi era. In 1943 he went to teach at the University of Chicago: at that time he was already regarded as a leading scholar in Orientalism. From 1957 onwards, he worked at the UCLA, where he founded the Center for Near Eastern Studies, which under his direction rapidly acquired prominence within the landscape of American Middle East Studies. We will see how, within this institutional scenario, von Grunebaum was not merely representative of the way German philosophical and humanistic assets of academic knowledge were integrated into American postwar social sciences but, more specifically, of how a markedly culturalist continental-European approach could be considered immediately applicable to the field of political science in the United States. Aided by a little more historical perspective, I will try to modify an approach such as Laroui's, whose limit, consistent with the function of Orientalism's critique, is to pose the question in the rather ahistorical terms of the flaws of culturalism (or cultural essentialism).

Textual references are drawn here from the last collection of essays published by von Grunebaum, a kind of *summa* of his own hermeneutics of Islam, first published in 1962 (though I will refer to the 1964 revised edition) at a time when his own prestige and influence were at their peak at an international level. He was widely recognized as the old ("late-classic") student of the Islamic Orient engaged in transmitting his body of knowledge to the new breed of American Middle East Studies' scholars practising a blend of political sociology and political science (see the analysis of the second circle, below). It was also a time, however, when Orientalism began to be considered as an issue for its own sake, especially by scholars of Arab origin, as to its status of knowledge which claimed universal validity. Von Grunebaum did not shy away from the beginnings of critical consideration of the studies of the Islamic Orient, as shown by his participation in the 1961 Brussels' *Colloque sur la Sociologie Musulmane*.

What makes the essays in the 1962 collection particularly worthy of analysis is that they no longer incorporate the unquestioned character of Orientalism as a science. It is not by chance that the single contribution based on the paper presented at the Brussels' colloquium holds a central place in the collection. In this essay von Grunebaum revealed a profound consciousness of the specific historical conjuncture of the early 1960s, with its dominant model of universalism suspended between triumph and vulnerability. Even more, he was probably aware that a major crisis was close: "It may well be that our comprehensive, or universalistic approach will lose its attraction . . . And, above all, the sustaining aspiration of our cultural community may change." (von Grunebaum, [1961] 1964a, p. 54). Under the tangible justification constraint that governs the speech of the authoritative Orientalist, this essay has the merit of making explicit the epistemic premises of the first circle.

The single statement that drew the greatest attention and the most virulent critique, as it has been considered the epitome of how von Grunebaum conceived of Islam, and, above all, of his own method of interpretation (see Arkoun, 1964, p. 114; Laroui, [1973] 1974, p. 87; Waines, 1975, p. 118; and Said, 1978, p. 297), is to be found in this study:

> It is essential to realize that Muslim civilization is a cultural entity that does not share our primary aspirations. It is not vitally interested in analytical self-understanding, and is even less interested in the structured study of other cultures, either as an end in itself or as a means toward clearer understanding of its own character and history (von Grunebaum, [1961] 1964a, p. 55).

To stop at this statement, or to make this the exclusive focus of a judgement on von Grunebaum, would prevent us, however, from taking a wide analytical advantage from the richness of clues included in his study (significatively entitled *An Analysis of Islamic Civilization and Cultural Anthropology)*, which has the merit of highlighting the crucial links between the problematic tackled and the method used.[2]

Let us begin with the long, final footnote of the essay, which mentions the scholarly controversy on the evaluation of Islam within the Heidelberger Weber circle. This is particularly useful to elucidate the background to the link between problem and method in von Grunebaum's hermeneutics by looking at the author's explicit recognition of his historical affiliations. He remembers the dispute mentioned in Chapter 6 between the Orientalist scholar who probably had the strongest impact on Weber's view of Islam, Carl H. Becker, and the theologian Ernest Troeltsch. At stake was, as von

Grunebaum sees it, the appraisal of "the essential participation of the Islamic *Kulturkreis* in the destiny of the West" (von Grunebaum [1961] 1964a, p. 97 n. 66). Von Grunebaum seems to subscribe to the winning position of Troeltsch, who rejected the thesis of Islam's relevance, thereby decisively contributing to the formation of Weberism. This became the necessary paradigm for both a universal sociology constrained by a comparative perspective, and an increasingly sociologized Orientalism, that explictly began to look at Islam from the viewpoint of the centrality and uniqueness of Western modernity.

In spite of the fact that his scholarship manifested the highest degree of sociologization ever pursued by Orientalism until that time, Carl H. Becker reflected the limits of Orientalism's capacity to draw the most consequent methodological conclusions from the paradigm of Western uniqueness. His historicist argument in the controversy was vulnerable in sociological terms, once sociology had established a Western-modelled concept of modernity as the standard regulating any judgement of other cultures. Referring to the contention, von Grunebaum does not miss the opportunity to make it clear that his own hermeneutics are indebted to this dispute and to its outcome, as shown by his concomitant quotation of Weber's Foreword to the RS (see Chapter 6), which solidly establishes the "objective pre-eminence" of Western culture.

Let us turn now more directly to the argumentative apparatus employed by von Grunebaum in order to tackle the problem of Islam's alleged inherent deficits. In logical terms, his discourse starts by taking firm root in the terrain of Western self-understanding. He recognizes "the recurrent intellectual and social crises characteristic of the West for at least the last four or five centuries" as a vehicle for self-renewal. This virtue is held to go hand in hand with the core of modern Western uniqueness, "the ever-widening control and understanding of the inner and outer world". But Islam's crises are basically different, since they are not inscribed in this progressive dialectic: "their" crises are only one basic, inherent and "pervasive" Crisis, that is the negation itself of any chance of subjective self-regeneration. In Muslim societies we merely observe the fabrication of self-images for the immediate sake of political ends (von Grunebaum, [1961] 1964a, pp. 45–6). In trying to explain how in those societies there is no real change in the Western sense, von Grunebaum pictures the Islamic pseudo-change as "a leap from one absolute to another". The changeless character of the absolute model is further seen as sanctioned by the dogma of the final revelation through the Prophet Muhammad, which pinpoints the closed, inward-looking character of Islamic ethics.

From other essays previously published by von Grunebaum we know that the starting formula for the identification of the primary "aspiration" of Islam is the quest for correctness in life, thinking and social organization. The semantics of such models of correctness are seen as rooted in the Medinan period of the Prophet's life (Waines, 1975, p. 116), following a reductive option in the hermeneutics of Islam, whose reasons and consequences have been preliminarily addressed in Chapter 1 (see Chapter 6 for Weber's own version). This Medinan centrality should also explain – according to von Grunebaum – why the Muslim world is not interested in the kind of Other's knowledge stimulated by the quest for Self-knowledge so familiar to Westerners. To the Muslims,

> the non-Muslim world is interesting enough but, in a sense, obsolete
> . . . The testimonial to the lasting and universal adaptability of
> the faith and its unadulterated (though unspecifiable) cultural
> implementation still takes the place of an analysis of the contem-
> porary scene and Islam in it or of the nature of Islam in successive
> periods and different places, which is not merely a device quickly
> to project tomorrow's programme onto the screen in the guise of
> a past realization (von Grunebaum, [1961] 1964a, pp. 56–58).

And, *as a consequence*, we have the typically Islamic political short-cut: "this attitude leads to an extreme concern with power and success in history, or, more precisely, with success in history as the validation of revelation." (p. 58). The shift to a political dimension is seen then as the product of a tension inherent in Islam: the original factor is Islam *per se*: politics is derivative from it, in the sense that it does not originate from a process of modern structural differentiation, or of modern intellectual distinction. This conclusion neatly expresses, without major alterations, the core argument of the conflationism that we can attribute to classic Orientalism at large, including its pre-Weberian, late nineteenth-century form (see Chapter 6). The following passage condenses in a masterly way the classic Orientalist-conflationist formula within the framework of an acute Weberist awareness:

> The pursuit of an ideal political life (early projected into the reality
> of the first forty years of the *hijra* . . .) in disregard of the actual
> situation has become the permanent drama of Islam. The primary
> cause for this unresolvable tension between norm and fact is the
> Muslim identification of the temporal and the spiritual planes. The

faith (or faith *per se*) is a political value; in fact, it is the only political value and decidedly the only value that gives the *civitas Islamica* its *raison d'être* (pp. 65–6).

The step necessary for legitimizing such a deductionist path is the liquidation of the eighteenth century as an era of no-change for Islamic history[3] (for the importance of this century see Chapter 3). The change which occurred in Muslim lands since the beginning of the nineteenth century is unmistakably heterogenetic, as von Grunebaum states in another essay from the same collection (von Grunebaum, [1960] 1964b, p. 21). The ensuing "reactivist" historical model (see Chapter 3) is defended against any claim from within the Muslim world that such change was the product of internal renewal (p. 20).

In a third essay von Grunebaum provides a more refined formulation of the argument for Islam's inherent deficits, supported by the use of a category that he supposes to be interculturally valid, i.e. "classicism". After defining this as a cultural attitude of universal import, he subsumes under this label "most of the Islamic reform movements", from Hanbalism to the Muslim Brotherhood. A "close resemblance" with Western Renaissance and post-Renaissance classicism is recognized (von Grunebaum, [1962] 1964c, p. 112). At this point, von Grunebaum seems very close to crediting those Islamic movements with the capacity to reformulate a civilizational aspiration following at least "proto-modern" canons (see Chapter 3). The category of classicism, however, here fulfils the function of dictating the limits of the modern potentialities of such expressions: first, Islamic reformism cannot go beyond classicism, unlike Western cultural movements; second, for Islam, classicism is not an option among others, suggested by a particular historical conjuncture, and facilitating the construction of the new through reference to the past: it is, rather, the intrinsic hermeneutic dimension of Islam. From Hanbalism to the Muslim Brotherhood, the model of reference to the past is virtually identical. No trajectory of reformism is recognized. The most significant element of continuity with classic Orientalism is the refusal (or incapacity) to focus on the varying social conditions of concrete manifestations of thought.

The synthetic statement that we can attribute to the first circle as represented by von Grunebaum is that, as a result of a negation – explicit or implicit – of the very possibility of a social differentiation usually conceptualized as "modern", there is no genuine political-intellectual thought in Islam. In the end, Islam as such is political, so that a construct like "political Islam" is a mere tautology and does not deserve to be handled as a separate question.

Von Grunebaum was himself conscious that his own hermeneutics of Islam had to be located within a space of interpretive contention, as he writes at the end of the pivotal essay of the collection (von Grunebaum, [1961] 1964a, p. 96): "Our methodology will not be lost, but many of our results and much of our manner of presentation will imperceptibly but inevitably turn into source material from which those who come after us will recapture our aspirations." The most immediate interpretive shift foreshadowed by von Grunebaum's testament affects the question of the implicit model of Eurocentrism. In von Grunebaum's most important direct reference to Max Weber, recalling the first part of the Foreword to RS, he takes a position on the basic question summarized by Weber's opening statement of the Foreword (see Chapter 6), where the German sociologist pinpoints the inevitability of a heuristic Eurocentrism, but also warns against adopting a normative one. Von Grunebaum's position takes for granted the universalization of Western modernity, whose merit is, according to him, to decrease "the importance of the cultural dividing line between 'East' and 'West' with regard to the future" (von Grunebaum, [1961] 1964a, p. 97 n. 66). This statement appears to embody a stance of neutrality between a heuristic and a normative Eurocentrism, but slides towards the second, which was consolidating as a major feature of the second circle at the same time as von Grunebaum published the essays here analysed (see below).

Once modernization theory consolidated its grip on postwar Middle East Studies and replaced philology with a new social-scientific methodology and vocabulary, the formula of the universal path of modernization allowed for revising the first circle's contention regarding Muslim societies' non-propensity to "political development". The task of defining the extent of continuity and change between the "old" European Orientalism and the "new" American Area Studies has proven to be highly controversial.[4] For the scope of the present work, the second circle is relevant, at first glance, for denying the core tenets of the first circle and its conflationist model. The second circle's thesis is that Islam as a whole is residual in the modernization processes that Middle East societies undergo. As a consequence, Islam's political-intellectual impetus is marginal, considered partly as a "transitional" expression of modernist élites of the turn of last century, partly as the language of forces trying to resist modernization. As a foremost case of the deconflationist line of argumentation followed by the second circle, I will consider textual material written by Manfred Halpern,[5] that reflects a mature stage of development of the circle represented.[6]

The first prominent element in *The Politics of Social Change in the Modern Middle East* (Halpern, 1963) is the author's emphasis, in the

Foreword, on his motivation for conducting the study. He mentions the need for policy-oriented research on the Middle East (whose rough correspondence to the core of the universe of Islam was taken for granted), deemed urgent in spite of the lack of solid corpuses of data concerning the societies of the region. The basic rationale of the study is in a sort of "parsonization" of late-classic Orientalism, or rather in a synthesis between mainstream Weberist sociology, as embodied by Parsons (see Chapter 6), and Middle East Studies imbued with Weberism, as represented by von Grunebaum.

Untrained in Oriental languages and in methodologies of textual analysis, a social scientist of Middle East Studies like Halpern still had to rely on the Orientalist production, which he was unable to complement or make superfluous through survey data, as attempted in another work belonging to an earlier stage of maturation of the second circle: Daniel Lerner's *The Passing of Traditional Society. Modernizing the Middle East* ([1958] 1964). Notably this renewed dependence on classic Orientalism (the sacred triad of English-writing Orientalists, Wilfred Cantwell Smith, Sir Hamilton Gibb and Gustave von Grunebaum, is explicitly and repeatedly invoked, especially for their interpretations of Islamic reformism) is to a large extent the consequence of acknowledging the limits shown by Lerner's findings, consisting of the tripartite grouping of individuals (examined independently of their class location) as "modern", "traditionals" and "transitionals".[7] We will gradually see how the introduction of a Parsonian systemic optic into a field of transcultural import,[8] as well as of a consolidated, theoretically unchallenged, dualism of the kind "traditional vs. modern", prepared the ground for overcoming the static, monodimensional character of the hermeneutics of Islam during the 1970s (see Chapters 8 and 9).

The heading of Chapter 2 (*The Challenge of the Modern Age to Islam*) still reflects a Grunebaumian affiliation, and in fact Halpern's "Islam" is given by what was maintained by the first circle. However, a theoretical awareness of what "the modern challenge" consists of finally makes the exegesis of Islam – here mostly implicit – overtly dependent on the variability of the modern developmental factors animating the political scenario. In the second circle the scheme works in just the opposite way to the first, where the fair degree of familiarity with the already dominant social-scientific paradigm of modernization did not yet result in an overt subjection to it.[9] It would seem that Halpern's attempted operationalization of system theory with reference to the Other, as well as its redefinition first as modernization theory and then as a policy-oriented tool to be applied to the Middle East and North Africa, makes the ever-present emphasis on the reality of modernization in Muslim lands the basis for a kind of negative hermeneutics of Islam, whose essence and fate are finally constructed through a contrastive reference to the dynamics of the inescapable challenge of modernity.

The "negative" character of this interpretive model rests on a characterization of Islam as a series of gaps, which echoes Weber (see Chapter 6). However, at the historical juncture in which the second circle thrived this negativity could no longer be regarded as absolute and "essential". The developmental approach suggested by modernization theory had at least the merit of admitting, in principle, the possibility of major discontinuities within the evolution of an Islamic framework of reference: "Can any closed system like Islam be made to mesh with an open and dynamically changing society, yet succeed in remaining a closed system?" (Halpern, 1963, p. 34).

The mere formulation of this crucial question already shows the type of trail the second circle seeks to follow in order to transcend the definition of Islam fabricated by the first circle. The limits within which the question can be answered are evidently dictated by considering Islam as a "closed system", hence through its preliminary and wholesale classification as a traditional culture. However, the next step radically diverges from von Grunebaum's theory on classicism, which helped to justify the "introverted" character of Islam. Halpern asserts: "if the modern Moslem must contend with an inherited system that was fixed and closed, he also received from the past an uncommonly flexible style for dealing with a world in motion" (p. 34).

Halpern seems to doubt whether the final product of modernization, "such a changed Islam", will still be an entity that one could call "Islam", since "the road to modernization for all societies involves a march without a final prophet, a final book, or even assurance of final success" (p. 35). Halpern's argument is that modernizing Islam purports its gradual overcoming. He takes pains to provide some valid specifications of this general claim. At this point his approach emancipates itself from the generic vision of modernization as Westernization, which was still dominant in von Grunebaum's work. Halpern's position marks instead the universalist apex of modernization theory applied to the Middle East, as it conceals the normatively Eurocentric power of the notion of modernization under the universalist claim that, independently of how the change began, "it has become a native movement" (p. 36).[10]

In an effort to ground his argument on an analysis of social forces,[11] Halpern attempts to demonstrate why the two main currents that claim to speak on behalf of Islam within the political arena – Islamic reformism and what he calls "Islamic neo-totalitarianism" – are doomed to failure and cannot carry the weight of the modernizing movement. First, *'ulama'* reformism is a desperate effort to make Islam fit the requirements of modernity "at a time when orthodox Islam has already lost its fervor, influence and clarity" (p. 120). This conclusion automatically derives from the concept of Islam as a closed system, its "endemic weakness" being due to the fact that "analytical philosophy has always seemed impious to the orthodox Moslem – a sacrilegious and ultimately doomed effort to lay bare God's essence, meaning and purpose" (p. 125). The reformist undertaking is seen as having virtually failed very early, with al-Afghani and 'Abduh (cf. Chapter 5), thereby opening the way to "the triumph of secular leadership": "For the Moslems who are now taking the leading roles in Middle Eastern life, the battle has moved from the realm of religion into the realm of politics" (p. 129). Political development tends to negate Islam. Islam by now matters only in terms of its trajectory of disappearance in the wake of modernization; however, "[if the] war is over . . . there will still be battles", and the political sociologist of the Middle East can no longer disregard, as the first circle did, how "traditional Islam reacts by transforming itself into a religio-political totalitarian party" (p. 130).

This swift step towards the consideration of such a pathology of modernization, after having clarified that this is a phenomenon which merely affects the present transitional phase, obscures, however, a crucial breach in Halpern's argumentation. This is where he mentions the Consensus of the Community as being itself susceptible to a kind of transformation which does not usher in the "end" of Islam, but its "modernization": "Increasingly . . . the insistence on the hallowed consensus is itself becoming a force for change as the pressure for conformity comes no longer from one's ancestors but from one's peers. Novel ideas can be accepted in the name of national unity" (p. 132). Although expressed in a very sketchy form, this statement hints at the fact that the passage from the Consensus of the Community to a "consensus of communication" (see Chapters 3 and 5) is not entirely, even not primarily, due to exogenous forces. This admission does not have an autonomy of its own, but rather appears to serve the purpose of excluding "neo-Islamic totalitarianism" (along with the aborted Islamic reformism) from the modernized consensus.

Such a claim is, nevertheless, only legitimized by the ultimately normative character of Halpern's approach, for whom political modernity can and should be attained through "secularist" paths. It is remarkable that Halpern's attempt at directly portraying the kind of movement that would later (after the 1973 crisis) be made object of attention in terms of "political Islam" (see Introduction and Chapters 8 and 9), leads to the questioning of the validity of the exclusivist rationale. It also makes an overt object of contention out of the tension between the negation of the modern affiliation of Islamist movements, as a result of their religiously grounded past-orientedness (von Grunebaum's "classicism", for Halpern more simply "resurrecting" tradition), and a de facto recognition of their modernity, as far as they seemed capable of articulating social needs that are a result of modernization.[12]

The unsolved contradiction that pervades Halpern's dealing with the Islamist phenomenon (a curious phenomenon indeed, since it is doomed to failure by history – p. 148 – but whose "potential . . . continues to grow": p. 153) is revealed by the following:

> To call them "extreme nationalists" is to mistake them for secular politicians. No nationalist in the Middle East, however extreme, is likely to join the leaders of Islamic totalitarian movements in saying that "my religion is dearer to me than my family and clan. My religion is the first country that I take shelter in" (p. 135).

Hardly any other Islamist statement could be clearer in rejecting traditional loyalties and constructing modern ones. Yet Halpern's admission that the grounding of the Muslim Brotherhood meant the transformation of "chiliastic, reformist and uprooted modern elements . . . into the ideology of a modern political movement" (p. 137) condenses too early into the reassuring conclusion that they are the "Middle Eastern version of fascism" (p. 136). That Islamism belongs to the pathology of modernization (a motive that will be central to the third circle: see Chapter 9) is only slightly further specified through the assertion that "the [Muslim] Brotherhood is itself a symptom of uprootedness, yet cannot accept modern uprootedness as the precondition of modern liberation" (p. 138).

The second circle was responsible for consolidating the ontological character of the schematic "traditional vs. modern" dichotomy. This dualism was still very much in evidence at the threshold of the 1973 crisis (as evident in Palmer, 1973), and we will see how the new polarization between the third and the fourth circles will revolve around this same dichotomy, without seriously challenging it, and thereby stiffening into a sterile contest of judgement about whether political Islam is modern or not.

NOTES

1   We should remember the acute insights and light irony of Mohammed Arkoun's review of the major collection of essays by von Grunebaum (Arkoun, 1964), which already contained the main thrust of the objections later raised against the Austrian scholar by other authors. Arkoun formulated his position in a cautious vocabulary more attuned to the climate of incipient critique of Orientalism that preceded its actual crisis (on Arkoun see Conclusion).

2   Since the author seems to see the problem at stake, consistently with classic and especially late-classic Orientalist views, as the interpretation of Islam's genetic failure, it has been proposed to explain the method-problem complex in von Grunebaum by reference to Hegel, and to his evaluation of Islam as a basically adialectical cultural unit (Turner, 1984, p. 195). The conclusion drawn is that Hegelism, is the main influence behind von Grunebaum's hermeneutics of Islam. This is correct, however, only in as far as Weberism is always imbued with some degree of Hegelism. Nevertheless, as shown in Chapter 6, Weberism is a legacy that cannot be reduced to Hegelism alone.

3   "By the eighteenth century Muslim society everywhere, and in every area of endeavor, was in serious decline" (p. 61).

4   Binder (1976) stresses the change, Said (1978) the continuity; Rodinson (1980) takes an intermediate position.

5   That von Grunebaum and Halpern suitably reflect the passage from classic Orientalism to neo-Orientalism has been already recognized by Said. The conditions of the passage have not, however, been commented upon by him at particular length. "The strength of [von Grunebaum's] hold on the new Orientalist . . . is due in part to its traditional authority, and in part to its use-value as a handle for grasping a vast region of the world and proclaiming it an entirely coherent phenomenon." (Said, 1978, p. 299). Following this statement, Said quotes a couple of sentences from an article written by Halpern, considered symptomatic of the intellectual clumsiness of the new Orientalism. This procedure is insufficient to unveil the intricacies and breaches of Halpern's argument.

6   While classic Orientalism is a purely European enterprise, the second circle has several adherents among Arab scholars. During the 1960s, these scholars did not figure, however, in the forefront of the hermeneutic contention, as they did after the 1973 crisis within the third and fourth circles (see Chapter 9).

7   For a reconstruction of Middle East Studies inspired by modernization theory, as well as of the extent of their links to late-classic Orientalism, see Zartman, 1976, pp. 269–73.

8   See Halpern's sentence: "The cumulative growth of ideas, production, and power generated outside the Islamic system has penetrated that system and

is tearing apart its repetitive patterns of balanced tension" (Halpern, 1963, p. 25).

9 His "cultural anthropology" was predominantly the product of the late-classic Orientalist's adaptation to the new format and methodological orientation of Middle East Studies.

10 For Halpern modernization consists of the structural element of "social change" and the policy element of "exercising effective leadership". A general recipe for this, reflecting the normative character of the approach, would be "fashioning a social structure that can accommodate newly emerging social classes and new relationships among individuals . . . forming political institutions resilient enough to overcome the present crisis of uncontrolled change, and capable of transforming further changes into evolutionary, stabilizing development" (p. 37).

11 This is missing in other works produced within the same cultural and academic climate, squeezed as they were between a behavioural and an institutional approach (see Zartman, 1976 and Binder, 1988, pp. 24–84). The choice of Halpern's text is due not only to its unquestionably representative and authoritative character but also to the way it re-elaborates the crucial claims of the previous circle and anticipates the main lines of contention between those following.

12 This opposition between an "exclusivist" and an "inclusivist" concept of modernity will re-emerge under altered conditions in the polarization between the third and the fourth interpretive circles (see Chapter 9).

CHAPTER 8

The crisis of Orientalism and the *return of Islam*

This chapter should elucidate the delicate, historically critical passage from the polarization between the first two circles still inscribed within a linear hermeneutics of Islam to the emergence of the bidimensional hermeneutic field of "political Islam" as a consequence of a thorough metamorphosis of the transcultural space. This change was set in motion by the crisis of "Weberism" (see Chapter 6) that began during the 1960s.

An essay by Anouar Abdel-Malek published in 1963 (the same year that Halpern's book was published: see Chapter 7) provides the first diagnosis of the problem of Orientalism's essentialism, as well as of the related focus on units of language or religion detached from factors of social development (Abdel-Malek, 1963, pp. 113–14).[1] The Arab scholar had the merit of making clear with argumentative strength that the question transcended the level of academy, and that there was a significant link between the crisis of Orientalism and the collapse of the colonial system: "the crisis strikes at the heart of Orientalism: since 1945, it has not been just the 'field' that has run away from it, but also the 'people', yesterday still 'object' of study, but by now sovereign 'subjects'" (p. 109). Besides the content of this claim, which the Egyptian scholar attempted to support through an analysis of the development of Orientalism and its shift into post-Second World War neo-Orientalism (cf. Chapter 7), it is noteworthy that as an Arab intellectual he consciously attempted to upset the status quo in the transcultural space, so paving the way for the later enterprise by Edward Said. The superficially optimistic character of Abdel-Malek's critique lay, in contrast to what Said was to do (see below), in challenging the ethnocentrism of Western universalism whilst maintaining a thoroughly universalistic approach based on a generic Marxism, adopted as an alternative to the dominant Weberism. Abdel-Malek's diagnosis failed to address the actual core of the problem, as represented by Weber's crucial role in the long-term displacements of the West's essentialization of Islam (see Chapter 6).

The examination of the first explicit attempts to analyse Weber's view of Islam from an explicitly "critical" perspective can be useful for elucidating when, how, and in which cultural climate the Weberist equilibrium within the transcultural construction of Islam began to be shaken in a way that generic critiques of Orientalism could not do autonomously. Maxime Rodinson's *Islam et capitalisme* (1966) attacked Weber's interpretation of Islam as ideologically functional to establishing the superiority of Western rationality and, in the final analysis, the Western monopoly upon modernity. It is true that Rodinson's essay showed a tendency to oversimplify Weber's arguments, taking these out of the context and the rationale of the work of the Heidelberger sociologist (Schluchter, 1987, pp. 86–8). All these flaws notwithstanding, or even by virtue of them, the critique performed by the French scholar heralded the emergence of an urgent will to liberate Orientalism from the suffocating embrace of Weberism. If levelled not against Weber, but against Weberism, most of Rodinson's criticism is correct.

The next major critique of Weber's study of Islam appeared some years later. The change in motivation and perspective in Bryan S. Turner's *Weber and Islam* (1974) shows that by that time Weberism had begun to be recognized as a problem for its own sake (although it was not given such a name). Turner's original intention was: "to write a very general work on Islam which could be directed at undergraduate sociology students" (p. 1). So he came to the idea of "using" Weber, but this turned out to be impossible without oversimplifying Weber's sociology, and thereby falling, as we would say, into Weberism. Such a task required, on the contrary, a reinterpretation of Weber and of his view of Islam, an operation that was almost automatically a challenge to Weberism. The post-Weberian sociology of religion had not been innocent of justifying Weberism, both in general terms (through the propagation of a rough theory of secularization: see Chapter 3), and more specifically since it never approached Islam directly in a comparative perspective. Whereas Rodinson defied Weberism directly, while seeking to criticize Weber, Turner provided an attempt to restore the "true" Weber, beyond Weberism.

Turner's book was published shortly after a major world crisis occurred, centred on the oil embargo and the logarithmic leap in crude oil prices following the Arab–Israeli war of October 1973. The way in which this crisis was staged and narrated by Western mass media laid the bases for a profound metamorphosis of the transcultural space between the "West" and "Islam". My goal is to examine the constructions of Islam produced in the West which impinged upon general discourses of "crisis" while instrumentalizing references to the Arab Middle East, the core of the "world of

Islam", and increasingly the locus irradiating economic and political crises impacting on Western welfare and security.

The link between these two different dimensions of crisis is not evident in itself. I will attempt to approach both the contingent representation of the events that were subsumed under the label "crisis" by the most powerful sources for world news, the Western mass media, and the general meaning of crisis as a critical breakthrough in the unfolding of intellectual modernity (see Chapter 2). Such a type of turn is characterized by the awareness of a gap which appears unbridgeable by resort to "normal" tools of knowledge. The central factor determining a crisis is thereby a sort of "will of distinction", which produces forms of intellectual discourse suitable for legitimizing the rupture and suggesting new paths of normalization. This is the definition employed by the historian Reinhart Koselleck (Koselleck, [1959] 1988), who analysed the epitome of the modern intellectual breakthrough, the Enlightenment, when the word crisis was just beginning to acquire a socially diagnostic and predictive meaning (p. 161).

We are instead focusing on a critical juncture where the use of the label "crisis" reveals an unprecedented intensity. However, the link between the two different critical junctures is given by the fact that, since the Enlightenment, conscious intellectual elaborations of feelings of crisis have marked the highest points in modernity's unfolding, because it is only through discontinuities that the very special tradition of modernity can keep itself alive (cf. Touraine, 1992; Lash and Friedman, 1992; Eder, 1993, pp. 175–82). In this sense, a "crisis" does not witness the occurrence of an ontological discontinuity of paradigms or epistemes, but rather the necessity of thinking *in terms of* discontinuity: a crisis produces new types of discourses or at least induces new uses and combinations of extant categories and terms.

We can now turn to analyse the crisis of 1973, in order to explain why this crisis, beyond the evidence of its underlying "hard facts" (that we do not need to recapitulate here in great detail), induced a change within the transcultural constraint of using Islam for defining Western identity. The scenario of crisis was legitimized and stabilized by the use of this word in various contexts and with shifting meanings on both sides of the transcultural space. These different significations were often inconsistent with each other, but the unity of the scenario was independent of logical coherence. It was warranted by another sort of cogency, resulting from the power of the techniques of communication at work in propagating it: beyond all possible meanings given to the word "crisis", it is the operation of their reduction to an "event", and its staging according to aesthetical canons of spectacularity, which is relevant for the metamorphosis of the transcultural space. This calls into question the power of representation by the principal media, whose reading of the crisis, both in formal and substantial terms, was dependent on their capacity firstly to dramatize and then to reduce to simple, familiar and reassuring narrative patterns – targeted at the broader Western public – a hermeneutic potential for examining problems of worldwide inter-connection, or of "global" import, that had obviously been accumulated over time, especially in the 1960s.

The success of this globalizing perspective cannot be considered simply as the natural product of ongoing structural transformations in the world economy. The success of theories focusing on global factors should be related to the gradual but relentless demise in the West of grand social theory, able to account for social change, a crisis which became evident in particular from the late 1960s to the mid-1970s. This process has affected both propagators and foes of the adoption of a "post-modern" perspective for stabilizing the sense of a crisis of valid knowledge as applied to society. The paradox is that the crisis in theories of social change, including modernization theory (see Chapter 7), matured precisely at a time when in "peripheral" parts of the world something "political" was being staged that showed similarities to patterns of revolution which since the end of the eighteenth century had been familiar to Western Europe, where they appeared to have receded for ever, after the disillusionment that followed the enthusiasms of the 1968 youth movement. The apex of this paradox, as experienced during the second half of the 1970s, was reached with the Iranian revolution in 1978–9, an event whose explanation was impervious to any major theory of social change available in the West, however recycled or reformulated. A first major consequence in social theory during the late 1970s and early 1980s was that within growing theories of globalization a steady shift was recognizable from emphasis on structural factors towards the establishment of the centrality of communication.

Theorists of globalization themselves point to the 1960s as the phase when globalization processes reached a critical point. Since then, the wide-spread consciousness of the existence of a "Third World", as well as the idea of "multiculturalism", went hand in hand with two broad phenomena that should be considered in their reciprocal relationship: growing "uncertainty" and "consolidation of global media system" (Robertson, 1990, pp. 26–7). The net result of their interaction can be generally defined as the constraint to engage in "the definition of the global situation" (Featherstone, 1990, p. 6). This "global constraint" seems to be located at the very source of all discourse – whether originating in the media or of a more genuine intellectual nature – affecting the transcultural space in the crucial conjuncture here analysed.

A thus-defined globalization dictated the conditions for representing the crisis as a way of bridging the gap created by the tension between an increasingly recognized uncertainty and the quest for orientation, i.e. the need to "possess a map" (cf. Robertson, 1990, p. 19), an impulse often supported by a sort of "neo-religious", or at least "neo-cosmological" mood (see also Robertson, 1992).

Among the many layers of relevance of the 1973 crisis for the metamorphosis of the transcultural space, the first, and more obvious, is that the geopolitical scenario of crisis was objectively one of contention, compromise and alliances between Western and Arab governmental actors. However, from the point of view of Western public opinion, this was no more than world politics manoeuvres reflecting a much higher stake: the global dangers of further political "instability" and risks of new wars in the Middle East entailing direct superpower involvement, a preoccupation that added to the even deeper concern over energy supplies and their prices.

The staging of a crisis as revolving around a "meaning event" within this scenario, and the legitimate concerns of the man in the street mediated by the new global perspective, cannot be understood without specifically addressing the role of the major Western media. It is not by chance that a first authoritative recognition, by a historian, of the power of the media to make history through the creation of events dates back to the year preceding the crisis here examined (Nora, [1972] 1974). This novelty relativizes my previous discussion of the recurrent meaning of "crisis" in the unfolding of modernity as conforming to Koselleck's scheme, that envisages intellectual critique as genetically connected to crisis, or even its cause. In the era of mass media a crisis depends on its staging for it to become visible to the wider public. This operation needs a significant event that has to be clearly connected with the structural crisis of development, and suitable for narration according to simple, culturally available, patterns, where the role of the bad guys can be identified with the widest possible consensus. This is no longer an intellectual operation, but one that requires more encompassing and penetrating media resources and techniques.

Nevertheless, one should recall that the centrality of the media is no simple matter of the pervasive character of a technology, but is also dependent on the more general, and still intellectually mediated, cultural trend of "going global". Here I am not discussing the general role of the media, but their function in "crisis" situations, when an event is staged that goes beyond routine. Those analyses of globalization in the field of mass communication which avoid an exclusive focus on technological innovations, cannot avoid drawing attention to how the evolution of mass-media technologies, along with the qualitative upgrading of their pervasiveness on a world scale since the late 1960s, was first paralleled by an increasing awareness of the importance of flows of information, and then by the "growing interest in comparative cross-cultural . . . and image studies" (Mowlana, 1990, p. 225). This was certainly the case with Edward Said (see also below): "There was widespread consciousness of the immense power of the means of production of representations – images, media, all of these sorts of things." (Said, 1988, p. 33). It should be noted that the missing link between media power and cross-cultural sensitivity is provided by a staged crisis, which can act as a powerful medium in inducing not only awareness and study, but the possibility itself that such studies, as in Said's case, attract the attention of the intellectual community at large, in so far as this community already thinks, acts and reacts within the same horizon of crisis.

As a result, the new quality of media intervention is to be seen as part of a deeper change in the very conditions of production, diffusion and consumption of discourse, or of what could be called a transformation in the "episteme" of an age (cf. Foucault, [1968] 1991). This is a type of change that potentially affects every discursive formation and influences the modalities themselves of defining the objects of knowledge (p. 56). The metamorphosis that affected the scenarios of crisis dealt with here led to the eradication of the category of modernity from a field of relatively high consensus of definition, and to the consequent dislocating effects on the game of reconstructing this concept, as well as to the compensation for this loss of epistemic solidity through reference to processes of globalization.

It is legitimate to suspect that the sensitivity of the leading media to crisis-related issues was in no way sudden, and that the staging of a major crisis in the Middle East was well-prepared. A leading journalist, Edward Mortimer, reported how, in the spring of 1973, the editor of *The Times* of London called him and said: "Edward, would you do the Middle East?" Mortimer, who had not yet covered that region, recalls:

> Even before I departed on this quasi-presidential "swing" I had written, and *The Times* published, two leading articles on events in the Middle East . . . Once I had got back to London and published my impressions of the Palestinian problem in three signed articles, my accreditation as an "expert" was complete (Mortimer, 1981, p. 492).

Not surprisingly, this was the prelude to Mortimer's later production of a book on the political impact of Islam. In itself, the instant making of a

Middle East expert out of a distinguished correspondent on European affairs might signify only that the dominant media were well prepared to shift forces in covering what would quickly become the "area of crisis" *par excellence*. But this was only the first step, as we will see, within an escalating media involvement in reifying the "crisis" through its relocation in the West's relations first to the Arabs and then to "Islam".

In the immediate aftermath of the Iranian revolution, the first book, written by another journalist, in a popular-scientific style and explicitly addressing the "phenomenon" of politicizing Islam (see Introduction), retrospectively confirms the impression of a strong continuity between the concern of the Western public for the party ("the Arabs") considered responsible for threatening their security on a number of levels during the 1973 crisis (the war, the oil embargo, the price-raising), and the later identification of an ideological source of threat against Western values ("Islam"):

> Since about 1973, in the aftermath of the Arab–Israeli war of that year, it has been gradually borne in on the minds of Western observers that something "new" was brewing out of Asia . . . It was, of course, the oil embargo imposed by Muslim countries, with its resultant scarcity of fuel oil, that drove the point home to every single Western citizen through sheer physical discomfort and inconvenience. Since then evidence of a *political resurgence of Islam* [emphasis added] in many Muslim countries . . . has accumulated with increasing speed (Jansen, 1979, p. 11).

Several investigations of the characterization of Arabs and Muslims by the Western media during the 1970s and later seem to converge in highlighting such a continuity. Some of these studies may have retrospectively accentuated the fact that the 1973 crisis already manifested an attention on "Islam", or more probably on the Arabs as Muslims. This overestimation is due to the absence of a strictly quantitative definition of the research results. This is, however, marginal for the scope of this analysis, which concerns the trajectory in the "making of a theorem" that was relevant for initiating a transformation in the transcultural space.

Let us first look at Said's book, *Covering Islam*, published in 1981, three years after *Orientalism*. Besides being a well-documented study, *Covering Islam* has the merit of testifying to the causal relationship between the modalities and outcomes of the staging of the crisis on the one hand, and the making of a "monument" of the metamorphosis of the transcultural space, as represented by *Orientalism*, on the other. It is more than a hypothesis that a new media discourse on the Islamic Orient arose after the 1973 crisis, and that only as a consequence of it was a fresh, mature wave of Orientalism critique, as opposed to the circumscribed academic controversy on Orientalism of the mid-1960s (see Abdel-Malek, 1963 and Gabrieli, 1965) set in motion, inaugurated by the appearance of the *Review of Middle East Studies* in 1974–5.[2] It is quite clear, as we will see, that the Saidian critique reacts to the added dimension acquired by Orientalism through its expansion into a new media discourse, although the theoretical tools of the critique are drawn from the general repertoire of the intellectual discourse of crisis.

One introductory statement in *Covering Islam* (Said, 1981, p. x) gives enough clues for understanding the motivational terrain which prompted Said to deal with "Western and specifically American responses to an Islamic world perceived, since the early 1970s, as being immensely relevant and yet antipathetically troubled, and problematic." Moving from the analysis of this feeling of attention and anger in the Western public, Said swiftly concludes that it was the sudden OPEC price rise in early 1974 that set in motion a rapid process of condensing in "Islam", and of subsuming under its supposed domain of influence all that before was said or predicated in relation to groups identified according to national criteria, such as Arabs and Iranians (p. 33). Coherently with the core argument of *Orientalism*, Said does not hesitate to explain this phenomenon through the deeply-sedimented, rather defensive and "primordial" Western image of Islam, which was waiting to be resuscitated from the West's historical memory in order to fuel the construction of narratives in large and small media which blamed Islam for the West's troubles:

> Only Islam seemed never to have submitted completely to the West; and when, after the dramatic oil-price raises of the early 1970s, the Muslim world seemed once more on the verge of repeating its early conquests, the whole West seemed to shudder ... Then in 1978 Iran occupied the central stage (p. 5).

Even if Said might have neglected the gradual character of the shift from the Arabs to Islam as the target of Western anger between 1973 and 1979,[3] there is enough evidence that the watershed moment in the emergence of discourses on the politicization of Islam was not, as widely maintained, the Iranian revolution.[4] The stage was already set, and the roles already assigned, by the media's reading of the 1973–4 crisis, so that the impact of the 1978–9

"Islamic turmoil", again associated with the rise of oil prices, cannot be interpreted as an independent influence. A good evidence of the making of a theorem along the axis "crisis-oil-Arabs-Islam" is provided by a study on *The TV Arab* (Shaheen, 1984) based on eight years of analysis of television broadcasting in the United States. The examination begins with the 1975–6 TV season, including entertainment programmes, documentaries and cartoons which have the Arabs as a target. This analysis is complemented by interviews with broadcast executives and producers. The focus of the study is on the "Arabs", taken in isolation from an explicit reference to "Islam". It shows how Arabs are depicted as billionaires, bombers and belly-dancers: "In today's films and television shows, Arabs do not pursue women only, but a host of things, like American real estate, business and government officials" (p. 13).

The study nevertheless highlights how, from the beginning of the period considered, there was at least an implicit reference to the Arabs as Muslims. The investigation illustrates the formation of three equations that well represent the basic structure of the theorem: first, OPEC means Arab with a negative connotation; second, Iranians are Arabs ("nearly everyone I interviewed thought Iranians are Arabs"); third, all Arabs are Muslims (p. 14). What holds together the equations of the theorem, and gives it an unmistakably Orientalist flavour – in a Saidian sense – is an interpretive element not visible at the surface of the equations: the imputation of irrationality to Arabs and Islam.[5] Pending a precise content analysis of the shift in the use of concepts and images in the Western media for defining the new role played by Arabs as Muslims on the world politics scenario, one can hypothesize that after the 1973 crisis the explanatory deficit towards the question "why did all this happen?" *began* to be filled with references to "Islam". As late as 1976, the leading Orientalist Bernard Lewis claimed that Islam has always been political, thereby suggesting where the solution to the theorem might lie.

This assertion summons back the thesis of the first circle under altered world political conditions, as displayed by the title of Lewis's article, *The Return of Islam*. This consisted of a dense description of how Islam was beginning to move again. By melting the scholarly and the journalistic view-points, Lewis's intervention provided a milestone on the trajectory of emergence of the hermeneutic field of political Islam during the 1970s. I have attempted to show the passage from an ethnic to a religious identification of the Arabs through the making of their image as crisis-makers. Lewis's article certainly played a fundamental role in encouraging and legitimizing this process, as it appeared primarily aimed at restoring the view of an historical continuity in the Islam-inspired processes of politicization, against a background of alleged Western misunderstanding, during the 1950s and 1960s, of many political phenomena especially in the Arab portion of the "world of Islam" as manifestations of a secular nationalism.[6]

It was, however, the October War of 1973, according to Lewis, which offered the strongest proof that the ideological force engaging Arabs in political action, by now clearly of immediate concern to the West (and obviously Israel), is of a "strikingly religious" nature (Lewis, 1976, p. 48). Lewis's first conclusion is that "Islam is still the most effective form of consensus in Muslim countries" (p. 48). This seems to conform with what Halpern wrote at about the same time, nuancing his earlier modernizing optimism (on the second circle, see Chapter 7) and sanctioning "the weakness of the counter-tradition in Islam" (Halpern, 1977, p. 90).

Lewis's argument seems at first sight inspired by the will to regenerate the strength of the classic Orientalist appreciation of the necessarily "religious" character of politics among Muslims (on the first circle, see Chapter 7). As Lewis himself knows, however, this cannot be a mere restoration, since after the 1973 crisis the concern for the Middle East is no longer exclusive to the scholar, but attracts the attention of the media and the public. Thus, the old-style Orientalist, the legitimate heir of von Grunebaum, now has to look to the future and warn the Western public that "[Islam] will be increasingly effective as the regimes become more genuinely popular." (Lewis, 1976, p. 48). He finally indicates the reservoir of supplementary political potential provided by what he explicitly calls a "resurgent Islam", and concludes by transplanting the question of Islam's politicization in the same symbolic and emotional terrain that the Western media had begun, late in 1973, to exploit with increasing rhetorical skill: "Both the Saturday people [the Jews] and the Sunday people [the Christians] are now suffering the consequences" of Islamic resurgence (p. 49).

What is prominent in *The Return of Islam* is the tension set up between Lewis's claim that "Islam from its inception is a religion of power" (p. 49), his appeal to Western public opinion to take this into full account after the evaporation of the universalist and modernizing enthusiasm, and the prediction that Islam's inherent political character will be intensified by mass participation in politics. This was an almost prophetic prefiguring of the irruption, three years later, of pro-Khomeini crowds onto Western TV screens. For these reasons we should situate Lewis's theorization of a "resurgent Islam" within the same hermeneutic context where the theorem crisis-Arabs-Islam was shaped, helping to redefine the West's post-crisis identity. This phenomenon was acutely recognized by Clifford Geertz, who wrote in 1982, the revival of Islam . . . tends to divert attention from its referent to itself. The question becomes whether there really is such a thing out there in "Islamdom" demanding special explanation or whether there is not, and our sense that there *is* grows out of tuning in late to a historical process, faith-driven politics, that has been going on for a very long time and has come to our attention only because it has begun directly to touch our interests (quoted in Lawrence, 1987, p. 16).

"Revival" or "resurgence" (and the like) are the sort of catchcategories paving the way to a reconflation of the two alleged dimensions of Islam as religion and politics, thereby inducing a transformation of the older, derivative conflationism of the first circle to one that can be formulated, as we will see in the analysis of the third circle (Chapter 9), according to more analytical social-scientific criteria. It is my claim, however, that the measure of the political, and its consecration as an autonomous hermeneutic factor within the interpretive field of political Islam, is not primarily established by an objective assessment of which political acts are performed in the name of Islam in Muslim societies, but by the way it provides a contrastive image for a redefinition of Western political subjectivity in times of crisis. Islamic, "faith-driven politics" begins to be a phenomenon in the moment the authorized (mainly Western) observer feels the urgency to reflect on it. It is this "resurgence" of Western attention towards "Islam in movement" that marks the passage from a linear hermeneutics of Islam to the bidimensional hermeneutics of political Islam: Islam is no longer a civilization of the text and law closed on itself, but a global issue on the Western political agenda.

Whatever the stages in the unfolding of the theorem crisis-Arabs-Islam had been through the 1970s, by the end of the decade there seems to have been a striking convergence among the most important media, leading sectors of the academy and the policy-advising establishment on producing interpretations rigidly inscribed within the logic of the theorem. Such a convergence could not pass unnoticed by the great inquisitor of the integrated, political character of Orientalist discourse. Said reminds us how the forging of the label "oil and turmoil" was possible by making explicit the alleged role of Islam. Before crystallizing as a journalistic formula, "oil and turmoil" appeared as the title of a report issued in the fall of 1979 by the Special Working Group on the Middle East of the Atlantic Council (Said, 1981, p. 15).

Until then, the function of Islam in the chain of crises had not yet been autonomous and dynamic enough in the Western perception: it was its strict association with turmoil which gave it an impulse of its own. This general evidence is confirmed by a detailed content-analytic study consisting of a comparative examination of *ABC Television* news and the *New York Times* coverage of Islam and Muslims from 1979 to 1987, and whose main result is that "crisis events" ranked first in both media (al-Zahrani, 1988). The most significant element of continuity before and after the Islamic revolution in Iran is precisely in the pervasive presence of crisis as an unquestioned, constraining category, when speaking of Arabs and Islam in their relations with the West.

Said's accusation that Orientalist scholarship is the real cause of the perverted distortions in "covering Islam", as it failed to voice credibly what Islam is really about (Said, 1981, pp. 21–5), might appear justified, if we accept that not so much the raw material, but the existing frameworks of explanation which journalists translate into their own language had to be of academic origin. This view is coherent with the highly compact definition of Orientalism that Said conveys in all his works, envisaging a unitary matrix underlying each genre of representation of the Orient, from travel literature to philology to poetry. It is not surprising that Lewis's theorization of *The Return of Islam* was a privileged target of Said's indictments.[7]

What Said neglects, however, is the way in which, within an epistemic environment already pervaded by the spirit of crisis, the mass media were the only source capable of delivering a plausible message out of disparate signs, because only they held the tools to make the crisis tangible and readable, to make a story out of it through narratives fitting the audience's expectations. Most remarkable, however, is that these media altered the actually valid, paradigmatic knowledge produced by the academy. The story narrated was increasingly to contradict the still alive, although weakened, modernization theory, as it focused on the backwardness factor associated with Arab-OPEC blackmailing strategies, and later explained backwardness by reference to Islam, once regarded by theory as a negligible obstacle to modernization in the Middle East (see Chapter 7).

Nonetheless, this passage, realized with the blessing of top-level Orientalist authorities like Bernard Lewis, signified, from a certain point of view, the rescue of the core rationale of modernization theory, once purged of its interventionist encrustations – a meaningful shift than cannot be reduced, as Said reduced it, to an eruption of media-mediated, primordial stereotypes on Islam resulting from the scientific failure of neo-Orientalist models, unreally detached from their object of study and only functional to Western interests. At the core of Said's misunderstanding of the reasons that engendered this theorem is his paradoxical use of an anachronistic concept of academic scholarship at the same time as he was actively contributing, through his own campaign, to an unprecedented challenge of this idea of academy within Middle East Studies.

In spite of the emphasis here laid on the distinctly new role played by the media, it is essential to keep in mind that the academy was in no way extraneous to this game of projecting "crisis" into the Middle East, nor did it play a merely ancillary role, by acting rather defensively and reactively. "The crisis is *there*, our crisis depends on *their* chronic crisis-making": this pattern of exorcizing the West's (and the global) crisis was used as a way for circumscribing and keeping under control the mounting critique against Western scholarship charged with the study of the Islamic Orient. The account, however anecdotal, given by one former president of MESA from the tribune of its annual meeting, Yvonne Y. Haddad, could hardly be more telling:

> Several MESA members met in October to organize a two-week summer institute for high school teachers on the general subject of teaching about Islam and the Arab world. Having determined the overall topics to be addressed, we decided to leave one session open to deal with whatever might be "the crisis of the day". Someone asked, "but what if there isn't a crisis?" Such a possibility seemed quite unthinkable to most of us. "I'm sure there will be something", said one person. And another, for good measure, added, "and if there isn't, we can make one up" (Haddad, 1991b, p. 1).

At this point Haddad feels compelled to ask the painful question: "What is this Middle East to the study of which we have devoted our lives? Have we somehow created an entity for our own needs and purposes that may not correspond to reality?" Through raising such questions the game of crisis-staging opens up a new space for critique.

The general criticism of the Western path of historical development and the more specific one levelled at the Western game of legitimizing this path through stylizing a countertype ("political Islam") should not be kept strictly separate, since the latter is in large part the consequence of the former, depending on both the modalities of the ("post-modern") critical turn in the dialectic of modernity and the reduction-exorcization of the crisis performed through its staging by mass media. The resulting metamorphosis of the transcultural space is best epitomized by the peculiar axis constituted by Michel Foucault and Edward Said.

These two authors are jointly mentioned in several works concerned, from different perspectives, with recent developments in intellectual cultures (see Binder, 1988; Turner, [1983] 1991; Norris, 1992). There are certainly several reasons for this association. My purpose here is, nevertheless, to point out a specific motive which relates both scholars to the change in the transcultural space. To this end, I will juxtapose textual material originating from a crucial passage in Foucault's own venture into critical modernity and which explicitly affects the question of "what is Islam today?", with Said's main intellectual campaign directed against Orientalism, whose target was easily defined from the beginning, and which had only to be carried out by the right author, at the most convenient moment, with suitable discursive tools. Rather than emphasizing straightforward analogies or oppositions, we should concentrate on a delicate tension between the two authors that has passed unnoticed. It is the tension between their common terrain of reproblematizing questions of knowledge and control according to a genealogical perspective as a way of studying the present, and, in this way, intervening in it (see Introduction), on the one hand, and their being positioned very differently within the transcultural space, on the other.

The years from the mid-1970s to 1978 saw the progression of a crisis in Foucault's own path of knowledge, due to a tormented reflection on the significance of intellectual criticism and the way it might be rooted in "enlightened" modernity. The fact that this crisis appeared, towards the end of 1978, to be provisionally absorbed by Foucault's rather sudden engagement in understanding the Iranian revolution (in a more or less consciously managed game of displacement of the critical question of modern political identity) is certainly paradigmatic of a more general cultural mood in the West, which was more than the expression of post-modern disorientedness or a passing fashion. Foucault's experience condenses, in an undeniably original manner, an attitude that was visible first of all in France (see Eribon, 1989, p. 30) but to some extent in the West at large. It consisted of opposing to the standard, media-mediated staging of the "crisis" in terms of "Islam" (or of "Islam" in terms of "crisis") a more thoughtful mode of representing Islam by which intellectuals, while adapting to the canons of spectacularity dictated by the media, attempted to reimpose their own discursive centrality, as grounded on the hermeneutics of critical modernity.

The year 1977 was very probably a major turning-point in Foucault's own evolution. A profound intellectual crisis was set off by the feeling of having been misunderstood after the publication of *La Volonté de savoir* in 1976, and despite its unprecedented success on the market (Eribon, 1989, pp. 292–3). At that time he began to reflect on the meaning of Enlightenment and revolution in Western history, while practising what has been called "philosophical journalism". The common denominator between the field of reflection and the genre of discourse was Foucault's own articulation of the modern question of how thought is tied to the present. It is probably not purely chance that this kind of emphasis coincided with his recognition of a first real failure in his publishing career, due to the reception of the above-mentioned book. From that moment on, the most significant products of his work were no longer to be found in books, but in what might appear to be minor texts: lectures, pieces of "philosophical journalism" and even interviews.

Foucault's 1978 lectures began to offer some tangible points of anchorage for his strategy to exit the crisis and to find a new point of equilibrium. Foremost is the lecture delivered in April 1978 at the *Societé Française de Philosophie*, curiously bearing the double title *What is criticism?* and *What is Enlightenment?* (see Szakolczai, 1993a, pp. 49–50). Here Foucault places himself in the Kantian tradition, in attempting to find a significant link between modernity, critique and crisis in the Enlightenment. However, the French philosopher was not able to overcome his crisis through a conventional solution. We can hypothesize, with the benefit of historical perspective, that Foucault was looking for the right way "to pose problems". This is the result of an analysis of the last two years in his life, 1983–4 (see Szakolczai, 1993b), when he went back to analysing the same text that had occasioned his reflections in the above-mentioned lecture of 1978: Kant's formulation of an answer to the question *Was ist Aufklärung?* ("What is Enlightenment?"), posed by a Berliner journal in 1784 (see Chapter 2). At that stage, "philosophical journalism" appeared to Foucault as a solution of format, probably a provisional way of fixing, amidst the storm of crisis and critique, the affirmation of intellectual modernity, but certainly not a futile one. It is not inappropriate to deduce that during 1978 Foucault already saw in it a particularly exciting genre of discursive enmeshment (see Foucault, 1979a), so well rooted "in the reflection on 'today' as difference in history and as a motive for a particular philosophical task", which was precisely where he saw the novelty and the attraction of the Kantian text (Foucault, 1984c, p. 38).

It is possible to argue that the study of, or even the obsession with, *Was ist Aufklärung?* during 1978 was due to the occasion it offered Foucault to reaffirm a tradition of modernity. He continued to work on this kind of self-genealogy of modern thinker in the following years, but at that stage he seemed unsure about how and around which categories to locate this tradition. These quandaries certainly enhanced the attraction of "philosophical journalism" as the peculiar moulding of the two components, philosophy and concern for the present, which he saw as indissolubly united in making up modernity.

Foucault's coverage of the Iranian revolution has already been submitted to a careful analytical investigation (Stauth, 1991) which recognizes that at the core of the concern of the French thinker there was the problem of assessing "revolution in spiritless times", and that the resulting appraisal is to be inscribed within the evolution of Western perceptions of Islam during that period. This study, however, too quickly postulates the "ambiguity" of Foucault's operation, thereby neglecting the textual and contextual clues which suggest significant ties between his personal-intellectual crisis, the more encompassing critical turn of Western intellectual culture during the 1970s, and the media-mediated staging of the "crisis" with its increasingly privileged focus on "the role of Islam". Stauth's study has the merit of trying to connect Foucault's interest in the Islamic revolution of Iran with his "political theory", as gravitating around *Surveiller et punir* ("Discipline and Punish"), published in 1975. This is, however, a quite static term of reference, which obscures the extent to which Foucault's intervention in Iran was delicately embedded in a critical passage of his intellectual path through which he appeared to go consciously beyond his elusive work on "power-knowledge" of the early 1970s.

A more dynamical perspective should be adopted in assessing and defining the hermeneutics of Islam in which Foucault indirectly engaged while reporting from Iran. At the origin of this enterprise we find a curious double inversion: first, of the relationship implied by "philosophical journalism" – it no longer meant performing journalistic work from the perspective of philosophy (as he had already done well before studying Kant's text), but producing philosophical discourse through journalism. That Foucault did not dismiss philosophical journalism as mere feuilletonism, but upgraded it through precisely this inversion, is shown by the genesis of his writings on the Iranian revolution. This story also offers some clues for explaining the reason of the other significant inversion, from reflection on the West's present towards reflection on the present of one portion of the "other" world.

Having been requested by the Italian newspaper *Corriere della sera* in 1977 to write "philosophical" articles, after the Iranian uprising had began to capture his attention Foucault submitted the counter-proposal to conduct a journalistic investigation on the event. He spent a week in Iran in September 1978 and another week a month later, producing two series of articles published in the Italian daily after each stay. The first series recounts Foucault's encounter with the upheaval that raised the banner of the "Islamic government" and is by far the most interesting. I will analyse the product of this first experience through a more condensed and cogent account, represented by an article published in *Le Nouvel Observateur* in the middle of October 1978 (Foucault, 1978a). The French-magazine piece has the particular merit of giving an initial assessment of the revolution after Foucault's first trip, expressed in a mood of passionate expectation for the second sojourn that, instead, did not yield any strikingly new insight (Eribon, 1989, pp. 298–304). As this article best embodies Foucault's position during the uprising, it must be analysed in conjunction with two other texts, a talk and an article, written after the revolution had succeeded and had begun to show its truculent face.

Foucault seems to oscillate in evaluating the role of "Islam" in this eruption of political spirituality. Whether Islam counts as a real force or just as a cover for other interests is not, however, the primary issue. The question is whether it represents the force of tradition as resistance to tyranny, or the force of an assertive, forward-looking utopia. Foucault is careful not to raise this question by invoking the tension between "tradition" and "modernity". It is by keeping this polarity in the background that he attains in some salient passages a dense formulation of the revolt's meaning. This is no revolution in the conventional-analytic sense of the term, but rather comes close to what this is in its very essence, as "the uprising of a whole nation against a power that oppresses it" (Foucault, [1979] 1988, p. 212). On closer scrutiny, however, his evaluation of the Iranian revolution goes much further, to the extent that it seems to fit the sense highlighted some years later, as he again, and more intensively, commented upon Kant's *Was ist Aufklärung?*:

> The question which seems to me to appear for the first time . . . is the question of the present, of the contemporary moment. What is happening today? What is happening now? And what is this "now" which we all inhabit, and which defines the moment in which I am writing? . . . For the philosopher it will no longer . . . simply be the question of his belonging to a human community in general, but rather of his membership of a certain "we", a we corresponding to a cultural ensemble characteristic of his own contemporaneity (Foucault, [1983] 1986, pp. 88–9).

There is little doubt that an entity approximating the definition of this "we" was recognized by Foucault among the Iranian population rebelling against the shah. The paradox is that the "we" is found among "them". It is as if the question "What is Enlightenment?" were posed in conjunction with another major question, matured in the context of the emergence of a modern intellectual distinction: Montesquieu's "How can one be a Persian?", which expresses the puzzle of the modern mind in being confronted with a radical otherness (see Chapter 2). In a certain sense, Foucault makes use of the latter question in order to answer the former. It is, not surprisingly, a contingent answer imposed by the fact that the redefinition of a modern Self appeared to Foucault as dependent, in that historical conjuncture, on understanding the driving force behind the Iranian upheaval and its astonishing success. Unlike the Kantian situation, the articulation of a modern political discourse through the philosopher seems to be, in that particular moment, impossible by reference to his own post-revolutionary society, where it is no longer possible to find the right sign, a valuable event:

> A sign of what? A sign of the existence of a cause, a permanent cause which throughout history has guided men in the way of progress . . . The Revolution as spectacle and not gesticulation, the Revolution as a focus of enthusiasm for its witnesses and not as a principle of upheaval for its participants . . . Never mind whether it succeed or fail, that is nothing to do with progress, or at least with the sign of progress which we are looking for (Foucault, [1983] 1986, pp. 89–94).

Revolution is seen as a high point in the unfolding of modern political subjectivity, and in this regard Foucault did not shy away from comparing the meaning of the Iranian uprising with the significance of the French revolution highlighted by Furet in a famous book published (coincidentally) in 1978, in which revolution is depicted as the supreme event and experience (Foucault, [1979] 1988b, p. 214). Behind Foucault's intervention on the Iranian stage there is much more than the concern for an actual issue. There is the spark of a solution to a multifaceted crisis, which can be subsumed under the question: "Has the spirit of revolution really disappeared from history?"; "Where has it gone?" It is the question of the fate of the political spirituality of modernity, or, to use a category which began to be reshaped and to gain a central place in Foucault's own discourse on modernity precisely in those critical years, the question of "subjectivity", intended in its transindividual dimension.

At this point, Foucault can no longer postpone the question of the "role" played by "Islam" in this movement of the spirit. During the uprising he began to suggest an answer:

> At the dawn of history, Persia invented the state, and later trusted its recipes to Islam: its officials served as cadres of the Califate. But

from this same Islam it has derived a religion that has given to its people indefinite resources for resisting the power of the state. In this will to an "Islamic government" should we see a reconciliation, a contradiction, or the threshold of a novelty? (Foucault, 1978a, p. 49).

Foucault's question was well formulated for discovering that the Islam at work on the most genuine of the political stages in Iran was not the manifestation of a political short-cut of the kind envisaged by the main trend in the Western essentialization of Islam, as the suppressor of subjectivity:

In rising up, the Iranians said to themselves – and this is perhaps the soul of the uprising: "Of course, we have to change this regime and get rid of this man . . . But, above all, we have to change ourselves. Our way of being, our relationship with others, with things, with eternity, with God, etc., must be completely changed and there will only be a true revolution if this radical change in our experience takes place." I believe that it is here that Islam played a role . . . religion for them was like the promise and guarantee of finding something that would radically change their subjectivity (Foucault, [1979] 1988, pp. 91–3).

It is impossible to overlook how what Foucault sees as the spirit of the Iranian uprising, supposedly connected in no casual way to "Islam", recalls one of his rare attempts to define modernity:

Thinking back on Kant's text, I wonder whether we may not envisage modernity rather as an attitude than as a period of history. And by "attitude" I mean a mode of relating to contemporary reality; a voluntary choice made by certain people; in the end, a way of thinking and feeling; a way, too, of acting and behaving that at one and the same time marks a relation of belonging, and presents itself as a task (Foucault, 1984c, p. 39).

Foucault is obviously not theorizing on "modern Islam", nor making a study on the "resurgence" of religion as a vehicle of politics. It is probably not by chance, however, that through his particular engagement in a strikingly new event taking place in the very middle of a global scenario of multiple crises, he is able to offer a crucial contribution to the Western intellectual discourse on Islam:

I feel embarrassed to speak of the Islamic government as an "idea" or an "ideal". But as a "political will" it has impressed me. It has impressed me in its effort to *politicize* [emphasis added], in response to actual problems, structures *indissolubly* [emphasis added] social and religious (Foucault, 1978a, p. 49).

Despite being constrained by the bidimensional hermeneutics of political Islam as any other Western observer at that time, Foucault's own mental stance in "going Oriental" by looking at what was happening in Iran was best suited for profitably investing the "empathy" factor (a component central to the classic Orientalist way of essentializing Islam: see Waardenburg, 1963) in an enterprise whose final outcome is foreign to the mainstream Orientalist (and, even more, Weberist) propensity – as updated by Bernard Lewis – to deny Islam a potential for developing a dynamic subjectivity (see Chapter 6).

One cannot discount as purely formal the aestheticizing modalities that governed this enterprise and made it possible. But one cannot agree with those critics of Foucault who tended to reduce his engagement to a mere intellectual evasion in purely aesthetic terms. We have to recognize a more profound reason, one significant for the metamorphosis of the transcultural space. One must only recall how, in defining modernity, Foucault later appealed to Baudelaire's formulation, according to which it consists of "the attitude that makes it possible to grasp the 'heroic' aspect of the present moment . . . not a phenomenon of sensitivity to the fleeting present . . . [but] the will to 'heroize' the present." (Foucault, 1984c, p. 40). Here a concept of modernity is shaped where the aesthetic and the ethical dimensions are indissolubly merged. Did Foucault recognize a spark of such modernity in the Iranian revolution? More probably, it was *his* experience of empathetically narrating the Iranian revolution that came close to this definition of modernity. It is the Iranian *revolution as* recounted by the leading Western thinker Michel Foucault that marks a displacement (and a rescue at the same time) of the tradition of modernity.

Foucault himself, however, did not make much effort to conceal the power of fascination: the scenario was intriguing because it seemed to be genuinely non-Western, thoroughly "Oriental", with the enigmatic figure of the bearded, venerable elder at the centre stage, invoked by the masses as their liberator, and patiently waiting his turn while sitting in the periphery of Paris: "everything showed that one believed in the force of the mysterious current linking an old man, exiled for fifteen years, and its people invoking him. It is the nature of this current that has fascinated me." (Foucault, 1978a, p. 48).

The "mysterious current" was probably perceived by Foucault as the secret of the revolution. This was assessed as an extraordinarily fascinating experience (Foucault, [1979] 1988, p. 219) in that it could not be read according to canons familiar in the West, where the meaning of revolution must always be inscribed within a "huge effort to fit the upheaval within a rational and manageable history" (Foucault, 1979b, p. 2). As a consequence, the French thinker could not avoid feeling uneasy when hearing from the very protagonists of the uprising that what was happening was perfectly translatable into the categories of Western experience:

> One often says that the definitions of Islamic government are inaccurate. They have instead appeared to me with a very familiar, but, I have to say, very little reassuring limpidity. "They are the basic formulas of democracy, bourgeois or revolutionary," I said, "we haven't stopped reiterating them since the eighteenth century; and you know where they lead to". But they promptly replied: *"The Koran had issued them before your philosophers, and if the Christian and industrial West has lost their meaning, then Islam, instead, will be able to preserve their value and efficacy."* (Foucault, 1978a, p. 49).

From the very beginning of his Iranian adventure Foucault paid close attention to the difficulty of managing the balance between universality and uniqueness in interpreting the event he was observing. But this difficulty did not seem to embarrass him. His entire reading of the Iranian revolution is original and influential in so far as it does not try to suppress one element to the advantage of the other: what Foucault wanted to see confirmed was the idea of a displacement, yet of the survival, of political spirituality. The conclusion he seems to draw is that there can be no history without enchantment, as he writes in his last article on the Iranian issue:

> Nobody is entitled to establish that these confused voices sing better than the others and tell the profoundest truth. It is enough that they exist to give a sense to listening to them and trying to find out what they want to say. Moral question? Maybe. Question of reality? Sure. All disenchantments of history won't do anything. It is because there are some voices that human time has not the form of evolution but precisely that of "history" (Foucault, 1979b, p. 2).

The net result of Foucault's attention towards the Iranian revolution lies, however, in the extent to which his engagement was nurtured by the force of fascination, that acted as an instrument for diluting such a universalist perspective, as well as in his reluctance to celebrate what he experienced in Iran as a modern staging of an utopia or an ideal (as we would say, and as many Iranians involved in the revolt actually told Foucault). The French thinker was rather eager to see at stake "something very old and also very distant in the future" (Foucault, 1978a, p. 49). The formal dilemma between modern and traditional, past-orientedness and future-projection is simply made obsolete by the unique strength of the revolution as "fact" and as "will": "People rebel, this is a fact: and it is in this way that subjectivity comes into history and gives it its spirit." (Foucault, 1979b, p. 2). One really wonders whether this representation of an absence of tension, of harmony with history, or with its supposedly "true essence", could hold together without Foucault's own aesthetic feeling for what he was experiencing:

> Now what struck me in Iran is that there is no struggle between different elements. What gives it such a *beauty* [emphasis added], and at the same time such gravity, is that there is only one confrontation: between the entire people and the state threatening it with its weapons and police (Foucault, [1979] 1988, p. 216.)

This is, however, a peculiar kind of uniqueness, not simply of an event approached with empathy, but of the very experience of Foucault as the Western intruder, who never tried to disguise his reportage in the form of objective observation. And it is true that its outcome, the stress on Islam not as Law, but as anti-Law, or creative subjectivity, runs counter to the core tenets of the Orientalist tradition, committed to consider Islam, at least in its allegedly orthodox version, strictly dependent on a rigid hermeneutics of Text and Law, that excludes any access to a hermeneutics of the subject. Foucault's intervention sanctioned the irreversibility of the crisis of Weberism as well as the absence of an alternative paradigm, since a valid knowledge of Islam could not be sustained by simply updating its power of fascination.

The French philosopher was publicly accused by an Iranian woman of confusing spirituality with religious fanaticism. "One would say that for the Western left obsessed by humanism, Islam is desirable . . . elsewhere." (Foucault, 1978b, p. 26). This attack, expressed in crude and resentful terms, alludes to the sort of displacement we have observed in Foucault's reportage, and it is a bit surprising that he reacted quite defensively, without taking up the question of displacement. His generic reply corresponds, in its first part, to the common denominator of each construction of "political Islam" since Bernard Lewis's intervention, whereas in its second part it spells out only the minimal condition for considering political Islam independently of the deleterious influence of the TV theorem: " . . . the problem of Islam as a political force is a problem essential to our epoch, for the years to come. The first condition for tackling it, regardless of how intelligently, is not to begin by putting hatred into it (Foucault, 1978b, p. 26)."[8]

It could appear paradoxical that the progressive, Western-located Arab intellectual, Said, made such a display of scholarly indebtedness to Foucault (see Said, 1978, p. 3) in the same historical conjuncture when the latter's own intervention in the Iranian revolution manifested a fresh, intellectually fashionable variant within the repertoire of Orientalism. It is evident that the two undertakings were independent of each other, since Foucault was experiencing his own crisis as a crisis of criticism, whereas for Said criticism preserved all the regenerating potential of an intellectual tool suitable for deconstructing and unveiling discourses of domination. As to the declared Foucaultian affiliation of Said's work, this clearly concerns the "pre-crisis" Foucault, or rather that distinctive combination between the "archaeological" work of the 1960s (Foucault, 1966 and 1969), unveiling the statics of power-knowledge, and *Surveiller et punir*, which tackled the dynamics of social control. We should remember that Said wrote *Orientalism* in the years 1975–6, when Foucault's personal and intellectual crisis had not yet openly erupted. In this sense, the articulation of "critique and crisis" in *Orientalism* is certainly obsolete from the viewpoint of Foucault just examined. However, Said's book and Foucault's texts on the Iranian revolution were published at about the same time and captured the attention of the same sort of intellectual audience, and this is why it makes sense to place them in the same hermeneutic context.

Said's campaign was animated by the conviction that the crisis provided the scenario that made a critique of the Western Other-understanding more urgent, and easier to be staged by addressing the part of the public dissatisfied with the platitudes of the media theorem. It is not by chance that an author that was both a literary critic and an Arab scholar working in the West, seriously concerned with questions of identity, was so successful in making a "case" out of Orientalism. Despite all previous analyses of Orientalism and associated debates on it (see Chapter 6), a grand controversy was only originated by Said because he cumulated a feeling of anger at the "otherization" of the Arabs after 1973, according to the theorem previously sketched, with a particular, professional sensitivity for the semantic and linguistic dimension of this otherization.

The Western representation of the Arab (or, later, of the Arab as Muslim, or even – mistakenly, as in the case of the Iranian revolution – of the Muslim as Arab) is the original motivation for Said's own engagement in a genre of discourse that did not exactly coincide with his primary discipline, literary criticism. As early as 1970 he wrote *The Arab Portrayed,* in the wake of the Arab–Israeli war of 1967 (Said, 1970), and towards the end of 1976, when the book *Orientalism* was virtually finished – though not yet published – he made it publicly clear from the columns of the *New York Times Book Review* that his target was the media theorem blessed and upgraded by Bernard Lewis, whose article came out in that same year (Said, 1976). The connection between the theorem and the struggle for crushing the Orientalist axiom according to which "they [i.e. the "Orientals"] cannot represent themselves"⁹ is clear in the juxtaposition between the following argumentative blocks:

> Television, the films, and all the media's resources have forced information into more and more standardized molds. So far as the Orient is concerned, standardization and cultural stereotyping have intensified the hold of the nineteenth-century academic and imaginative demonology of the "mysterious Orient." This is nowhere more true than in the ways by which the Near East is grasped . . .
>
> The life of an Arab Palestinian in the West, particularly in America, is disheartening. There exists here an almost unanimous consensus that politically he does not exist, and when it is allowed that he does, it is either as a nuisance or as an Oriental (Said, 1978, pp. 26–7).

Denouncements of the pamphletistic character of Said's work, his plain mistakes, wholesale judgements, and finally his lack of competence in analysing Orientalism, might have rightly pointed to a constitutive weakness of this book. These accusations do not diminish, however, its value in consecrating an epistemic rupture. The innovative strength of Said's fresh problematization of Orientalism is to be seen, within the post-crisis climate, in its capacity to reduce to a common denominator the scattered elements of former critiques of Orientalism, and thereby grounding a virtually new tradition of discourse. This merit was sustained by Said's firm will to mark a new intellectual and public *presence* suitable for attaining the goal of challenging the Western paradigm of knowledge of the Islamic Orient. In other words, Said was able to create a counter-theorem.

He was to a large degree aware of the extent to which his undertaking was both old and new. He paid tribute to Anouar Abdel-Malek as the one who "perfectly characterized . . . the Orientalized Orient" (p. 96),[10] but the scope *and* the style of Said's enterprise were well beyond a simple "characterization":

> For contemporary students of the Orient, from university scholars to policymakers, I have written with two ends in mind: one, to present their intellectual genealogy to them in a way that has not been done; two, to criticize – with the hope of stirring discussion – the often unquestioned assumptions on which their work for the most part depends (p. 24).

Let us try to reconstruct a significant sample of Said's core statements, formulated so as to imitate the style of the drastic essentializations performed within the Orientalist tradition, that he has to challenge on its own terrain. After postulating the "constant interchange between academic and general imaginative Orientalism since the late eighteenth century" (p. 3), that during the 1970s condensed into a compact theorem, Said unequivocally denounces the self-reflexive foundations of the science of the Islamic Orient: "Orientalism is . . . a considerable dimension of modern political-intellectual culture, and as such has less to do with the Orient than it does with 'our' world" (p. 12). Or, even more sharply: "The Orient is an integral part of Europen *material* civilization and culture" (p. 2).

The materiality of Orientalism is in its "mode of discourse with supporting institutions, vocabulary, scholarship, imagery, doctrines, even colonial bureaucracies and colonial styles", much more than in what is supposed to be its "object". Therefore, we should consider labels such as "Occident" and "Orient" as social products of a sort of "imaginative geography", emanating from mechanisms of intellectual regulation, whose ultimate logic is that "every discrete study of one bit of Oriental material would also confirm in a summary way the profound orientality of the material" (p. 2). In this regard Said has spoken of the Orientalists' ability to issue "summational statements" (p. 245). But even more important is the epistemological status that the entire Western society, including its allegedly anti-systemic components, has attributed to such statements and to the use of the adjective "Oriental", since " . . . one could speak in Europe of an Oriental personality, an Oriental atmosphere, an Oriental tale, Oriental despotism or an Oriental mode of production, and be understood." (Said, 1978, pp. 31–2).

The Orient as a discursive category overarching the production of meaning in disparate discursive formations is the first of three strictly related core claims conferring a distinctive flavour to the book *Orientalism*. The other two are stigmatizations of the ordering function of the opposition between rationality and irrationality (the "motif of the Orient as insinuating danger", of "rationality undermined by Eastern excess": pp. 55–7) and of the explanatory power of the "reactivist" paradigm ("So impressive have the descriptive and textual successes of Orientalism been that entire periods of the Orient's cultural, political and social history are considered mere responses to the West. The West is the actor, the Orient a passive reactor": pp. 108–9).

The foundation of a counter-theorem, and not a reform of Orientalism resulting in its de-orientalization, is all that we should search for in Said's book. His invocation of "a rigorous methodological vigilance that construes Orientalism less as a positive than a critical discipline" (Said, 1986, p. 216) shows a determination not to leave Orientalist scholarship unchecked and unchallenged. The term "vigilance" is a good keyword, a preliminary condition, for attempting a relocation and a management of essentialism, which is all we can do, since one cannot suppress it without at the same time giving up any claim to knowledge (see Chapter 6). Said is, however, not interested in going that far, and in his praise of scholars such as Rodinson and Owen we should not see more than an understandable search for allies from within the fields of Orientalism and Middle East Studies: after all, Said sees in their works only "instructive correctives brought from the contemporary human sciences to the study of the so-called Orient" (Said, 1978, p. 327).

It has been rightly emphasized that the spread and market success of *Orientalism* are proof of its very particular status (Johansen, 1990, p. 72). The secret of this performance was in the book's capacity to strike out efficiently against the "guilt complex . . . inherent in much of Western culture, political systems, scholarship". The resulting "essentialist approach to European culture" (p. 73) cannot be simply denounced as a scholarly failure, almost an inevitable side-effect of the commercial exploit. It is precisely this essentializing operation that makes the work so central in the metamorphosis of the transcultural space. This anti-Orientalist essentialization, taking root in the very core of the Western side of that space, is the key to the cumulative effects attained by Said's book in the climate of "critique and crisis", through shaking the previous transcultural equilibrium under the aegis of Weberism. Retrospectively, Said has had no difficulty in admitting the motivation that lay at the origin of his initiative: "This I took also to be an attempt to act as an interlocutor rather than as a silent and inert Other." To this end, the "political" Foucault of *Surveiller et punir* of the mid-1970s was no doubt the most suitable model (Said, 1988, p. 32).

Nevertheless, for Said the strength of criticism is not limited to the theoretical power of a deconstructionist approach, but culminates in the rhetorically skilled foundation of a persuasive counter-discourse for the use and delight of one circumscribed, but significant portion of Western intelligentsia vulnerable to a guilt complex towards the non-Western world. It has recently been acknowledged, in a work dedicated to intellectuals and critique, that

> Said's argument owes something of its persuasive force to his command of large-scale narrative structures, that is to say, his gift for marshalling so much detailed evidence into a powerful indictment of Western attitudes and policies which wouldn't make the point so effectively if treated in a more dispersed or piecemeal form (Norris, 1992, p. 141).

Since the target of Orientalists has been an entity called "Islam", Said's challenge is potentially devastating, because "the negation of Orientalism turns out to be the negation of Islam" (Binder, 1988, p. 120). Saying that the result of Said's undertaking would be the "dispersal of Islam" (p. 121) is also going too far. Said's aim is no blind deconstruction but to defend the right of anything associated with Islam to be other without being otherized through a judgement on the degree and quality of its rationality, the right of Muslims to reconstruct Islam – to the extent they wish to do it – without depending on a Western preconstruction: an evidently utopian purpose, because of the inevitable interdependence between Western and indigenous constructions of Islam (see Chapters 3 and 4).

Said performs this task through a conscious use of those rhetorical instruments, including obsessive repetition, which he saw – in examining other history-making texts such as Marx's *Eighteenth Brumaire* (Said, 1983) – as a privileged tool of expression of a worldly meaning (see Norris, [1982] 1991, pp. 88–9). As a result of this well-managed rhetoric of radical social criticism, whose vehemence springs from an underlying utopian impulse, Said's making of a counter-theorem was comparable, in terms of its essentializing force and ability to capture the attention of the right kind of audience, to the shaping of a compact theorem through the crisis-staging by the principal Western media. As the theorem stated that there is a precise relationship between the Arabs and their animating essence, "Islam", the counter-theorem responded by unveiling a precise relationship between the

Orientalists' job and the regulating function of the idea of the "Orient" in sustaining the consolidation – especially through the prism of a discourse of crisis – of Western self-understanding.

Compared with Foucault's *Archaeologies* of Western knowledge, Said's book is certainly disappointing. This is understandable, since an accurate "archaeological" study of Orientalism, as involving a hermeneutic space responding to increasingly transcultural constraints, and where more disparate discursive formations intertwine than in the cases studied by Foucault during the 1960s, is too complex a task for performance with the tools of radical literary criticism. Said's intention was, however, symptomatic of the ongoing metamorphosis in the transcultural space, in that he appeared willing to render Foucault's archaeological focus less parochial. We should remember that beyond the words of praise and indebtedness addressed to Foucault, Said also accused him, in an essay not primarily concerned with Orientalism, of being,

> unaware of the extent to which the ideas of discourse and discipline are assertively European and how, along with the use of discipline to employ masses of detail (and human beings), discipline was used also to administer, study, and reconstruct – then subsequently to occupy, rule and exploit – almost the whole of the non-European world (Said, 1983, p. 222).

This quotation suggests where the main hermeneutic dislocation between the two authors lies. For Foucault, the Orient could only be an occasion to be seized in order to provide responses to the feeling of displacement of the spirit of modernity: it was instrument, but no "question" in itself. Said, instead, insisted in making a question out of it, and he no doubt succeeded, although this question-raising swiftly crystallized in a new discursive formation: the critique of Orientalism.

In the same period when Foucault was trying to assess the historical and intellectual roots of modern criticism, Said did his best to concentrate critical power on the subject of Orientalism. Said was dismayed at seeing how an old Western tradition of knowledge had produced, through the manipulative strength of the mass media, a huge potential for otherizing the Arabs and Muslims, so jeopardizing the very possibility of Arab citizenship in the US-dominated "global village". In his assault on a tradition of Western thinking, Said bravely and consciously operated within a horizon of representations.

Foucault, instead, provided a highly innovative version of the Western embarrassment of being confronted with the Islamic Orient, intrigued not by the idea of engaging in an archaeology of Western essentialism which would touch its ultimate layer of definition (the construction of the neighbour as the Other), but by an "event", a revolution (*the* event for a Western intellectual) that was staged, strangely enough, in the Orient, and thereby was valuable, by contrast, in pointing out the present stagnation of Western subjectivity, incapable of renewing its political spirituality. Two different, but interdependent, processes or traditions were called into question by the interventions of Foucault and Said: the development of a Western subjectivity, and the evolution of the Western construction of a convenient Other. At one point, however, the two different discourses of the French *penseur* and the Arab intellectual converge: on the possibility of *recognizing* Islam as "true" and autonomous, capable of developing a dynamic subjectivity, not merely a shadow civilization.

The crisis lay in the fact that, in both cases, a tradition appeared to have used up its stabilizing force, and the obvious absence of a ready-made alternative fostered the formation of a "post"-climate. The epistemic break was no prelude to a "paradigmatic revolution" in the Kuhnian sense. The only alternative to TV and academic neo-Orientalism was a generic "post-Orientalist" mood. This climate of insoluble crisis accompanied a metamorphosis of the transcultural space, its emancipation from the solid and simple certainties condensed in Weberism.

NOTES

1 Another well-known attempt at criticizing Orientalism by a Muslim scholar located in the West (Tibawi, 1964) is less relevant for us, because it was largely still inspired by a traditional apologetic mood.

2 This publishing initiative was launched by a group of scholars who had become "increasingly dissatisfied with the state" of Middle East Studies, and whose aim was "to encourage the production of theoretically relevant work informed by a critical appreciation of the Middle East and its history." (Asad and Owen, 1975).

3 In any case, Said's attention towards how the Arabs and their supposed cultural assets were portrayed in the West goes back to the June War of 1967, and has probably been uninterrupted since then (see Said, 1970).

4 This conviction has been repeatedly expressed from the presidential tribune of the Middle East Studies Association (MESA) annual meeting (see Esposito, 1990; Haddad, 1991b, and Eickelman, 1992).

5 This has been a persisting motif in picturing the Arabs as Muslims that also inspired Western representations of the Islamic Orient during the Gulf War in early 1991. The role played by the media was in that case one of selecting and reshaping the images which best symbolized such an allegedly inherent irrationality (Gerhard and Link, 1992). The anti-Saddam crusade as narrated by the most influential Western media may well have fulfilled the function of exorcizing this Islam-centred obsession of crisis incumbent on Western welfare and security since the 1973–4 events: such an appraisal transcends, however, the scope of the present study.

6 Lewis attempted to unveil two Arab nationalist groups, Nasser's "Free Officers" and Arafat's *fatah*, in their alleged Islamist affiliations, via over-stressing their constitutive links, at the time of their births, with the Muslim Brotherhood.

7 A prominent example of the clash between the two authors is in the MESA debate on "The Scholars, the Media and the Middle East", held on 22 November 1986 (see Said, 1988, p. 33).

8 It has been pointed out, in terms less blunt than in the Iranian woman's objection to Foucault, that the intellectual focus of what I have conceptualized as the transcultural dimension of "crisis" is precisely a "phenomenon of Western admiration for the political spiritualism of the East" (Abaza and Stauth, [1988] 1990, p. 220). This diagnosis has led to a stigmatization of the "fascination of Islam" as the vehicle through which "Western social scientists and intellectuals, who were similarly impressed by Muslim revivalism, have too crudely and too quickly evoked perspectives and arguments which aimed at a decomposition of secular intellectualism in the Middle East" (pp. 220–1).

9 This is the opening quotation of *Orientalism*, transposed from Marx's *The Eighteenth Brumaire of Louis Bonaparte*.

10 The reading of Abdel-Malek's critique of Orientalism (1963) probably played an important role in helping to shape the conceptual basis of Said's own engagement, that matured before the Arab-Israeli war of 1967 (see Said, 1988, p. 33).

CHAPTER 9

From Islam to politics,
or the reverse?

In the case of the second circle the interpretation of Islam's politicization was still contained within a monodimensional perspective, in which the "political" was derivative of the negative, disturbing function of Islam's presence in the modernization process. But we have seen how in the "post-crisis" era, and by virtue of the logic that governed the representation of this crisis through the Western media, the political has gradually acquired the status of an autonomous dimension (see Chapter 9). This process unfolded via the category of Islamic "resurgence", or of its virtual equivalent, "revival". Following the 1973 crisis, there were clear signs from within the academy that the perceived weakness of the modernization paradigm was producing a tendency to problematize anew, no longer according to the negative-derivative perspective of the second circle, the relationship between Islam and social change. One major symptom of this shift was the launching of a project, at the University of Chicago, jointly directed by a former representative of the second circle, Leonard Binder, and a Muslim scholar of Islamic studies, Fazlur Rahman. "The project sought to find an alternative to the prevailing paradigm which predicated that an increase in social change necessarily caused a decrease in Islamic religious commitment." The joint venture was completed before the Iranian revolution (Binder, 1988, p. ix).

The Western perception of an "Islam in movement" was obviously no absolute novelty, as "the fear of a 'revolt of Islam', of a sudden movement among the unknown peoples whom they ruled", has affected the Western colonial enterprise since at least the end of last century (Hourani, 1991, p. 301). However, this fear was not yet at the core of the emotional apparatus animating Orientalist studies, which focused on a rather static hermeneutics of cultural-religious units (see Chapter 4). The emergence of the hermeneutic field of "political Islam" grounded on the perception of Islam's renewed capacity to move, made explicit since the mid-1970s a reflex that had long remained latent within the Western view of the Islamic Orient, and above all had not yet been given a full-blown form.[1]

165

Islam "as such" was not able to polarize and subsume under its hermeneutic power a wide range of other categories or slogans, each with a history of its own. It was considered either intrinsically political, or ineluctably bound to political marginality. The absence of a dynamic field of problematization depended on the unquestioned strength of the two sets of categories and institutions that supported, in the West, the compact idea of Islam: on the one hand the category of modernity and the enterprise of a "modern distinction" (see Chapter 2); on the other, the category of the Islamic Orient and the enterprise of an "Orientalist distinction" (see Chapters 4 and 6).

"Political Islam" becomes the hub of an autonomous interpretive field in the very moment it ceases to be a tautology. A bidimensional field of this type enlarges the space of contention and multiplies the voices entitled to engage in problematizing the relationship between Islam and the political. The linearity, embodied in a standard vocabulary and tools, of a relatively closed discursive formation (such as the two primarily involved in the hermeneutics of Islam: Orientalism and the Islamic sciences as centred on *fiqh*: see Chapter 4) is then put under severe stress. All discourses intervening in the interpretive field of political Islam, including those institutionally originating from the representatives of these two formations, begin to make sense in a much wider and more integrated semantic context than those proper to specialized disciplines. First and foremost, the post-crisis interpretive circles are confronted with the hermeneutics of critical modernity, whether they cope openly with this intellectual challenge – as reactualized by the epistemic break matured since the late 1960s – or attempt to domesticate or even exorcize it.

The sheer quantitative dimension of the emergence of the hermeneutic field of political Islam is impressive. Bibliographic surveys of contributions published in Western languages during the 1970s and the 1980s which address political Islam yield a thousand titles or more (Lücke, 1993, pp. 17–18 and Haddad, 1991a). This figure is even inadequate, since it is drawn only from the sources identifiable through standard bibliographic tools. From a work that surveyed contributions published in German and in English, it clearly appears that the events of 1978–9 centred on the Islamic revolution in Iran and its aftermath multiplied the quantitative weight of the contributions, but it is also evident that in the period 1974–8 scholarly interest already attained a level contrasting sharply with the virtual silence on political Islam during the years immediately following the Arab defeat in the 1967 war with Israel (Lücke, 1993, pp. 21–9), though from an intra-Arab perspective this event represented the first highly symbolic turning-point in the maturation of an Islamic "awakening" (see Chapter 10).

A salient feature that characterizes the corpus of texts that we have subsumed under the catchcategory of "political Islam" is that the authors' evaluations differ deeply with regard to what the phenomenon, in its socio-political shaping, is really about. What is most interesting, however, is that hardly any scholar seems to question the unity of the object of inquiry (see Lücke 1993, p. 5). This tension between heuristic uncertainties and a high consensus in identifying a definite "phenomenon" or problem is further demonstrated by the propensity of more than half of the analysts to introduce their works through a reassessment of the labels in use (p. 191). Sometimes this operation also suggests that the author is conscious that the intricacies of the definitional game are indeed the first, problematic layer of the phenomenon to be coped with.

A common-sense objection to discussing the tense relationship between this perceived phenomenon and the related field of interpretation could be that all that happened between the mid- and late 1970s was a tangible, unprecedented mobilization under the banner of Islam, and that the corresponding attention of observers, situated at various levels – insiders and outsiders – simply followed up this fact, as usual. But this is no more than half the truth, since it is legitimate to maintain that since the 1930s this kind of mobilization has been virtually continuous (as in Egypt's case: see Chapter 3), in the sense that its seeming regression was more a function of political fortune and public visibility than of an actual decline in the actors' motivation. It has been claimed that if one sees a continuity between the Islamic movement of the 1930s and the 1970s, the cognitive validity of the concept of "resurgence" is jeopardized (Davis, 1987, p. 49). Bernard Lewis's message (see Chapter 8) was able to spell out the contradictory foundations of Western constructions of political Islam, since he rightly tried to emphasize the elements of continuity, but also made mostly explicit the need to begin to protect Western interests through a fresh consideration of the phenomenon and of its potential evolution. The result of his argument is that the stress on the continuity of political Islam inevitably slides towards the warning before an incoming resurgence. The measure of "Islamic resurgence", or the like, is given by the consciousness, perception and fear of the Western observer.

The hermeneutic field of political Islam is here conceived as the general form of problematization underlying the different interpretive responses it encompasses (cf. Foucault, 1984a, p. 389). In order to offer a historically sound typification of all following circles according to the criteria sketched in the Introduction, I should first of all exclude that the game of creating, using and destroying different definitions of "Islam in movement" can provide crucial elements of differentiation among various interpretive models. It is pointless to discuss at any length any such definition, because what matters here is more their basically equivalent hermeneutic "exchange value" than their shifting, discursive "use-value". It has been pointed out that "we introduce copulatives (the revival of Islam, the militancy of Islam, the fundamentalism of Islam) wildly and randomly to come to terms with something that will not be simply understood or quickly subdued." (Lawrence, 1987, p. 16). As noted before, what is common to all these labels is their pointing to movement, whose crudest metaphors are hydraulic, meteorological or even seismological (Clément, 1983, pp. 91–2).

The first documented, explicit use of the label "political Islam" by an influential author as a substitute for roughly equivalent definitions dates back to the immediate aftermath of the Iranian revolution (Abdel-Malek, 1979). Since then, "political Islam" seems to have gradually acquired, especially in very recent times, a certain prominence, due to its higher neutrality and precision in identifying the problem of the relationship between "Islam" and the "political" (cf. Ayubi, 1991 and Roy, 1992). As a label, political Islam is successfully replacing, or sometimes complementing, other definitions, mostly of vaguer or more value-charged nature, or else not general enough, like "Islamic fundamentalism", *intégrisme islamique*, "Islamic radicalism" or even "Islamic revival" or "resurgence". This process can be considered proof of a learning process in the specialized literature, a search for a categorization platform that more neatly reflects the interplay of the two dimensions involved.

On the other hand, from the perspective of the present work political Islam is more than a topic or catchcategory mentioned explicitly in the texts analysed. Besides its actual, primary interpretive strength, it is a unifying symbolic package helping capturing the feeling of an unbridgeable gap between the analytic-denotative function in the use of labels for defining phenomena of politicization of Islam, and the symbolic-connotative power that conditions the *view* of an "Islam in movement", a power decisively enhanced by mass-media intervention. Through this basically non-logical, visionary intensity, "political Islam" becomes a kind of umbrella category, embodying a reservoir of added and partly concealed meaning that conditions the application of all other categories evoked by the interpreters: above all, the category of "modernity".

It is now my task to examine the contention, within the interpretive field of political Islam, revolving around defining the direction of Islam's movement. We will see how this dispute almost immediately leads to a judgement on the extent to which Islam's politicization is compatible with modern social and ethical standards. As modernity embodies an idealized historical trajectory, Islam's movement, especially – but not only – when viewed from a Western viewpoint, cannot escape such a judgement. In the case of the first circle, this was implicit, since the object under examination was a static Islam: the absence of movement made an explicit judgement superfluous. Similarly, the second circle, although recognizing some movement in Islam, considered it unavoidably "transitional", at odds with history, thereby devoid of any appreciable direction.

The object of the contention between the third and the fourth circles is not the hypothesis – widely maintained and shared, with shifting accentuations, by virtually all the post-crisis interpretive circles – that some critical socioeconomic or socio-cultural factors contributed to the relative success of movements of Islamist inspiration. The problem is how to interpret the movement, as "a defensive and non-constructive reaction to drastic change", according to a rationale laid down by the second circle, or alternatively as "creative, innovative, and active responses to change" (Hegland, 1987, p. 3). This is the interpretive crux where the notion of "fundamentalism" is called into question, as an instrument for a conceptual upgrading of the "movement" link between Islam and the political, which terms like "resurgence" can illuminate only superficially.

Initially transposed to the Islamist realm from a reference to a circumscribed current within American Protestantism, the label "fundamentalism" gradually acquired, during the 1980s, the status of an acknowledged category in the Western sociology of contemporary religions (see Robertson, 1989; Lawrence, 1987 and 1989; Riesebrodt, 1990 and Marty, 1992). This term has consolidated its social-scientific status through its comparative application to contemporary developments within all monotheist religions, in order to account for the "modern rejection of modernity", or at least a very ambiguous instrumentalization of it, in the name of allegedly unchangeable religious "fundaments". In this sense, "fundamentalism" has been widely employed in connection with hermeneutic and social phenomena attending the alleged crisis of modernity (see Chapter 8). Thus, resort to this category for interpreting the politicization of Islam through reference to a broader sociocultural background has gained a degree of academic respect, which goes well beyond its widespread circulation and use in media representations.

Apart from the fortunes of "fundamentalism" as the marker of a critical turn,[2] it is important to bear in mind that the demise of modernization theory in the context of a more general questioning of the taken-for-granted value of modernity, has opened up a much wider space of interpretive contention concerning the admissibility and quality of any judgement on modernity. While Enlightenment modernity represented a confident act of taking root in history through conceiving and experiencing the present as the locus of progress, or the workshop of the future, the critical "post-modern" turn points out the need to reopen the universe of hermeneutic possibilities that the Enlightenment tended to close by virtue of its intrinsic dialectic (see Chapter 2). The overall logic of the post-modern breakthrough is represented by the striving towards freely reconstructing one's own place within modernity among a much wider range of options than previously allowed.

Each model of construction of political Islam, from the third circle on, is dependent on this exit from the teleological trajectory of modernity. This has increasingly become an "essentially contested concept", even a void and meaningless notion, if taken alone. It is still very meaningful, however, when associated with other categories which predicate it or are specified by it. We will see how the judgement on the modern character of political Islam is built upon this kind of game of redressing and enhancing the meaningfulness of modernity as well as its function as hermeneutic marker, through its variable association with the factor "Islam" and with its "political" dimension. We are going to see how in the confrontation between the third and the fourth circles, the definition of what is at stake in the dispute is relatively straightforward, so that the argumentative devices adopted by their purest representatives examined here are easily comparable through linguistic analysis (see Introduction).

It is my intention, however, to elucidate as far as possible not only the historical-diachronical process of hermeneutic derivation among circles, but also their constitution, in a synchronic interaction, of a largely integrated discursive network. In order to highlight this interdiscursive dimension, one must enhance the visibility of a common semantic within the interpretive field of political Islam, going beyond the tendencies towards fragmentation and the pursuit of side issues, a semantic allowing for effective communication, more than a simple reassertion of one's own position, or that of one's circle. As a consequence, I will privilege, from the third circle onwards (hence from well within the Western part of the transcultural space), a subcategory of interpreters who are presumed to possess a high degree of motivational homogeneity. These are intellectuals of Arab origin, albeit of varying cultural and religious backgrounds. For these interpreters, political Islam can never be a question seen from outside, but inevitably recalls the problem of the historical formation of an Arab–Islamic framework of reference: a question situated at the crossroads between the intellectual's own position *vis-à-vis* contemporary Arab polities and his quest for a viable identity and citizenship in world society. In coincidence with the crisis of the transcultural equilibrium, Arab scholars based in the West enjoyed growing attention and earned greater recognition. It is not surprising that, from the third circle on, Arab authors become increasingly central, while they played no part at all in the first circle, and were not prominent actors in the second (see Chapter 7).

The second circle had been capable, prior to the outbreak and staging of the crisis, i.e. at the beginning of the 1970s, of revising the linear, monodimensional character of standard modernization theory, and of taking into account crisis factors in the political development of Arab societies (see Binder, 1971). But it was not before the late 1970s that the emerging impression of a "failure to modernize" in Muslim societies began to be associated with Islam's "return" or "resurgence" (see Chapter 8), thus presenting the former as the cause of the latter. The third circle asserts that this alleged resurgence of Islam is the expression of a conscious reaction to externally induced models of modernization and development. Political Islam is accordingly depicted as the most acute form of a new, typically Middle Eastern pathology of anti-modernizing impulses. The indebtedness of this interpretation to the second circle's thesis is clear enough, but it is also evident that the third circle has inherited from the first a vision of Islam as intrinsically hostile to modernity.

Although the third circle was and is well represented within the academy, its most typical sources of irradiation are the mass media. To put it more clearly, this circle seems to be given life by a stratum of (scholarly and non-scholarly) "Middle East expertise", acting both within the mass media and policy-advising establishments. Although it is possible to identify refined versions of this circle's arguments, its most basic attitude consists of an overreaction to the most recent political events variably (often tenuously) associated with Islam, and of obscuring the need for historical depth in the analysis. This inclination results from a sense of urgency leading to alarm in the face of the perceived threat emanating from political Islam and directed against the values of modern secularism, as embodied in the West and its path of development.

Within the large production of Bassam Tibi, a political scientist of Syrian origin who grew up in Germany, we find a differentiated but very representative case of the argumentative model which draws towards a conclusion of this type, and is intentionally addressed to a public broader than a mere academic one.[3] As Tibi makes clear in the very beginning of the Foreword to his first main work on political Islam, *The Crisis of Modern Islam*, among the two sets of variables intervening in the phenomenon the principal one is "Islam", an entity that has, nonetheless, to be submitted to a social-scientific scrutiny (Tibi, 1981, p. 7).[4] The adoption of this perspective requires, differently from the first circle, the explicit consideration of factors of mobilization grounded on structural reasons (Tibi, [1981] 1991, p. 65). The contemporary sociocultural mechanisms of Islam's politicization, which Tibi prefers to synthesize in the formula of "reislamization" (p. 29), are assessed as a particular case in the process of Third World reactivation of autochthonous, pre-industrial cultural assets as a response to the Westernization carried out in the absence of any thorough industrialization process (p. 14). This reaction against the penetration of Western culture, along with its scientific and technological superiority, is attributed a "defensive" character (p. 17). Tibi revises the second circle's universalist, ahistorical perspective by seeking inspiration in the strand of literature on political development concentrating on the inevitable pathology of modernization, and by employing a simplified version of the concept of "civilizing process" by Norbert Elias. This combination becomes the vehicle for reaffirming Western uniqueness, as well as the key for shaping a "maximalist" (see Chapters 2 and 5) concept of modernity (pp. 38–41). In spite of the demise of Western optimist views of modernization, Tibi found support, years later, in Habermas's redefinition of modernity as an unfolding project (Habermas, 1992b). Although consciously Eurocentric, this definition is, nonetheless, not maximalist. The evolution of Tibi's search for authoritative supports of the view of modernity he needs to underpin the third circle's argument shows a growing capacity to accommodate a non-maximalist concept, more attuned with the post-crisis intellectual climate. In this sense, the model of the third circle is not dependent – as the first two circles were – on a Weberist-maximalist notion of modernity.

As a consequence of the worldwide globalization of the civilizing waves irradiating from Western Europe, a "modern acculturated Islam" (also called "Islamic modernism", basically coinciding with the current more correctly identified as "Islamic reformism": see Chapters 3 and 5) arose, which remained, however, a circumscribed and élitist undertaking and was unable to provide a solid bridge between the Western and Islamic cultural codes, nor prevent the aggravation of "cultural anomie" (Tibi, [1981] 1991, p. 31). Tibi's own use of this sociological concept consists of pointing to the "identity crisis that functions as the social-psychological background to the Islamic resurgence", in the wake of "asymmetrical processes of interaction in the cultural sphere on an international level". According to Tibi, it follows logically that the way out of anomie can only be in a "return to the indigenous cultural heritage", which in turn produces "a militant and comprehensive rejection of all foreign adoptions" (Tibi, 1983, p. 7). This is what he terms a "deacculturation" process, the final expression of which is "reislamization".

The formula of reislamization, or "repoliticization of Islam" (Tibi, [1981] 1991, p. 62), derives – Tibi continues – from neglecting the structural reasons for the crisis, and from the concomitant appeal to Islam as the solution for every social problem, entailing the building of an Islamic state (p. 46). Tibi questioned the possibility of classifying this form of "defensive" response as a fully-fledged political ideology, since this would automatically imply the recognition of some modern quality in the politicized Islam. He has no doubt, however, that when assessed as a political ideology "Islamism" should be distinguished from Islam, the latter being a normative or, more broadly, cultural system (Tibi, 1983, p. 5). This is a very important distinction, because it allows the author to detach himself from the standard deduction of Islam as politics from Islam as norm, and finally from Islam as religion, carried out by the first circle.

In this way Tibi can recognize that the politicization of Islam is precisely the consequence of a clash between the symbolic-communicative system and the modern world, hence something new. The relationship between the ideology and the underlying cultural system is indeed very close, since the defensive character of the former depends not only on structural factors, but on cultural standards unsuitable for modern tasks. Tibi is eager to highlight that Islamists adopt these standards for judging what is, or is not, morally and socially acceptable. This is in turn considered by Tibi as a proof of the pre-industrial character of Islam as an all encompassing cultural system (Tibi, [1981] 1991, pp. 45–6),[5] whose definition the author curiously transposes from what Islamists themselves maintain it to be.[6]

This reconstruction of the mechanism of politicizing Islam becomes less linear when Tibi feels compelled to deliver a more markedly developmental, and historically sound, justification of the repoliticization of Islam, especially when he has to cope with the fact that the strand of "Islamic modernism" represented by the reformer Muammad 'Abduh (see Chapter 5) was later followed by the success of "Islamic fundamentalism".[7] Tibi's adjustment of Halpern's view that Islam's way out of politics was historically inevitable has the interesting consequence that the Syrian scholar can no longer, as Halpern did, consider the two Islamic currents as embodying different responses to "modern challenges", both equally doomed to failure though each characteristic of a distinctive historical phase. Whereas to the American social scientist it was sufficient to address and damn them separately, Tibi has to cope with the task of clarifying their relationship in the long-term shaping of reislamization, which is expected to reveal the direction of Islam's movement. Tibi's resulting reconflationist formula is built on the necessity of reconciling a vision of Islam's indissoluble unity between religion and politics – a view typical of the first circle – with the developmental perspective inherited from the second circle. As the latter concentrated, in its deconflationist path, on the theoretical underpinning of Islam's way out of politics, Tibi has to reconstruct the trajectory of Islam's way back to it.

The consequent stress on the *re*politicization of Islam (see Tibi, [1981] 1991, pp. 61–78) suffers, however, from an inherent ambiguity, since it depends on the adoption of the Lewisian perspective of the "return", without being capable of justifying this developmentally. Sometimes Tibi tries to fill this gap by suggesting that the conditions for politicizing Islam have always been available throughout history. This amounts to exhuming the claim of the first circle for Islam's inherent political character.[8] It is basically a "repoliticization of the sacred" (Tibi, 1983, p. 4), that constitutes today's political Islam. Sometimes, instead – and quite contradictorily – it seems that the repoliticization of Islam results specifically from the strong "deacculturationist" impetus of Islamic fundamentalism, whereas the first weak politicization was constituted by "acculturationist" Islamic modernism (Tibi [1981] 1991, pp. 60–5). This pattern of definition of the "repoliticization of Islam/reislamization" attenuates Tibi's dependence on the argument of the first circle, as updated by Lewis (see Chapter 8).

The former solution, the closest to the first circle, seems, however, to outweigh the latter in Tibi's argumentative model, as he finally defines the re-politicization of Islam as a "cultural backward-looking" phenomenon (p. 62). His reshaping of the formula of resurgence allows in the final analysis for a synthesis between the first and the second circles that is more systematically cogent, although symbolically weaker, than the one found in Lewis's warning. The latter pattern of interpretation seems to emerge, instead, every time that Tibi cannot avoid mentioning "Islamic modernism", but is in fact employed with all the caution and vagueness that characterizes his confrontation with this phenomenon, which he would like to isolate from the process – that he considers deleterious – of politicizing Islam, but finds difficult to set apart completely from the later fundamentalism (pp. 58–75).

The passage where Tibi overstates, probably consciously, the success of 'Abd al-Raziq's "secularist" discourse[9] (see Chapter 5) seems to depend on the need to underpin, on an emotional and perceptional level, the justification for the emphasis on *re*islamization that he finds it difficult to support argumentatively: "*Yet* we experience *anew* from the early 1970s a *re*vitalization of Islam [emphasis added]" (p. 67), where the author obsessively insists on the subjective and observational impression, dominated by a reaction of surprise towards the return of Islam (see Chapter 8). Some years later Tibi felt obliged to recognize, albeit reluctantly, the continuity between Islamic modernism and fundamentalism in their relation to modernity, on the grounds of their common concern to preserve the textual fundaments while confronting modern knowledge (Tibi, 1992, p. 100). Tibi's embarrassment in dealing with the stream of thought centred on Muhammad 'Abduh is probably due to his feeling of involvement in the difficult process of defining a "secularized" Islam (Tibi, 1981, pp. 8–9), the feeble traces of which during the last hundred years can only be located within "Islamic modernism".

The resulting question, from Tibi's perspective, is whether Islam is likely to appropriate modernity – i.e. not merely to react defensively to it – without losing its "substance" (Tibi, [1981] 1991, p. 20). In raising this question, he is drawn to mention von Grunebaum's emphasis on the incapacity of Islam to modernize in an originally Islamic fashion (pp. 20–1), one major *leitmotiv* in the hermeneutics of Islam produced by the first circle. Tibi accepts without hesitation the standard "reactivist" historical interpretation (see Chapter 3), well rooted in both the first and the second circles, according to which modern history was introduced in the Islamic Orient by Napoleon's occupation of Egypt (p. 56–9). As a consequence of the confrontation with Western colonialism, no ideology within Muslim lands can be assessed as purely autochthonous. Tibi admits that the "revitalized" culture is influenced by the foreign culture against which it is forged. However, he insists that the adoption of foreign elements conforms to a culturally defensive logic. The label "Islamic Republic" itself, reflecting Islamism's grandest historical success in the Iranian revolution, would demonstrate how such a logic animates the politicization of Islam, since the formula manifests an attempt to appropriate a typically European institution, the "republic" (see also Chapter 8), by specifying it through an autochthonous attribute, "Islamic" (pp. 18–19). Whereas Halpern tended to emphasize that in spite of having its origin in the West, modernity is no longer an exclusively Western endowment, Tibi seems to end up taking an ambiguous position with regard to the problem of the transferability of modern Western knowledge and world view. In a Habermasian mood, this is seen as part of an indivisible "project" (Habermas, 1992b). Through most of his works, Tibi adumbrates that it is possible to take up the project at the same time as he warns, however, how pointless any idea of transfer can be, when appropriate structural and cultural conditions are absent (see Tibi, 1991, p. 216).

As to the related, crucial question of whether "modern Islam" can be the basis for a framework of reference in Muslim societies, as a rough equivalent and an integration – but not a mere imitation – of national frameworks in Europe (see Chapter 3), thereby functioning as a successful political ideology, he seems inclined only to recognize a certain degree of transient effectiveness of Islam in helping to absorb the impact of rapid social change (Tibi, 1983, p. 12). In the final analysis, for Tibi the relationship between Islam as a symbolic-communicative system and as an ideology is negative. "*Islam does not know any reformation nor any tradition of Enlightenment* [emphasis in original]." ([1981] 1991, p. 185). Tibi explicitly considers the absence of a Reformation-like process in Islam as the main reason for the negative character of this relationship (1985, p. 74).[10]

More recently Tibi has manifested a propensity to attenuate his claim that the relationship between Islam as a cultural system and as a political ideology is inevitably negative in character, and to accept that a possible Enlightenment in Islam should not necessarily disavow the underlying, "traditional" symbolic-communicative system (Tibi, 1991, p. 275). In spite of such an interpretive shift, Tibi is consistent in negating the existence, over the last one hundred years, of a viable Arab–Islamic framework of communal reference (see Chapter 3), as he denies Islam the capacity of a not merely defensive coping with critical modernity (according to the definitions provided in Chapter 8).[11] The contemporary, enduring hegemonic position of fundamentalism in the Arab–Islamic world – Tibi believes – demonstrates this incapacity. The perspective of the third circle is in the end one that isolates "fundamentalists", roughly corresponding to our seventh circle (see Chapter 11), from the rest of the native portion of the interpretive field of political Islam. He denies them any significant interdiscursive competence *vis-à-vis* all other positions, and tends in the final analysis to overestimate Islamic fundamentalism's strength in the present and the future (Tibi, 1992, p. 17).

The crucial question of the hermeneutics of critical modernity has been tackled more directly by Tibi in more recent essays. He recognizes, at least in very general terms, the crisis of Western knowledge and world view, as a crisis of the modern Western undertaking of defining the Self and essentializing the Other, as well as its impact on what I have called the transcultural space between the "West" and "Islam" ("crisis is the general in our context": Tibi, 1991, p. 265). Tibi, however, insists on sharply distinguishing between the Western "crisis of modernity", and the "crisis of autochthonous traditions" in the non-Western (including the Arab–Islamic) world. Here there cannot be any crisis of modernity for the simple reason that there has been, despite globalization, no modernity at all. Even more explicitly, Tibi warns us that to see a close relationship between the two crises is precisely what Islamic fundamentalists illegitimately do (Tibi, 1992, p. 15).

It is true, according to Tibi, that there is a transcultural connection between these two disconnected types of crisis, but he adds that constructing this link is a surreptitious undertaking performed by those involved with "post-modernism". Tibi tends to restrict, coherently with his purposes, the meaning of post-modernism, adopting the drastic, discrediting definition given by Habermas: a movement aspiring to pose an end to Enlightenment, and even a revolt against modernity. It is simple for Tibi to relocate "reislamization" within the context of post-modernism, accused of jettisoning the Enlightenment critique of religion and promoting a restoration of pre-modern world views (Tibi, 1991, pp. 202–6). Islamic fundamentalism – as Tibi now, in accordance with a dominant trend, explicitly calls the political and theoretical current previously subsumed under the label of reislamization – perfectly fits the portrait of the post-modern trend, and coherently develops this into a markedly anti-Western, *ergo* anti-modern ideology (p. 209). This is not surprising – Tibi concludes – since the "project of modernity" has not touched Islam in any significant measure.

The Habermasian definition of this project borrowed by Tibi is no structural-functional, maximalist notion of modernity, such as the one shaped along the Durkheimian–Weberist path that delimited mainstream sociology (see Chapters 2 and 6), but is close to a minimalist definition of intellectual modernity (as developed in Chapters 2 and 3) that stresses the emancipation from tradition through the emergence of public discursive mechanisms for discussing questions of common interest. We will see how, though based on this same definition of modernity, the judgement on the modern character of political Islam delivered by the fourth circle is almost diametrically opposed to that of the third circle.

In Tibi's opinion, what ultimately distinguishes Islamic fundamentalists is their inherently ambivalent relationship to modernity (Tibi, 1992, p. 51), their "dream of a half-modernity", as they want to appropriate its scientific and technological assets, without being willing or able to join in its "project". It is interesting, however, that he denounces at the same time the fundamentalists' selectivity towards modernity as a whole *and* towards Scripture (p. 39). This recognition of scripturalism's selectivity is contradicted by Tibi's insistence on the fact that the modern deficit of Islamic fundamentalism is also due to the Muslims' alleged blind credence in the written word (p. 42). Tibi fails at this point to differentiate between the symbolic cogence of scriptural references and their limited influence on the building of argument within fundamentalist discourse (a point to be developed in Chapter 11).

Tibi's own judgement on the modernity of political Islam appears conditioned by his hermeneutic location, from where modernity can be seen only as a given and indivisible, "take-it-or-leave-it" property. He seems at least partially conscious of the tension between different dimensions of modernity, as reflected by his final image of political Islam as "modernly anti-modern". The more recent essays written by Tibi reflect the (at least implicit) need to respond to the objections of the fourth circle, which took shape during the 1980s, about the modern character of political Islam (see below). He remains firm, however, in denying the Islamic fundamentalists any competence to articulate a modern, publicly regulated, intellectual discourse (p. 64): "The return to Islam is not based on discourse" (p. 66).

In sum, Tibi comes close, as did Halpern (see Chapter 7), to admitting that there is something genuinely modern in the "rejectionist", anti-modern act of politicizing Islam, i.e. of making it into a political ideology. The basic concerns of the third circle for the anti-Western and "anti-secular" character of Islamic fundamentalism prevented him, however, from clearly recognizing this modern feature. Such a recognition would lead into the orbit of the fourth circle. It is this subtle difference in the judgement on the modernity of political Islam which cleaves the third and the fourth circles. Surprisingly enough, it is *not* the adoption of a completely different notion of modernity which allows the fourth circle to reverse the judgement on modernity produced by the third, but rather the trail and the direction followed for constructing a relationship between "Islam" and the "political" in the definition of political Islam. The fourth circle opts for a deconflationist model that assumes, in analogy with the second circle and differently from the first and, to a large extent, from the third, that we should not start by looking at Islam, but by directing our attention to what happens on the political stage.

Sami Zubaida, a political sociologist of Iraqi origin based in the United Kingdom, provides us with a good example of the argumentative logic of the fourth circle, which leads to a drastic reversal of the third circle's final judgement on political Islam and its modernity. In the Introduction to his collection of essays, written during the 1980s, on *Islam, the People and the State*, he immediately makes clear his intention to counter the interpretation of the " 'return of Islam' . . . as the assertion and triumph of this distinct essence". Conceiving his task as part of an anti-essentialist campaign, he promptly asserts his intention "to argue that the Islamic phenomenon in politics is the product of particular political and socio-economic conjunctures."

(Zubaida, 1989a, p. ix). The turn-about of the relationship between the two categories of variables represented by "Islam" and the "political" is evident, and Zubaida is anxious to make clear how this reversal is associated with the claim that,

> current Islamic movements and ideas are not the product of some essential continuity with the past, but are basically "modern". Even when they explicitly reject all modern political models as alien imports from a hostile West, their various political ideas, organizations and aspirations are implicitly premised upon the models and assumptions of modern nation-state politics (p. ix).

I will analyse, in particular, two different essays in the collection, whose sequence is interesting because in the first one the author employs, in dealing with "the quest of an Islamic state", the widely-used term "fundamentalism", while in the second article, written a couple of years later, this label is carefully avoided because of the close association it had acquired, by the late 1980s, with the third circle. Zubaida thus replaces "fundamentalism" with an explicit use of the concept of "political Islam", assessed as more neutral. It may not be entirely casual, however, that in the above-mentioned, short Introduction, the author uses the label "Islamic politics" in the first sentence, and employs it again shortly after as synonymous with "political Islam" (pp. ix–xi), as if he were aiming at transforming Islam from the predicated essence into a variable attribute.

Zubaida is much more determined than Tibi to lay emphasis on the continuity between the current of thought centred around Muhammad 'Abduh, which he refuses to define as "Islamic modernism" – a label that points to an acculturationist impulse – and "Islamic fundamentalism". The crucial feature they have in common is their arbitrary construction of a " 'sacred history' as a model for the modern state", with only "a very tenuous connection to the holy sources" (Zubaida, [1987] 1989b, p. 46). In insisting on the modern continuity in the trajectory of Islam's politicization, Zubaida highlights, in opposition to Tibi, an increase in the modern character of political Islam: ". . . of all the political parties operating in recent Egyptian history the Muslim Brotherhood is one of the most modern in assumptions and operations" (p. 50).

Even more significant is Zubaida's intention to make the judgement on modernity independent of an explicit appropriation of its Western European prototype: "[The Muslim Brotherhood's] rejection of European cultural forms does not necessarily represent a rejection of modernity *per se*, but can be seen as a reconstruction of modernity according to Islamic models and motifs." (Zubaida, 1989c, p. 157). In a similar mood, he considers the label "Islamic Republic" in Iran in its assertively modernist (because of "republic") character (Zubaida, [1987] 1989b, p. 59), instead of assessing it, as Tibi did, as the result of a culturally defensive impulse. The reason for this divergence is that Zubaida is inclined to admit only an instrumental relationship between grass-roots Islam and Islam as a political ideology,[12] while according to Tibi Islam as a "pre-industrial culture" was the principal conditioning force behind the ideology of "Islamic fundamentalists".

The essential profile of Zubaida's judgement on the modernity of political Islam is best revealed in the first of the two essays, where he did not yet feel obliged to distance himself from the third circle's easy use, or abuse, of the word "fundamentalism" for identifying political Islam. Zubaida tries there, instead, provocatively to reverse the implicit meaning of fundamentalism by arguing that "all 'fundamentalism' is modern in that it attempts to reconstruct the fundamentals of an ideational system in modern society, in accordance with political and ideological positions taken in relation to current issues and discourses." Here the modernity is a function of the capacity to operate selection and abstraction for the sake of gaining influence on the present through the production, diffusion and finalization of a public discourse. This concept entirely fits Habermas's definition of modernity, also adopted by Tibi but employed by him as a tool to deny the modernity of political Islam.

It is evident how the opposition in the final judgement on political Islam between the third and the fourth circles is not caused by the passage from a maximalist to a minimalist concept of modernity,[13] but by the shift from an exclusivist to an inclusivist perspective on processes of modernization. The fourth circle appropriates and intensifies the universalist-inclusivist view of the second circle (see Chapter 7), as it no longer excludes Islamist voices from the modern consensus of communication. This revision is accomplished by questioning the "reactivist" claim, reiterated by all three previous circles, that the possibility of a modern path in Muslim lands was itself a consequence of Europe's direct impact, as initiated by Napoleon's occupation of Egypt.[14] This more open attitude of the fourth circle, nonetheless, tends to remain in the background: in demonstrating the modernity of political Islam attention is paid to contemporary socio-economic or sociocultural dynamics in Muslim societies, in their contradictory unfolding, marked by an enduring dependence on the West. Rejected is the abstract view of a linear modernization process, that the third circle has inherited from the second and used to attribute to political Islam a basically anti-modern potential.

Moreover, we see that while the third circle tends to adopt "Islam" as the independent variable, the fourth claims the primacy of the "political". The divergence in the final judgement on modernity depends to a large extent on this basic difference, since it is the primary focus on the political arena that allows the use of an inclusivist concept of modernity. Zubaida feels committed to "social and political analyses following concepts and processes which are common to a general political sociology, applying to 'Islam' as much to the 'West'." (Zubaida, 1989a, p. x). The relative success of this universalist and inclusivist type of hermeneutics of political Islam is not only – and probably not principally – due to the underlying efforts of historical revisionism, but to the climate of growing influence of globalization theories (see Chapter 8), which attenuates the strong, distinctional meaning of Western modernity (see Chapter 2) and provides a swift and superficial settlement of the "post-modern" critical turn. In the climate of theorizing a planetary dimension of action and communication ("global village") within a process of intensifying and expanding production of discursive and visual meanings by mass media, permanently challenged by alternative codes, it makes little sense to label contemporary Islamism as non-modern or anti-modern (cf. Abaza and Stauth, [1988] 1990). However, in this case the resulting, positive judgement on the modernity of political Islam is issued almost by default, and is not the product of a reproblematization of the conditions for universalizing the political discourse of modernity.

The fourth circle crystallized during the 1980s as the standard alternative to the "reislamization wave" embodied by the third. The correspondence between each of the two circles, on the one hand, and the "theorem" and "counter-theorem" produced in the West as a response to the crisis of transcultural dimension, on the other (see Chapter 8), is evident and does not need to be illustrated in detail. Nevertheless, the following similarity is worth stressing: just as, on the one hand, the largely intentional mirroring character of the Saidian counter-theorem was tailored to the needs of a hegemonic contention within the Western part of the transcultural space, and was unsuitable to engender a real breakthrough, or revolution, in the paradigm of Orientalism as a science, the fourth circle, on the other, did not challenge the third through authentically radical arguments, as its derivation from the second circle also demonstrates. As we have seen, Tibi's more recent essays also reveal how part of the objections formulated by the fourth circle could be smoothly integrated into the model of the third, without disrupting the main trail of its argumentative path.

It is not surprising, therefore, that during the second half of the 1980s an effort has been made to resystematize the relationship between political

Islam and modernity in such a way as to make obsolete the contention between the third and the fourth circles. In an article published in the most prominent journal of research on the Islamic Orient, William Shepard has first attempted to build a typology of different political ideologies existing in the Islamic world, and has finally sketched a diagram in whose bidimensional spectrum he situates each. One axis is intended to measure modern-ideological intensity (or simply "modernity"), and the other the degree of commitment to Islam as a religion (classified as "Islamic totalism"). What Shepard calls "radical Islamism", in order to avoid the controversial term "fundamentalism", would then correspond to a combination of high values of both factors (Shepard, 1987, pp. 320-2). While the compatibility of this scheme with the argument of the fourth circle is evident, the diagram also accommodates the third circle's claim that "Islamic totalism" results from a defensive response to Western modernity. Precisely because the (compatibility with) modernity acknowledged to radical Islamism is different from its projectual dimension, that the third circle considers a monopoly of the West, this modernity can also be interpreted as an adaptive form resulting from the need to counter Western cultural penetration and its superiority grounded on the project of the Enlightenment.

If we accept that in Muslim countries the competence to articulate a political discourse of modernity is achieved through the prism provided by an Arab–Islamic framework of reference (see Chapter 3), and read Shepard's "Islamic totalism" as measuring the explicitation of a commitment to this framework, his elegant diagram is no more than a tautology. Or, at the very least, its usefulness is confined to identifying and measuring the idiosyncracies constituted by those public discourses that desperately try to be modern without being Islamic, thus failing to capture enough public support, or to be Islamic without being modern, so renouncing publicity, and indeed political effectiveness.

As a product of the competition between the third and the fourth circles, and in its attempt to determine systematically objective criteria for judging the modernity of political Islam, Shepard's undertaking ends up drastically suppressing the problematic character of the hermeneutics of political Islam, as well as of the underlying question of redefining modernity. Such a trend is the least suitable for helping to bridge the main gulf in the hermeneutic chain, at the crucial juncture between the fourth and the fifth circles, across both shores of the transcultural space, as it ossifies even more the concept of modernity and suppresses its interpretive variability. Thus, it aggravates the difficulties in shaping an autonomous circle, within the Arab–Islamic side of the transcultural space, that is really capable of rejecting any binary opposition between "Western modernity" and "autochthonous tradition", or the abstract collision between models (see Chapters 2 and 3), as well as of moulding and appropriating a concept of modernity not merely imitative of the West's (see Conclusion).

NOTES

1 This passage from latency to centrality can be described with the following words: "Emergence is . . . the entry of forces; it is their eruption, the leap from the wings to the center stage, each in its youthful strength." (Foucault, [1971] 1984d p. 84).

2 My understanding of the circumscribed analytic usefulness of this concept has been illustrated in Chapter 3.

3 Tibi's main works were originally published in German, but some have been translated into English, and have gained no little attention in the United States.

4 I will quote from the original, 1981 edition of *The Crisis of Modern Islam* only in the case of its Foreword, which has not been reprinted in the new edition of 1991, issued (the coincidence is not casual) shortly after the Second Gulf War. This corresponds to the original in all but some bibliographical annotations and a long additional, concluding essay.

5 In his essays Tibi repeatedly refers to Yusuf al-Qaradawi as the epitome of contemporary Islamist thought. We will analyse texts written by this author when examining the seventh circle ("Islamic solutionism": see Chapter 11).

6 This is a good example of the "short-circuits" regulating the communication between the third and the seventh circles (see also Chapter 11).

7 Tibi explicitly employs this term in his more recent works, after it had become established in the academic literature. Also in previous works, however, the basic logic of his argumentations was based on what fundamentalism would generally come to signify.

8 "In Islam political and religious functions are fused. The world is viewed theocentrically." (Tibi, 1983, p. 4).

9 Tibi considers 'Abd al-Raziq's work, coherently with his overall argumentation, the apex reached by Islamic modernism in its acculturationist quest for conciliating Islam and modernity, after which the successful trajectory of fundamentalism began (Tibi, [1981] 1991, p. 66).

10 We see how the reasons adduced by Tibi for Islam's alleged civilizational "failure" are more differentiated than in the case of von Grunebaum, and this shows why the third circle is no mere actualization of the first. The Austrian scholar tended to refer every historical manifestation of Islam back to its beginning (Waines, 1975, p. 119) and to analyse Islam's painful confrontation with the modern West as the measure of its essential deficits, and not as an autonomous reason for its "failure". However, an accurate assessment of the weight of endogenous vs. exogenous reasons for Islam's "modern failure" is not available in Tibi's work (Tibi, 1992, p. 12).

11 Tibi identifies *"shari'a* Islam", the Islam mediated by *'ulama'*, as the historical basis of reislamization (Tibi, [1981] 1991, p. 74), while he acknowledges that *"Sufi* Islam" showed a secular tendency, as it stressed inwardness and was hostile to the mediation, performed by the *'ulama'*,

between the believers and God (p. 182). However, he is not willing to hypothesize an autochthonous path of modern intellectual distinction in Islamic terms (see Chapter 3).

12 "Modern political Islam is not the product of a historical continuity with an essential Islam preserved in the hearts and minds of the people as 'popular culture', but quite the contrary, a modern ideological construction relating to current conjunctures of nation state and international politics, and distinct from the religious elements of 'popular culture'." (Zubaida, 1989c, p. 137).

13 Tibi does not change his judgement, in the moment he moves from a rough reception of Elias's maximalist concept of civilizing process to an extremely minimalist notion of modernity, as consisting of the capacity to produce a discourse.

14 "Modern Islamic political thought has to be seen in the context of a conjuncture between [Islam's own] historical background and the European impact." (Zubaida, [1987] 1989b, p. 43). This important interpretive shift is largely indebted to "revisionist" historiography, mentioned and commented upon in Chapter 3. Representatives of this current have also outlined an interpretation of political Islam conforming to – and attempting to enrich – the argumentative model of the fourth circle (see Schulze, 1985).

TOWARDS AN ISLAMIC POLITICAL DISCOURSE OF MODERNITY?

CHAPTER 10

The new politics of *al-sahwa al-islamiyya*

Although patterns of intellectual modernity in Arab Muslim societies are comparable with, and dependent on those in the West, the terms and rationales of modern political discourse within an "Arab–Islamic" public sphere can produce a hermeneutic dynamics engendering original options and forms of polarization. On the other hand, examining the three interpretive circles situated on the Arab–Islamic side of the transcultural space requires determining the degree of their subjection to the general constraints of the whole field of political Islam. The analysis in Part IV will have to pay attention to keywords used in Arab–Islamic discourses, as well as to the way they relate to Western categories, and how they are networked so as to give responses to the question of the relationship between "Islam" and the "political". More important, however, will be the assessment of the process through which the endogenous hermeneutics of political Islam frees some Arab authors from thinking in terms of this relationship and leads them to rethink the question in new terms. The result is a redirection of the inevitable essentialism (see Chapter 4) along paths of higher methodological awareness in establishing the degree of historical and normative specificity (as well as usefulness) of an Arab–Islamic political discourse of modernity.

For this purpose, it is worth reconstructing, at least schematically, a development that will help to understand the interplay of endogenous and exogenous factors in the genesis of the idea-slogan of *al-sahwa al-islamiyya* ("the Islamic awakening"). After supplanting the Arab *nahda* ("renaissance": see Chapter 4), the "awakening" has determinantly influenced the contention between the "solutionist" seventh circle and its "neutralist" rival, the sixth circle (see Chapter 11). Furthermore, it has provided the terrain where a further argumentative pattern has taken root proposing an alternative to the dilemmas of the polarization between conflationism and deconflationism on both sides of the transcultural space (see Chapter 12).

An interesting background of such processes is given by tracing a sort of arc linking the theorizing of 'Abd al-Raziq with the most original formulation of the Islamist, neo-*salafi* path by the Egyptian author Sayyid Qutb (1906–66). This requires an attempt to reread Qutb's work in the context of the new modalities of consensus within Arab–Islamic discourse sanctioned by the intervention of 'Abd al-Raziq (see Chapter 5). The following excursus on Qutb is meant as an interpretive reassessment, from the present work's perspective, of existing findings on his copious production. The study of this corpus is far from complete, and my rapid analysis here is not intended as a further gloss on the available investigations (for a recent one, see Moussalli, 1992), as has been the case in several contributions influenced by the dynamics of the interpretive field of political Islam, which invariably present Qutb as an early inspirer of Islamic resurgence or the like. Introducing Qutb as a prominent intellectual voice in the Arab–Islamic world as seen from Egypt should rather serve to fill the gap between the two critical periods of the 1920s (examined in Chapter 5) and the late 1970s/early 1980s.

The 1920s represented a crucial phase in the long-term incubation of the Western concept of political Islam, which was finally born during the 1970s (see Chapter 6). Now I should proceed in a parallel fashion on the Arab–Islamic side and analyse the argumentative models that go back to the 1920s, and were duly reshaped through the 1960s, before an epistemic break in the transcultural space occurred. However, it is impossible to keep such a symmetry, since the single important thinker who tried to reformulate radically the discourse of the neo-*salafiyya*, Sayyid Qutb, was almost entirely banished from the public sphere during the early 1960s, the most creative phase of his intellectual production. Therefore his representative character has been witnessed only *ex post facto*. It is even hard to say that he belongs hermeneutically to his time, unless we want to attribute his representativeness to the circumscribed "intellectual psychopathology of prison" that affected a whole generation of Islamists, whom the Nasserist state excluded from public life in the crudest ways, through imprisonment and execution.

We can view Qutb's argument as a step back from conflationsim, since it renounces the easy derivation of the necessity of the *dawla* for the sake of *din*, and concentrates on a deep elaboration of all that the latter implies. His hermeneutics of *din* are centred on the individual being and its transformation. The resulting character of Islam as *haraki*, characterized by movement and development (a view that differs from the media-mediated vision of an "Islam in movement" that will ground the interpretive field of political

Islam, to the extent that the former stresses the immanent dynamics of Islam as an ideology defined by human reason) is given by the permanent, creative reconstruction of *shari'a* as inspired by the divine *shar'*, but crafted by the individual conscience. Qutb converges with 'Abd al-Raziq in positing God's intervention as a preliminary condition for creating the movement, and in stressing that all which follows is determined by the personal efforts of Muslims. The unconditional submission of the Muslim to the *shar'* through an act of faith, the acceptance of Koranic *din*, is the path of access to creative freedom.

This effort is guided by the Islamic *tasawwur*, which I translate as "envisionment" or "imaginative appropriation", an act that mediates the acceptance of God's sovereignty (*hakimiyya*). This is accomplished via the personal work of the Muslim not merely on the sacred Text, but on himself and within social reality. This theoretical step completely fills the discursive space opened up by 'Abd al-Raziq's anti-traditional intervention through a comprehensive outline, in Islamic terms, of the dynamic relationship between subject and system in the interpretation and implementation of *shari'a*, which the movement of *islah* (see Chapter 5) had been unable to fit into strong and coherent patterns. With Qutb the idea of an historical unfolding of Islam as a system is solidly anchored within the expanding subjectivity of the active *tasawwur* practised by the individual Muslim (see Schulze, 1994, pp. 222–3). This is a theory that aspires to overcome the enduring primacy of reification over subjectification in the long-term making of an Arab–Islamic framework of reference (see Chapter 5).

There is a dimension of failure in Qutb's theory that is strictly related to his personal vicissitudes, which were dependent on the power structure that made the irradiation of a modernizing mythology the strongest imperative in Nasserist-inspired Arab politics, and gave the illusion of a swift implementation of the dream of *nahda* (see also Chapter 11). In this sense, it is true that Qutb's prison experience decisively influenced his last writings (see Ayubi, 1991, p. 137). He rejected the logic and thought of *nahda* overall through a radically alternative theorizing whose social-scientific weakness equalled its coherence and fascination, and led to a hasty closure of the positive hermeneutics of *din*. However, his radically neo-Islamic view of critical modernity was read reductively, in the era of influence of the interpretive field of political Islam, in terms of *sahwa* ("awakening"), which is *not* a Qutbian category. In this sense, to see in Qutb the "ideologue of Islamic revival" (Haddad, 1983) is a distortion dictated by the interpretive constraints of defining political Islam.

The paradox of Qutb's late writings is that they had no immediate impact on a corresponding, contemporary public arena. The fiction, at least, according to which influence can be exerted on the public is a crucial condition for intellectual activity (see Chapters 2 and 3), and Qutb's last works, most widely read during the 1970s, suffered from the virtual absence of this condition at the time they were written. Although Sayyid Qutb has certainly exerted an influence on the whole of the indigenous portion of the hermeneutic field of political Islam, there is not, surprisingly enough, one single author who can legitimately claim his legacy, nor was he anyone else's heir.[1] The *salafi* affiliation of Qutb is very tenuous, and in his attempt to transcend the historically-given *islahi* ("reformist") thinking he turns Islamic "reform", along with its inclination to a traditionalist-classicist stiffening, on its head. He makes theoretically explicit the future-projection of any real, uncompromising *islah*, and looks back in history only for the minimal, necessary invocation of the moment when Islam burst into history and "made a difference".

The idealized model of *al-salaf al-salih* ("the reputable ancestors") is different from the imaginative appropriations that Islam's movement permanently produces in history. According to Qutb, the scope of *fiqh* (Islamic interpretive "jurisprudence") is precisely the creative renewal of the "envisionment", guided by the criterion of authenticity: if *shari'a* is unchanging, its actual shape is given by human *fiqh* (Haddad, 1983, p. 71). The tension inherent in the Islamic *din* as movement and vision is given a positive expression through a stress on what it *ought to be* (p. 79). The systematic rejection of all existing forms of government as non-Islamic, not conforming to *din*, does not directly lead to the call for building an Islamic state, although the writings that Qutb produced in jail are more intensely animated by a sense of urgency to render Islam operative in society, as well as by the recognition that this could happen only by gaining political power (pp. 78–9).

This late reconflationist crystallization of Qutb's theory never condensed, however, into a quick-fix, "solutionist" formula that simply claims that Islam is the solution to all social problems, of the sort we will find in the seventh circle. The key category for Qutb was Islamic "system", *nizam* (p. 82–7),[2] not *dawla*, a word too compromised with the existing institutional configurations of power, which emanate from the worldwide *jahiliyya*, the state of pre-Islamic ignorance, under which Qutb grouped all things allegedly "un-Islamic", hence most aspects of the contemporary world, both within and without Muslim societies. The developmental character of Islam is preserved, on the subjective side, through resorting to the concept of *manhaj* ("method"), that reflects a stress on reason and creativity, whereas on the systemic side the non-contamination with all existing forms of rule (in

Arabic expressed through words derived from the root *hkm*: see Chapter 1) is sanctioned by the use of a neologism, *hakimiyya*, pointing to the very essence of the function of ruling, something close to "sovereignty": and this property is attributed to God alone, or is even what God, in the end, is all about. This is the point where Qutb's vision becomes unmistakably "secular": obviously not in the prevalent sense of the term based on the Western historical experience, but for its uncompromising rejection of all traditional loyalties based on personal obligations (see Chapter 3). The Muslim *shahada* (testimony of faith) demands a rebellion against any man-made form of power exercised over other human beings (p. 89), that is what politics is about. The final legacy of Qutb's hermeneutics of Islam as *din* is thereby an outright rejection of the task of problematizing the relationship between "Islam" and the "political". The accomplishment of Islam on earth would bring about the end of politics.

The first major impact of the unfolding of the interpretive field of political Islam on Arab–Islamic discourses is in the polarization between "solutionist" and "neutralist" circles. The seventh circle is here named "solutionist" because it conceives Islam as the solution to virtually every social problem by invoking the *shari'a* and the institution of an "Islamic state". The rival sixth circle is called "neutralist" as it asserts that Islam, while maintaining a normative power in the regulation of worldly affairs, does not provide any ready-made political recipe, i.e. is politically neutral (see Chapter 11). At the root of the polarizing dispute, we find – not surprisingly – a revival of the controversy over the work of 'Abd al-Raziq that took place in the post-Nasserist climate of the early 1970s, within the discussion of the legitimacy and necessity of an "Islamic state" (Wielandt, 1982, pp. 124–5). A second major presence in public debates taking place during the era of the "Islamic awakening" has been – even less surprisingly – Sayyid Qutb, considered the ideologue *ante litteram* of *al-sahwa al-islamiyya*. 'Abd al-Raziq and Qutb have been juxtaposed by Leonard Binder in his effort to judge the degree to which some liberal impulses of what he calls "the rejected alternative" (Binder, 1988, p. 128) in constructing a relationship between Islam and politics, i.e. a liberal orientation, can be found even in Qutb's "fundamentalist" theoretical corpus.

For the scope of the present investigation, however, the possible link between 'Abd al-Raziq and Qutb is interesting for a slightly different reason. Both the reception of 'Abd al-Raziq and the more immediate impact of Qutb have to be more carefully situated. They cannot be seen simply as the most illustrious precursors of contemporary Islamic "liberalism" and "fundamentalism" (or, according to my terminology, of "neutralism" and "solutionism"), but as the shapers of the basic terms and rationales of political-intellectual discourse within an Arab–Islamic framework of communal reference and universal projection (see also Chapters 3 and 5). As we will see, these terms have been used and redefined by Arab authors during the last twenty years according to contingent, and not generally valid, societal and discursive priorities, largely dictated by the constraints of the interpretive field of political Islam.

Due to their uncompromising formulations, 'Abd al-Raziq and Qutb represent the two most prominent landmarks on the road to forming an Arab–Islamic framework of reference. At the same time, and precisely because of the radical character of their argumentations, they happened to fulfil complementary functions: a "minimalist" formulation of the lowest common denominator for the new Arab–Islamic consensus of communication supplanting the traditional Consensus of the Community, performed by 'Abd al-Raziq, and a "maximalist" theorizing of how the new consensus should be filled, worked out by Qutb.

In particular, there is a logical link between the two authors in the passage from the hermeneutics which aim to purify *din* from what is *la-dini* (non-religious), to a coherent redefinition of the interpretive range pertaining to *din*, or emanating from it. Their contributions stand out because they cannot be read as conflicting with each other, since they are not mere examples of "deconflationist" or "conflationist" hermeneutics. They rather embody the two extreme logical points along an ideal trajectory, from positing to substantiating freedom and creativity of consciousness in Islamic terms. Both agree in saying that the *shar'* has nothing to do with human government, and that no viable Arab–Islamic framework of reference can be grounded when arguing ahistorically, as traditional *'ilm* did, in postulating a religious legitimation for the exercise of power. Both negate the existence in history of a government legitimized by *din*, see God's intervention through His *shar'* as a preliminary condition for creating the movement immanent to Islam, and stress that all which follows is determined by the efforts of individual Muslims.

A further characteristic common to 'Abd al-Raziq and the final Qutb is their high degree of isolation, at the time they wrote (albeit for different reasons), within the public arena, along with a belated success of the terms of discourse they used. As for Qutb in particular, it is highly problematic to see in him the theoretician of *al-sahwa al-islamiyya*. Whereas Qutb's thought, especially in its latest phase when it produced the most intriguing concepts for neo-Islamist discourse, was embedded in the tragic political and existential fate of a group of committed Islamist activists, the slogan itself of *sahwa* responds to a widespread need for re-reifying Islam as a banner for a normative discourse within an intense struggle conducted in the public arena since the mid-1970s. The agitation of *sahwa* was made possible by a growing degree of opening of the public sphere in Egypt, especially after the 1973–4 crisis, and most notably during the years of the Mubarak presidency. This process was not only significant for favouring the market success of "revivalist" writers (Haddad, 1991a, p. 10 and Gonzalez-Quijano, 1991), but also represented an important condition for a growing transcultural effectiveness of the interpretive field of political Islam, i.e. for rendering the West's construction of "political Islam" a major influence within the indigenous domain of intellectual debate.

NOTES

1 It is frequently stressed that Qutb's hermeneutics is indebted to the Indian–Pakistani author Abu al-A'la Mawdudi. This evaluation is acceptable only at first glance, and needs careful review.
2 This is a term not extraneous to Islamic traditions of learned discourse (see Gardet, 1978, p. 173).

CHAPTER 11

Is Islam the solution?

We will see in this and the following chapter how, by assuming and not further analysing (which is not the object of the present work) the entanglement of societal concerns underlying the widespread intellectual need to reformulate responses to the crisis after the "end of *nahda*", such answers began to revolve around the two keywords of *sahwa* ("awakening") and *turath* ("heritage"). Both are associated with *asala* ("authenticity"), but they end up embodying two opposite logics for tackling the crisis: the one suppressing it, the other consciously working on it. We will also see how, this basic difference notwithstanding, the discursively modern character of the first response cannot be denied if one adopts a "minimalist" concept of modernity (see Chapter 2). The suppressing mode to cope with the latter is not alien to, but compatible with, the dialectics of "critique and crisis" (see Chapter 8).

The most immediate meaning of *sahwa*, and the way it is most commonly translated into English, is "awakening". One of the most representative theorists of *al-sahwa al-islamiyya*, Yusuf al-Qaradawi, straightforwardly makes clear that *sahwa* is simply "Islam awakened", "a return to the source" (al-Qaradawi, 1982, p. 201). The simplifying and homogenizing character of the concept of *sahwa* as a tool of public communication and contention is evident here. Accordingly, the image used also shows plastic properties, as *al-sahwa al-islamiyya* is explicitly and directly related to the feeling of *naksa*, the "fall" (al-Qaradawi, 1988, p. 88) that marked the end of *nahda* (the Arab "renaissance"). In spite of the apparent similarity of image and meaning between *sahwa* and *nahda*, the degree of assertiveness of the former is much higher. *Sahwa* is not formulated as a will or feeling, but as a factual reality and an actual movement. It is the "return of consciousness and vigilance" after sleep or drunkenness, two metaphors reflecting the two causal dimensions that determined the crisis preceding *al-sahwa al-islamiyya*: the one internal, identified with the era of stagnation under Ottoman rule, and the other external, represented by the cultural dimension of European colonialism, which is held responsible for detaching the *umma* from its essence, thereby alienating and depersonalizing it (p. 17).

Though *nahda* and *sahwa* have almost the same meaning, al-Qaradawi takes the greatest care in not assimilating them. It is symptomatic that as possible synonyms for *sahwa* he mentions other terms (*yaqaza, ba'th*) but not *nahda* (al-Qaradawi 1988, p. 18). An explicit reference to the latter is made only in order to make clear that the Islamic *sahwa* does not dismiss the Arab *nahda* as such, but is engaged in transcending it. *Sahwa* is constructed as the "revealed", hard kernel of the ambiguous, too generic and contaminated *nahda*, and thereby as the pathway to the only possible "solution", after all other ways eclectically associated with *nahda* have failed (p. 108). The link to *naksa* is acknowledged more as proof of the unsustainable character of *nahda* and its virtual end, than as the profound cause of *sahwa*. "Materialist" interpretations of the origin of the "awakening" are rejected (p. 21), since they all emphasize mere contingencies, whereas *sahwa* is as necessary as Islam is true. A *sahwa* can only be Islamic (p. 23).

Correspondingly, the use of the category of *sahwa* coincides with the unfolding of the movement it pretends to describe, since this is something we all can see (p. 23). The new category appears to be a response to pressure generated by a modern critical breakthrough, but formulated in such a way as to reduce to a minimum the need to cope with its critical dimension. The core argument employed for performing this operation is that the Islamic *umma* can never die, since the Koran and the *sunna* of the Prophet are permanently preserved in the hearts of the Muslims, and if the *umma* falls asleep, it is "natural" for it to awake. The *sahwa*, the "awakening", is lifted to a founding *topos* of Islam as such, since its rise through Muhammad's teachings, is equated with a movement of awakening (pp. 18–21).

The success of the keyword *sahwa* coincided with the emergence of the hermeneutic field of "political Islam", within which the Western category of "resurgence" was being shaped (see Chapter 7). *Sahwa* seems to be almost a translation of the Western concept, grounded on the same impression of an "Islam in movement", but adding to it new meaning drawn from an endogenous interpretive perspective. It would be certainly useful to verify accurately whether the use of the term *sahwa* actually followed Bernard Lewis's intervention in 1976, but for our purposes here such a finding would not alter the evidence of a transcultural "short-circuit" between the autochthonous concept of *sahwa* and the Western-shaped category of "resurgence" or the like. This phenomenon has certainly enhanced the native feeling that undoubtedly *al-sahwa al-islamiyya* is taking place as a normal, physiological, automatic awakening. It is like an assertive response to the image of an "Islam in movement" that grounds the hermeneutic field of political Islam: "Yes, we are moving indeed!". The distributive economy of meaning within the conceptual pair *sahwa*-resurgence appears to be as follows: the Arab word indicates the "subjective-assertive", the English the "external-observational" dimension of the impression of an "Islam in movement". This relationship corresponds to the basic difference between the standard Orientalist conflation at the level of *is* (see Chapter 4), and the Islamist conflation, especially in the post-Qutbian era, that is much more rooted at the level of *ought to* (see Chapter 5).

The resulting "politics of *sahwa*" has to be situated within the general communicative background of the consolidation of a common "Islamic idiom" in the public sphere of Arab Muslim societies, that has contributed to blur divergencies of interest within the huge, metastatic middle class of countries like Egypt (see Binder, 1988, pp. 16–17 and Ayubi, 1991, p. 228). Within this process, metamorphosed and intellectualized forms of *'ilm* become the dominant sources of legitimation of discourse, since they remain, in their formal constraints, general enough to be appropriated by as many types of social actors as to jeopardize the claim that they are expressions of particular social groups. The argumentative models allowed within this discursive formation can vary without any rigidly corresponding difference in social location among representatives of different interpretive circles. This assessment is not contradicted by the observation that the ideological vanguard of *al-sahwa al-islamiyya* seems to be a sort of *Lumpenintelligentsia* of "new Islamic intellectuals" that took shape in Egypt during the 1970s due to the limited capacity of absorption of intellectual labour by the state, which declined after the Nasserist era (see Chapter 3). In spite of such shifts in the socio-economic location of the social and intellectual groups that most actively support Islamist forms of mobilization (see Roy, 1990, p. 264), it seems that the "higher" hermeneutic forms of production and legitimation of publicly relevant neo-Islamic discourse are still controlled by representatives of the *'ulama'* class willing to seize the newly emerged opportunities within the discursive arena to gain public influence and pinpoint their moral authority under altered social conditions (Eccel, 1988).

Two models allowed within such an expanded *'ilm* dominate the public sphere. They are linked to each other via an interpretive polarization centred on the dispute about the "Islamic state", *al-dawla al-islamiyya*, or sometimes the "Islamic government", *al-hukuma al-islamiyya*.[1] The Islamic state does not represent a clear-cut "public issue" in a stricter, almost technical sense, as it would be within a debate concerning the requirements or the goals of the state, in terms drawn from constitutional theory or political philosophy (though the dispute can well take root, in particular cases, within such a terrain). An important clue to the wider problematizing range of the controversy is the enduring symbolic centrality within it of the slogan *islam din wa-dawla*, whose signification is more complex than in the standard, simplifying translation of "Islam is religion and state" (see Chapter 3).

One inevitably hypothesizes the influence of the hermeneutic field of political Islam on this phenomenon of polarization-simplification of indigenous debates, since this field rewards with transcultural notoriety the voices that are more eager to provide responses to the question whether Islam has to move to politics or not (see Chapter 9). The two (sixth and seventh) autochthonous circles have clear historical affiliations, but their actual shape, the relationship between them and with all other circles, can be understood only in the context of the interpretive field of political Islam: the transcultural patterns of synchronic interaction contribute to their stabilization and to giving them a profile that the trajectories of their intracultural affiliations would not be sufficient to explain alone.

The public arena examined in this chapter is a basically Egyptian one, within which the polarizing dispute has been virtually continuous since the early 1970s (Ayubi, 1991, p. 212). The contention has been often conceptualized by Western scholars under the ambiguous label of "the debate on secularism" (see Chapter 3 for the reasons for this ambiguity). In the era of influence of the hermeneutic field of political Islam (see Wielandt, 1982 and Flores, 1993), this attention has been nurtured by the need to relativize the third circle's view of an inescapable, mounting Islamist hegemony (Flores, 1993). I look at the dispute in a basically different way, in order to see, in a genealogical perspective (see Introduction), how through this debate the long-term unfolding of the Arab–Islamic framework of reference has become stagnant, to what extent this stagnation is an effect of the constraints of the interpretive field of political Islam, and finally through which arguments a further interpretive circle takes shape that is able to transcend this polarization, along with the alternative itself between conflationism and deconflationism (see Chapter 12).

A first sign of the polarization dates back to shortly before the early 1970s, during a period coinciding with the disappearance of the public consensus previously cohering around the Nasserist option. The occasion for the start of an embryonic contention between "solutionism" and "neutralism" seems to sanction a return to the intellectual terms of discourse more popular in the period prior to the rise of Nasserism: subject to dispute has been the evaluation of the work of 'Abd al-Raziq, which almost automatically urged people to take a position in favour of or against the "Islamic state". It was, however, after 1973 that this sort of controversy began to take on a more definite form, and to become independent of a judgement on 'Abd al-Raziq himself (Wielandt, 1982, pp. 124–5). From this point on, the staging of the contention saw some authors (the "solutionists") claiming that Islam can provide a political solution to all social problems (according to the slogan *al-islam huwa al-hall*), while their challengers (the "neutralists") stressed the neutrality of Islam towards the form of goverment and the profile of the state. Such a scheme has continued to orient the debate at least until the end of the 1980s (Flores, 1993, pp. 32–3). The polarization has further progressed through also, if not principally, being carried out (despite an extraordinary boom in the production of books on this and related topics) in the columns of leading newspapers and even in public round-table discussions (see Gallagher, 1989, pp. 208–15 and Flores, 1993, pp. 37–8).

The two contenders here selected for the analysis of the controversy are Yusuf al-Qaradawi and Muhammad A. Khalafallah. An important parallel feature of their long-term engagement is that, although they have been eager to participate in the ongoing discussions in the Egyptian public arena of the 1980s, they provide one of the best examples of an exchange, more or less direct, performed on a markedly scholarly stage, i.e. at a level not exposed to the immediate pressure of persuading a wider public, and additionally situated within an explicitly Arab, not merely Egyptian, context of learned controversy. This discussion took place during a conference held in Amman in 1987 and addressing the topic of *al-sahwa al-islamiyya wa-humum al-watan al-'arabi* ("The Islamic awakening and the concerns of the Arab nation"). The following analysis of the contending circles as represented by these two authors will be enriched by looking also at some of their other writings.

Al-Qaradawi is highly representative of the seventh circle because he adds to an undeniable influence within the Islamist camp in Egypt and elsewhere (along with the corresponding theorizing of the basic tenets of "solutionism" beyond the sheer political slogan "Islam is the solution": see al-Qaradawi, [1974] 1977) the ability to elaborate and manage a lowest common denominator between the highly innovative Qutbian claim of Islam as "movement", and the preservation of a privileged role for the *'ulama'-fuqaha'* in the hermeneutics of Islam. I will focus on one major work, besides the essay delivered at the Amman conference, that fully manifested the centrality of his position within the Islamist current (al-Qaradawi, 1982). The relevance of the responses he delivered in this book is probably due to the fact that at the time he wrote, during the early 1980s, in the wake of the assassination of Sadat by the Islamist group *al-jihad* in October 1981, he felt under strong pressure, as one of the leading theorists of *al-sahwa al-islamiyya*, to clarify the independence of his solutionist position from the contingencies of political turmoil and from what al-Qaradawi himself called "extremism" (*tatarruf*). In this way the book placed itself at a delicate juncture of the transcultural hermeneutics, in as far as the Western impression of an "Islam in movement", of a "political Islam", was decisively shaped by the news-filling presence of such extremist groups. The transcultural relevance of this book seems confirmed by the availability of an integral English translation (al-Qaradawi, [1982] 1987).[2]

A necessary, preliminary remark concerns the fact that the seventh circle is no exception to the rule according to which each model of construction of "political Islam", i.e. each circle – starting from the third one – can be properly examined and understood only within the transculturally relevant "opening" of the hermeneutics of modernity (see Chapter 8). For the argument of the seventh circle, this opening has acquired the status of an acknowledged fact, that is unilaterally evaluated, in adherence to (and as a confirmation of) the Qutbian diagnosis of the moral bankruptcy of Western civilization at large. Surprising in this regard are the explicit references to the hippy phenomenon in the West, which al-Qaradawi compares with the Islamist youth devoting itself to the implementation of Islam on earth, and for this reason is accused of extremism. In both cases, he argues, the mere invocation of social factors to explain the phenomenon is misplaced (al-Qaradawi 1988, p. 22). The anxiety of the youth is considered as a vehicle for rediscovering authenticity beyond the ongoing changes that disorient contemporary man (al-Qaradawi, 1982, p. 142 and 1988, p. 22), hence for reappropriating a map for orientation in a world of turmoil. Although it is not stated explicitly, comparing the *sahwa* generation with the hippy generation (by which al-Qaradawi probably alludes to manifestations of protest by the Western youth in general, more than specifically to the hippy phenomenon) signifies that the impulse for distinction catalysed by discontent does not need, within an Islamic cultural environment – contrarily to what happens in the West – to shape a new symbolic repertoire at odds with the underlying culture or symbolic-communicative system. Rather, this impulse simply has to reappropriate inherited values and be inspired by them in order to reshape life models and make them compatible with the demands of society. These are the same values which are hypocritically professed by the society against which the Islamist youth revolts.

The *'ulama'* class, as supportive of, or quiescent towards, the power establishment, is notoriously not immune from the attacks of the Islamist youth. The reaffirmation and redefinition of the prerogatives of Islamic *'ilm* in general, and *fiqh* in particular, is therefore a recurrent issue in al-Qaradawi, and it is symptomatic, as we will see, that this difficult task is carried out by highlighting the public, intellectual function of a rightly conceived *fiqh*. The operation of emphasizing the centrality of the *fuqaha'* does not result, as one may expect, in a confinement of *fikr* (intellectual thought) within the strict boundaries of "traditional" *fiqh*, as it would appear to be on the grounds of the assertion that *fikr* is an emanation of the dogmas, *'aqa'id* (al-Qaradawi, 1982, p. 131).

Besides the well-known fact that the term for "dogmatics", or "doctrine" (*'aqida*) has widened its denotative field in modern Islamist discourse to encompass "ideology" and "theory", this stress on the centrality of *fiqh* and of the science of *usul al-fiqh* ("the sources, or fundaments of jurisprudence" or "legal theory", p. 150) is more of a formal-institutional nature. Highlighted is the alleged absence, in Islamic history, of a major break in the discursive mediation performed by the *'ulama'-fuqaha'* in spite of the emergence of Westernized intellectuals towards the end of last century (see Chapter 3). Al-Qaradawi justifies this centrality by emphasizing their technical skills in the definition of "true Islam", based on their capacity to select and identify the true fundaments, *usul*, and differentiate these from the non-essential ramifications and contingent applications, *furu'* (p. 89). This is a claim that, when read, as it should be, in the context of public communication in which it is produced and not of mere legal discourse, precisely conveys the essentializing function of selection and amplification of meaning, a typical task of the modern intellectual (see Chapters 2 and 3).

It is, however, significant that al-Qaradawi can define the category of the Islamic "propagandists and intellectuals" (*al-du'at wa-l-mufakkirun al-islamiyyun*) only through stressing their belonging to *ahl al-'ilm* – the administrators of Islamic knowledge (al-Qaradawi, 1982, p. 17 and 1988, p. 54) – thereby almost being a subcategory of them, more directly concerned with the actual social situation. As a consequence, the *'ulama'* are considered the only legitimate leaders *and* interpreters of the "awakening". The public intellectual competence of other kinds of authors in making sense of *sahwa* is, accordingly, contested. This can be assessed as a synthetical formulation of the post-Qutbian normalization: to dilute the revolutionary appeal of Qutb in the reified scenario of *al-sahwa al-islamiyya*, and to fix the latter as intrinsically dependent on the mediation of (however modern or modernized) *'ulama'*.

The case of extremism is taken as proof of the necessary pre-eminence of *'ulama'*, at the same time that it shows the extent to which Qutb's own radical stance can be reabsorbed and accommodated, but not antagonized, by the reaffirmation of their centrality. On the one hand – al-Qaradawi argues – there would be no extremism if the Islamist youth were guided by people competent in questions of *'ilm* (al-Qaradawi, 1982, p. 89); on the other, although it is indisputable that extremism is a concern for a wider range of social actors than the *'ulama'*, the attitude of fabricating judgements merely on the basis of the category of "extremism", instead of considering first of all the genuine impulse underlying the "awakening" Islam, is responsible for the proliferation of distorted interpretations of the phenomenon, which in turn legitimize undue repressions (pp. 11–20).

The whole work published in 1982 is aimed at reformulating the extent to which the impulse of the Islamist youth is motivated by a sincere commitment to *sahwa*, but is nonetheless contaminated by the corruption of the political environment and in particular of the rulers. Too many *'ulama'*, however, are not innocent in this situation, because of their complicity with, or acquiescence to, the power establishment (pp. 90–1 and 125–6): these are the reasons for the attacks against them by the *sahwa* youth. Al-Qaradawi is anxious to reaffirm the efficacy of the method of *'ilm* in spite of the failure of individual *'ulama'* (al-Qaradawi, 1988, p. 56).

The redefinition of the centrality of the carriers of *'ilm* is not an end in itself in al-Qaradawi's argumentation, but the crucial step for justifying a solutionist path. Through the reformulation of their role, the *'ulama'* are assigned a social task that fits a "minimalist" definition of the modern intellectual (see Chapter 2). They are entitled to the public interpretation and definition of Islam: any other unskilled mediation is no substitute for *'ilm* (al-Qaradawi, 1982, p. 90). More specifically, al-Qaradawi criticizes those ideologues of the extremist Islamist groups who reiterate the radical Qutbian reading of all Islamic history after its formative period, as well as of the historical institution of the Caliphate, as unauthentic (p. 100). This anti-radical critique is justified by reference to an evolutionist theory grounded on the allegedly supreme divine rule of gradualism, which governs the development of both the universe and of human society (p. 104).

Although this argument seems to lead to a banalization of Qutbian theory, and its diluting into a generic "philosophy of history", it is no obstacle to taking up Qutb's motif of Islam as the complete and perfect *manhaj* ("method") for human life, and to relaunch the principle of grounding the *hukm* ("rule") on God alone. This operation, however, is carried out with much less impetus than in the case of Qutb, in order not to prejudice the hermeneutic centrality of the *'ulama'*. This centrality is seen as deriving its legitimation from the *umma*, but also as hindered in its unfolding by the corrupt ruler, "whose Islam" is the product of an arbitrary selection of what suits his position of power, in disregard of the *'ilm* of the *imams* of *fiqh* (p. 133). The definition of "true Islam" should be the result of a public, critical discussion conducted by the leading *fuqaha'* (p. 144). Freedom of opinion,[3] as well as of manifesting opposition, is advocated as perfectly compatible with their guiding function.[4]

The rational legitimation of this interpretive-legislating leadership is dependent on the *fuqaha*'s ability to produce an "enlightened *fiqh*" for the rulings of Islam, distilled from its "authentic sources". As a product of this genuine hermeneutic effort, the *faqih* should "bring about such a kind of consciousness and *fiqh*" that escapes what is unessential and aims at reforming society (p. 145). The true *fiqh* is therefore always *al-fiqh al-wa'i*, the *fiqh* based on a deep hermeneutic consciousness. *Fiqh* and consciousness are inseparable from one another. It seems that the one defines the other, and the search for true meaning cannot depend on technical skills alone, in which case *fiqh* would drift away towards the handling of marginal issues, or on mere strivings of consciousness, which would produce distortions and extremisms. The only way to understand *shari'a* is by differentiating what is essential and what is secondary in it (p. 151).

This should not, however, as al-Qaradawi warns, legitimize arbitrariness in the search for "true Islam". A plurality of equally valid interpretations of its fundaments is excluded: *inna al-islam huwa al-islam* ("since Islam is Islam"). This strongly reifying assertion, and the corresponding argumentation, should be nonetheless interpreted as stating not so much that Islam *is* one, but that it should be interpreted and practised *in the assumption that* it is one, as the necessary condition for a consensus of communication within an Arab–Islamic framework of reference. Al-Qaradawi highlights that there are firm certainties (*qut'iyat*) in doctrine and intellectual thought (*'aqida wa-fikr*), which provide the platform for hermeneutic variability and social change, whose direction is determined by the goals of the community (al-Qaradawi, 1988, p. 55). In a more recent book dedicated to the problem of disagreement (*ikhtilaf*), the Egyptian *'alim* presents this as not only natural but necessary, to the extent that it does not affect the basic rulings of God's Will. In affirming this, al-Qaradawi goes beyond the general *islahi* ("reformist") commitment to *ijtihad*, and claims the necessity of giving publicity to the disagreement between *'ulama'*. This is even more necessary – al Qaradawi adds – in a globalized environment where easy access to others' opinions is complemented by growing divergencies. What in the final analysis cannot be questioned is the recognition of Islam as a principle of cooperation and consensual communication in the search for the common good (al-Qaradawi, [1990] 1992, p. 191).

The crucial point in the argumentation is that, along with the necessity of recognizing one "true Islam", we also acknowledge, or better develop, its socially all-encompassing character. This position is summarized in the statement that Islam has posed a value and has legislated on every domain of human action (al-Qaradawi, 1982, p. 174). Neglecting the obligations and the duties deriving from this regulating force would mean robbing Islam of its social dimension. The clearest example of this corruption is seen, coherently with the *islahi* ("reformist") thinking since 'Abduh (see Chapters 3 and 5), in the lack of social engagement of most Sufi brotherhoods, which reduce Islam to socially irrelevant rituals (pp. 177–8). Al-Qaradawi's critique is also levelled, however, against *al-du'at* ("propagandists") who show insufficient concern "for present problems and future aspirations" (p. 29).

Even if al-Qaradawi advocates a fusion of *salafiyya* and *tajdid* ("renewal"), he tends to lay a heavier emphasis on the latter, as this seems to be, at some points, equated with *sahwa* (p. 24). The evocation of the era of *al-salaf al-salih* ("the reputable ancestors") does not provide the platform for a backward-looking attitude, but serves as a reference to an idealized model of hermeneutic smoothness, given by the time when Muslims were capable of shaping simply crafted, binding interpretations, whilst keeping the degree of conflict within the community to a minimum, and so allowing the unfolding of innovative capacities (pp. 27–8). The idealized consensus is viewed as focussing on essential questions, and obtained through the real participation of the legitimate holders of the keys for interpreting the Law. This participation is after all a matter of subjective adherence, without which one cannot speak of implementation of *shari'a*, that is the symbolic core of the solutionist path. In one of the rare argumentative passages where a populistically coloured Qutbian influence seems at work, al-Qaradawi stresses how this implementation is above all a responsibility of the people (*al-sha'b*), well before it becomes a concern for the state (al-Qaradawi, 1988, p. 53). This stress is, however, superimposed by the argument that, as there cannot be *'aqida* ("doctrine") without *shari'a*, there cannot be *din* without *dawla* either (al-Qaradawi, 1982, p. 134).

Such a leap unveils the tough kernel of the solutionist version of conflationism, argumentatively sustained by the resentment against those who misunderstand and reduce the Islamic *din* to the Western concept of "religion": an older *islahi* motive (see Chapters 2, 3 and 5). Al-Qaradawi crafts this argument in a direct polemic attitude against the Western view of political Islam as centred on the formula of a "politicization of religion", nurtured by explanations mostly based on sociocultural, or even socio-psychological factors. Against this view al-Qaradawi is keen to reaffirm, again in a Qutbian vein, that Islam unifies theory and practice, spirit and form (pp. 134–6).

The axial passage of al-Qaradawi's argumentation lies in the development of a balanced reading of the relationship between individual duties and collective commitments. The former no doubt occupy a pre-eminent position in the doctrinally stricter terms of "obligation" (*fard*), but on this basis the author is prompt to specify that individual duties affecting the collectivity precede those of strictly individual import. This narrowly juridical consideration is not sufficient, however, for establishing the primacy of the societal dimension. This only attains a definite primacy through resort to a logical argument grounded on the invocation of the concept of collective utility, sustained by the almost purely ideological, no longer juridically grounded claim that "Islam . . . gives pre-eminence to social over personal relations" (p. 176).

This assertion is considered sufficient by al-Qaradawi for consecrating the "necessity" (*hatmiyya*) of the "Islamic solution" (*al-hall al-islami*), as consisting in the implementation of *shari'a* in all domains of life. The ensuing vision reflects a populist view of the *da'wa* (the "missionary" call for joining Islam, in this case the intellectually mediated "true Islam"), according to which concrete solutions to concrete problems are envisaged through direct contact with the "people" (pp. 220–1). This view almost automatically leads to the call for establishing an Islamic state, posited as a duty for the Islamic community and as a pivotal goal in the work of the *du'at* (those in charge of the *da'wa*). This assertion cannot, again, take advantage of any solid underpinning in the legal terms of *fiqh*. The ultimate obligatory character of the Islamic state is sanctioned through logical and ideological evidence and not through juridical argumentations.

Even more important, one can question whether there is a logical gap between the consideration of Islam as more or less synonymous with all that is socially good and endowed with normative force – hence to be implemented – and the call for an Islamic state. The populist flavour and vocabulary of the entire discourse is the only element that fills the gap: its logic is that even through a gradualist lens, the reform (*islah*) of the Community cannot be achieved without bridging the gulf between the horizontal and the vertical levels of societal organization (pp. 222–3). While examining the contending sixth circle we will see that behind the populist colouring of the solutionist path there is an option that is not fully justified by the logic of argumentation pursued.

As this is common to most political-intellectual stances, we should attempt to discover where the symbolic strength of the seventh circle lies, in spite of the logical incongruities of its discourse. The appeal of a certain sort of hermeneutics is never either a function of logical strength or of underlying interests, even less so in the case of the Islamist-solutionist discourse. The "re-enchanting", self-deceiving dimension of an argumentative path is what sustains it in the final analysis (see Chapter 2), and in the case of solutionism the category of *shari'a* is central in this respect. The call for the Islamic state, as is well-known, is strictly linked to the demand for enforcing *shari'a*. The definition of this concept, that is not less subject to interpretive variability than *islam* or *din* (see Chapter 3), is at the very core of the solutionist discourse, before it becomes overloaded, in purely logical terms, by the tension between the two axis, the vertical and the horizontal, of social organization.

According to the very essence of *al-sahwa al-islamiyya*, *shari'a* cannot be reduced to "cutting the hand of the thief", as al-Qaradawi stresses with bitter sarcasm, with evident reference to the most common, media-mediated views – in the West especially – of what *shari'a* is all about. After all, implementing *shari'a* does not exhaust what the Islamic "awakening" is or should be (al-Qaradawi, 1988, p. 56). At this point al-Qaradawi suspends the definition of *shari'a*, and it almost seems that its centrality is given precisely by this undetermined character (see Chapter 3). The ambiguous meaning of this concept in al-Qaradawi's argumentation makes it, in a Qutbian vein, the symbolic medium of Islam's unfolding in human history, or even of human history's unfolding as Islam. The reduced and diluted post-Qutbian version that intervenes in the framing model of the solutionist circle is finally centred, however, on the postulation of *al-sahwa al-islamiyya* as a natural, spontaneous awakening of Islam in terms of a return of consciousness, as well as on the definition of *al-haraka al-islamiyya* (literally: "the Islamic movement") as the activist core of *sahwa*, bringing to full awareness and articulating into a coherent vision the impulses inherent in the "awakening" (p. 107). This view attenuates the revolutionary potentialities of a Qutbian reading of *shari'a*.

It is crucial to stress again that within this theoretical scenario the attainment of the level of *dawla* ("state") is not so abrupt as the slogan *islam din wa-dawla* would allow us to think. The presumption that this is the immediate, logical consequence of demanding the enforcement of *shari'a* should be reassessed with more caution than usual, in order not to deform the model of the seventh circle. The recurrent accusation against solutionists (more from the Western side than from its neutralist contenders) is that the invocation of the Islamic state does not specify the constitutional model, or the political profile of such a state, so that one is led to fear that it will degenerate into the arbitrary and despotic rule of a clerical oligarchy. In parallel, it has been questioned which concrete, relevant changes the implementation of *shari'a* would introduce in the constitutional and legal system. On this point it has been rightly claimed that "the argument over the *shari'a* is not purely legal. It has become more a symbol than anything else: for lack of any other acceptable shibboleth, its enforcement is considered a distinctive feature of an Islamic state." (Flores, 1993, p. 35).

We should, however, try to modify this assessment, and in a certain sense to reverse it, by saying that the symbolic power of the call for enforcing *shari'a* is the hard kernel of the solutionist view, and that the invocation of the Islamic state is an important corollary of it, to the extent that it symbolizes the end of the violation, corruption and instrumentalization of *din* carried out by the existing *dawla*. It is undeniable that the solutionist formula covers a striving towards power or, more precisely, a project to redefine the existing patterns of social authority in order to achieve gains, as well as, if possible, underpinning these gains in the constitutional design, not unlike the Iranian case. However, the hermeneutic axis of the argument of the seventh circle, as well as its capacity to appeal to individual consciences and achieve public resonance is first in the symbolic construction and instrumentalization of the *shari'a*, and only secondarily in the accompanying invocation of an Islamic state. The call for enforcing *shari'a* functions as the discursive medium for envisioning Islam as the solution.

The combination of logical vulnerability and symbolic strength of solutionism has been countered by what one can call, by contrast, a "neutralist" discourse, according to which Islam is politically neutral. We will see, however, how the argumentative model of the sixth circle, while taking root on a logical terrain that enables it to unveil the contradiction of solutionism, ends up reveiling some logical inconsistencies of its own that must be filled in, again, with symbolic references. The sixth circle seems to be less touched than the seventh by the transformation of the last twenty years, as it would appear when comparing its basic arguments with the standard reading of 'Abd al-Raziq (that is, as I attempted to show in Chapter 5, highly reductive). Against this impression, one should warn that, first of all, the neutralist argument cannot be properly understood when abstracted from the "politics of *sahwa*" of the last two decades. Moreover, its argumentative path acquires an added transcultural dimension for being generally assessed in the West as the hermeneutic terrain of the "Islamic liberals", those who can express, or translate, Western values in an Islamic framework, thereby challenging the much-feared Islamist hegemony. Finally, the discursive patterns of some representatives of the sixth circle, similarly to those of the third one, are under the influence of "political Islam" as an explicit category, connotatively redefined in a way that is coherent with the argumentative frame of the circle. The term *al-islam al-siyasi*, as used in a famous book by

Muhammad Sa'id al-'Ashmawi (1987), is not so much the translation of the "external" impression of an "Islam in movement" (as in the case of the third circle, by virtue of its focus on socio-economic or sociocultural factors of mobilization), but rather of the perception, internal to the process of outlining an Arab–Islamic framework of reference, of a progressive "corruption" of "true Islam": "God has wanted Islam a religion; but [some] people want it to be politics." (quoted in Ayubi, 1991, p. 203).

If Islam makes an inroad into the political domain, it is bound to corrupt its genuine nature: this is, at first sight, the central formula of the sixth circle. Neutralism distinguishes itself for its emphasis on the separation between Islam as a religion and way of life (*islam din wa-dunya*) on the one hand, and the realm of politics and government on the other. It is problematic to equate neutralism with "secularism" in a Western sense (see Chapter 3), since the sixth circle takes Islam seriously enough as a sociocultural normative system and, under the pressure of solutionism, is even eager to discuss the extent to which it would be admissible or even desirable to define and construct an Islamic state or government. Neutralist arguments, including those concerning the Islamic state, are generally based on a higher degree of historical consciousness than allowed within the orbit of the seventh circle.[5]

Muhammad Ahmad Khalafallah shows a longer record of familiarity with such questions than most of his fellow "neutralists" who have engaged in public contentions during the 1980s. Khalafallah's elaboration of a deconflationist model dates back at least to 1973, when he published his book *al-Qur'an wa-l-dawla* (Khalafallah, 1973). Six years earlier he had already dealt with some aspects that are crucial to the vision underlying deconflationism, in the book *al-Qur'an wa-mushkilat hayyatina al-mu'asira* (Khala-allah, 1967). However, this work was still in a process of refining 'Abd al-Raziq's argument, and the simplistic differentiation there supported between *al-dawla al-madaniyya* (a translation of "secular state") and *al-dawla al-diniyya* (see Wielandt, 1982, p. 126) has no longer centrally featured in the more recent contributions examined here.

In his 1973 book, Khalafallah openly challenged the argument in favour of the Islamic state, by focusing on its weakest points in logical terms. He claimed that if there is an Islamic way to the constitution of the state, this cannot be direct, but should follow the accomplishment of the principle of *islah*. What was already clear in his book of 1967, and reiterated in 1973, is that the author acknowledges only the Koran for justifying any social strategy inspired to Islam (Khalafallah, 1967 and 1973). He is keen to stress that, although the Koran does not prescribe anything concrete about the state, it provides some guidelines that should be taken into account.

In the context of the contention with the seventh circle during the 1980s, this fundamental claim has been reformulated by Khalafallah in a sharp and slightly provocative way. He has stated that the very attitude of using Islam for predicating something else through the adjectival form *islami/islamiyya* (what we can call "attributional Islam") has hardly any basis in Islam as *din*. At least some of the concepts shaped through this attributional use of Islam have no textual basis, no footing in Scripture: among them there are keywords of the seventh circle such as *al-sahwa al-islamiyya*, *al-hukuma al-islamiyya*, *al-dawla al-islamiyya* and, last but not least, *al-hall al-islami* (the "Islamic solution"). The essay of Khalafallah, delivered at the above-mentioned 1987 Amman conference and in some passages directly tackling al-Qaradawi's model, bears the significant title *al-islam bayna wahda al-iman wa-ta'addud al-qira'at wa-l-mumarasat* ("Islam between the unity of faith and the plurality of interpretations and practices"). This title formulates the modern intellectual question of what "true Islam" is (or rather should be), and hints at an answer by claiming that its hard shell is *al-iman*, the personal dimension of commitment, or simply "faith" (see Chapter 1). This is supposed to embody what is unitary and untouchable, what is "sacred" in Islam, whereas all socially-bound readings and practices inspired by it should be situated at a more profane level, their social relevance notwithstanding (Khalafallah, 1988, pp. 149–50).

This position is summarized by stating, through a formula which clearly echoes 'Abd al-Raziq, that in order to understand Islam one should try to differentiate between what belongs to the realm of *din* and what is *la-dini*, meaning "non-religious", "profane", more than "secular" (p. 149). The first realm supposedly coincides with *al-iman* (Khalafallah, 1981, p. 140), but this identification rapidly turns into a major logical breach in the discursive path of neutralism. Khalafallah shows here his awareness of how insidious is the task of sharply separating the two domains, that are variably linked in social reality, if arguing in Islamic, and not liberal-secular terms. His way out of the impasse is by charging Western Orientalists with this "contamination" of Islam as *din*, as they are presented as the shapers of formulas such as "Islamic civilization" and even *islam 'aqida wa-shari'a* ("Islam is doctrine and lawful practice"), known to be an Islamist slogan (Khalafallah, 1988, p. 149). By so doing, Khalafallah fails to recognize the socially endogenous reasons for the inherent complexity of any definition of "true Islam" as the basis for an Arab–Islamic framework of reference.

After this indictment of Orientalism, Khalafallah promptly moves to address the problem of the Islamic state by directly tackling the argument of the rival seventh circle. This abrupt passage is significant for two reasons:

the first is that the author is incapable of pursuing in an autonomous, analytic way the question raised in the title and preliminarily approached at the beginning of the essay; the second is the apparent allusion to some strict continuity between the alleged Orientalist creation of "attributional" Islam and its use by solutionists.[6] Khalafallah is eager to show how the logical argument in favour of the Islamic state takes the upper hand in the framing model of the seventh circle, to the detriment of scriptural proofs. Here he seems to have scored a point in favour of his position, that tends to view "true Islam" as rooted in the Koran, and only to a limited degree based on the *sunna* of the Prophet (p. 150).

It might appear paradoxical that, on the basis of this argument, Khalafallah accuses al-Qaradawi of a too free exercise of *ijtihad*, as when the latter states that if one can perform a duty only in a given way, this way automatically becomes an obligation. Here the original duty is given by performing what is incumbent on the Muslim, and the "only way" refers to the institution of an Islamic state. Khalafallah's critique of the solutionist argument amounts to its simplification, since the invocation of an Islamic state is not independent of the more central call (loaded with symbolic, not merely logical significance) for the implementation of *shari'a*: a call which compounds subjective duties and systemic necessities. Through the ensuing argumentation, Khalafallah is neither able nor willing to capture this crucial and quite evident reason animating the rival claim, and in fact he insists on arguing on a merely logical level and raising the question: while it is indisputable that Muslims belonging to a certain community need a state, are we really sure that they *need* an *Islamic* state? Why pose the question of pursuit of "true Islam" in terms of government? Is this not rather a domain of purely social interaction, whose regulation God has permanently entrusted to man and his reason? (p. 151).

Khalafallah's argumentation becomes more penetrating when he accuses the seventh circle of overestimating the capacity of human reason to reproduce and represent God's Will. On the other hand, he is anxious not to deny, but to emphasize, the freedom of conscience and individual responsibility as rooted in *din* (see Chapter 1), and valid before God in the first instance. Immediately to project into a vertical dimension the corresponding domain of reciprocal conduct (*mu'amalat*), i.e. in a sociological jargon, of "social interaction", is, however, an unjustified short-cut.[7] The case of the particular rectitude and communal zeal of Muslims living in non-Muslim states is invoked as proof against the need for an Islamic state (p. 154).

Islam is deemed basically identical with other religions in that it is based on ethical principles: yet there is something more or something special in it. Khalafallah lists some such principles deemed as fundamental, and clearly transcending the level of *iman*. This is a point where he implicitly concedes that Islam is, beyond being an individual commitment to God, a blueprint for life conduct that inevitably affects the organization of the community. The list of principles culminates in the stress on *shura*, indicating the procedure of discussion which is necessary before taking political decisions. This is undeniably a principle that also affects the methods of *hukm* (rule, or exercise of power), and Khalafallah is willing to praise its place in Islam, although there is no specification in the Koran of the proper modalities for implementing it. The resulting emphasis on the enhanced communal dimension of Islam, compared to other religions, is, nonetheless, in no way considered a platform for formulating an Islamic doctrine concerning the form of the state. All principles, including the *shura*, are rooted exclusively in the individual conscience (p. 155).

In another contribution Khalafallah expands this argument into a radical critique of the clergy, accused of arbitrarily sacralizing extra-Koranic sources. This amounts to a critique of the self-constitution of the *'ulama'* as the guardians of a sacred heritage. This passage witnesses the importance of the conflict on the understanding of *'ilm* and the self-understanding of the *'ulama'* which underlies the intellectual confrontation between solutionism and neutralism. Khalafallah asserts: "I shall have to do with God alone." Through direct contact with God and only in this way, one can creatively shape solutions: this implies a critique of solutionism as an unauthorized conflation between the human and a putative divine realm unduly confiscated by the *'ulama'* (Khalafallah, 1981, p. 139). The precondition of any solution is consequently to distinguish sharply between the two realms.

Khalafallah carries the argument to its logical extreme, thereby shaping the final formula of neutralism, as he claims that the necessary implementation of all basic Islamic principles, including the *shura*, is no prejudice against any form of government or constitutional profile of the state: the alternatives between monarchy and republic, or democracy and dictatorship, are an exclusively societal issue. Not all representatives of the sixth circle would be willing to carry the argument so far. For al-'Ashmawi, for example, the principle of *shura* is the basis of "the government of the people; a government which they freely elect and in which they share; a government which they may change peaceably." This would be,

> [the] true Islamic government . . . not an Islamic government such as appeared in history but . . . another kind of government, one which would serve Islam rather than use it; . . . [that] will offer

Islam to all mankind as a way to God, a method for progress and a path of mercy. It will be the nucleus of a new ecumenical government, a core to a new united humanity (Al-'Ashmawi, 1986, pp. 12–13).

This represents a variation in closing the neutralist argumentation which adopts, in a slightly provocative way, an altered solutionist perspective, thereby challenging the seventh circle on its own terrain, at the level of the actual profile required by an Islamic state. Khalafallah is not far from a similar perspective, when he raises the question of social justice and distribution of wealth, thereby maintaining that a state that would endorse these issues could be legitimately called "Islamic". He uses this claim for demonstrating how solutionism does not offer any plausible solution to the most salient problem of communal relations and is thereby a void ideological formula (Khalafallah, 1988, pp. 159–60).

That the neutralist model does not dismiss an autochthonous, Arab–Islamic framework of reference is shown by its concluding claim that even in the absence of any reference to the actual form of state and government, the Koran necessarily provides the basis of an "order" or "system", *nizam* (p. 157). This affirmation, that echoes a central Qutbian motif, could be warmly supported by any solutionist, and proves why the sixth circle cannot be assimilated to liberalism in the Western sense.[8] Replying to the objections moved by the Sudanese *'alim*, the solutionist Hasan Turabi, as well as by the Moroccon philosopher Muhammad 'Abid al-Jabiri (a representative of the fifth circle: see Chapter 12) in the discussion that followed the presentation of his paper at the Amman conference, Khalafallah specified that his own plea was not against the Islamic state as such, but against propagating this as a religious duty. What is crucial for the neutralist position is to make clear that any discussion of the Islamic state is to be situated in the realm of human and historical contingencies. Even if we may agree on the general formula of an Islamic state – Khalafallah argues – its actual meaning depends on the orientation of the Muslims who ground the state, as shown by the profound differences among the three existing approximations of Islamic states: Pakistan; Saudi Arabia and Iran (p. 164). In this way the sixth circle eludes, however, the very core of the argument of the rival seventh circle, centred on the symbolic power and the collective-systemic dimension of the call for the enforcement of *shari'a*. Here the basic pitfall of neutralism becomes evident: the difficulty of being neutral with regard to the vertical dimension of the organization of social life, just as one cannot be neutral when reference is made to the normative structures of its horizontal cohesion.

The phenomenon of the apparent shift of some leading authors from the orbit of the sixth to that of the seventh circle in the course of the 1980s, far from being a sign of a tendential exhaustion of the former, reveals both the existence of a tenuous argumentative edge at the basis of the polarization, which makes a shift no dramatic jump in logical terms, and the higher power of attraction of the seventh circle the greater strength of its symbolic references. Two recent cases, those of Khalid Muhammad Khalid and Muhammad 'Imara, have been widely read in terms of a mere "conversion" to the hegemonic argumentation of solutionism, as a pure matter of "going Islamist". It is more appropriate, however, to consider the interpretive mechanism through which, within a pendular movement between the two strictly interdependent forms of Islamic reformism, the socio-political situation of the last twenty years has favoured a swing towards solutionism.

The alleged shift of Khalid towards a formal support of an Islamic state is certainly endowed with symbolic significance. In purely logical terms his argument (see Wielandt, 1982, p. 130) is nonetheless still virtually identical to that of some representatives of the sixth circle, such as al-'Ashmawi, and its emphasis on the *shura* (the alleged Islamic equivalent of democracy) as the key to constructing a true Islamic government. The major difference is that Khalid does not use this argument for antagonizing the solutionists, as al-'Ashmawi does, but rather for accommodating or even joining them, by stressing that democracy is among the crucial properties of any prospective Islamic government.

There is a passage in Khalafallah of particular relevance for directly approaching a salient question affecting the legitimation of reformed and intellectualized *'ilm*, and the new consensus grounded on it across the polarization between the two circles. Discussing the relationship between interest and interpretation, he claims that if the general interest (*maslaha 'amma* or simply *maslaha*) is at stake, the interpretation of the *faqih* (Islamic jurist) acquires a particular societal value. In posing the *maslaha* as a primary source, which can supersede the sacred texts in matters of *mu'amalat* (socially relevant dealings), he appeals to the Hanbali school and in particular to Ibn Taymiyya (Khalafallah, 1981, pp. 140–1). This medieval theologian-jurist, who represented a primary authority for the reformist programme of Muhammad 'Abduh and even more for the proto-conflationism of Rashid Rida (see Chapters 1, 3 and 5), has acquired during the last two decades the fame of a forerunner of "fundamentalism", as he appears to be a source of inspiration for contemporary Islamist groups (see Jansen, 1986). This is, however, a distorted view, since Ibn Taymiyya provides a good "traditional" authoritative footing to the broader *islahi* movement, given that he posed the Koranic prescriptions, identified with the domain of *din*, as not legislating into the details of communal life, and highlighted instead how the latter should be at the service of *din* (Gardet, 1978, p. 303): this can be considered as a call for interpretive and social creativity for the sake of enforcing God's Will.

This is quite clearly common terrain for the sixth and the seventh circles, and constitutes a further clue for showing how both are discursive offshoots within the same, broader tradition of *islah*, equally coherent with, its emphasis on *ijtihad*. They converge in supporting the autonomous judgement of individual Muslims and the need to take into account the requirements of the contemporary historical situation (Wielandt, 1982, pp. 128–9), as well as in highlighting the enhanced social dimension of Islam, in comparison with other monotheistic religions. However, the terms of discourse used, common to both circles, have reached through the disputes of the 1980s a degree of fixity and stagnation that is directly proportional to their incapacity to transcend the narrow *islahi* modalities of modern thinking, and to take up the challenge of the transcultural commensurableness of the political discourse of modernity.

NOTES

---

1 One could list several different categories of discussion which possess a denotative force virtually equivalent to that of "Islamic state": *al-khilafa, haqiqa al-islam wa-usul al-hukm, al-nazariyyat al-siyasiyya al-islamiyya, nizam al-hukm fi-l-islam* (al-Jabiri, 1982, p. 65).

2 As for most of the other texts in languages other than English quoted in this study, my translation of passages of al-Qaradawi's work is from the original.

3 The word used for "opinion", *ra'i*, also belongs to the traditional vocabulary of *fiqh*. In reformist *fiqh* the emphasis on the use of *ra'i* is a crucial tool for legitimizing the expansion of interpretive potentialities.

4 Evident is the closeness of this vision to the constitutional design of the Islamic Republic of Iran and its principle of the authority of the *faqih*, all the doctrinal differences between Sunni and Shii orthodoxies notwithstanding. The Iranian case is, however, never explicitly mentioned by al-Qaradawi.

5 For an extensive account of the production of the sixth circle in Egypt during the 1980s ("Islamic liberals") see Ayubi, 1991, pp. 201–15.

6 Among these, he sees no difference between the moderate wing represented by al-Qaradawi and the groups classified as extremist, such as *al-jihad*.

7 Khalafallah is particularly interested in recalling that the number of dealings regulated by the Koran is low, whereas the highest number of *suras* concern dogma and worship (Khalafallah, 1981, p. 140).

8 This obviously does not exclude that some of its representatives can assume public positions which are coherent with the tenets of Western liberalism; but this is a side issue for the topic of the present study.

CHAPTER 12

Social justice and cultural heritage (*turath*)

The fifth circle, or rather the search for it, is characterized by an attempt to transcend the dead polarization between the seventh and the sixth circles and the limits of their *islahi* framework. Focusing on the proper method for rationally authenticating the cultural "heritage" (*turath*) in order to articulate a viable political discourse of modernity not merely imitative of the West's, the fifth circle adopts a mobilizing ethos comparable to that of solutionism. This ethos is nonetheless developed through a social-theoretical rationale closer to the one of "neutralism", to the extent that the sixth circle has engaged in addressing the question of social justice and in some cases (as in Khalafallah's work) in beginning to work out methodically a redefinition of *turath*. Moreover, the fifth circle openly takes on the challenge of the transcultural commensurableness of "modernity", left unproblematized within the opposition between the Western-based third and fourth circles (see Chapter 9). The ambitious purpose implicit in the search for such an alternative circle, and the consequent high degree of indeterminacy surrounding this task, has given rise, since the late 1970s and early 1980s, to a sometimes disordered competition among authors aspiring to bring about the needed innovations in the modern hermeneutics of Islam without disavowing Islamic terms of discourse. I will attempt to reconstruct a single line of development, probably the most promising one, within the area where such interpretive efforts tend to crystallize.

It is not surprising that, in spite of the greater power of attraction of the compact and assertive vision of the seventh circle, the seeds for transcending the fixity of the polarization between "solutionism" and "neutralism" are more likely to be found in the ideologically weaker sixth circle. Khalafallah's argument departs from a purely neutralist logic as it makes clear that one should be neutral towards the form of the state, but that the Islamically grounded category of general interest (*maslaha 'amma*, or simply *maslaha*) implies a commitment to progress and social justice. This is the platform for envisaging an Islamic order that should necessarily have a social, or even "socialist" (*ishtiraki*) character. Quoting from *tafsir al-manar* written by 'Abduh and Rida, Khalafallah recalls, by pointing to the example of *zakat* (the obligatory alms, one of the basic "pillars" of Islam), that this social commitment is independent of any compulsion from above, but results smoothly from professing and practising Islam as *din* (Khalafallah, 1988, pp. 157–8.)

As a consequence, Khalafallah reproaches the solutionists for not having any solution to the crucial problems of the distribution of wealth and the fair retribution of work, whose centrality in Islamic terms he is very eager to demonstrate (p. 159). In fact, the accusation moved by Khalafallah against the seventh circle should also be read against the background of political contingencies, due to his affiliation with the leftist *tajammu'*. On the other hand, the history of the Nasserist repression of Islamists, and their support through the conservative Saudi regime, has rendered any explicit invocation of Islamic "socialist" values (a topic with which the Nasserist ideology was very familiar) almost a taboo within the orbit of the seventh circle. The association of parts of the Islamist movement with various forms of "Islamic business" during the last fifteen years might have complemented and strengthened this prejudice (Zubaida, [1987] 1989b, pp. 49–50). In spite of this trend, for the analysis of the seventh circle it could have been legitimate to opt for an author like Muhammad al-Ghazali, who, though not less influential, is certainly more socially radical than al-Qaradawi, and correspondingly better prepared to engage in discussions on social justice in Islamic visions of society: a topic that represents, after all, an important asset within the larger Qutbian heritage.

However, the formation of a hermeneutic gap which began to be filled by the fifth circle during the 1980s was not confined to social questions, but encompassed the problem of the relationship between the Arab–Islamic *turath* and the "globalizing", Western-centred modernity within the metamorphosing transcultural space, a reflection that the circular contention between neutralism and solutionism, and more in general between conflationism and deconflationism, was not able to produce. What constitutes the husk of *turath*? How can one sort out what is authentic in it and what is not? The reference to *turath* to be found in al-Qaradawi's writings simply helped to define what type of cultural asset *al-sahwa al-islamiyya* was expected to revitalize. In this way, *turath* merely embodies the taken-for-granted character of an authenticity marker (al-Qaradawi, 1988, p. 22). It can encompass very different directions and domains of thought, ranging from the conservative theology of al-Ash'ari to the progressive philosophy of Ibn Rushd (p. 26). It is not, however, the problem of what, but of *what for*, which can make a difference in the use of *turath*, and al-Qaradawi, in his generic view, is very far from conceiving the cultural heritage in innovative terms.

Differently from al-Qaradawi, Khalafallah is able to elaborate an embryonic methodological position in coping with *turath*, that he defines in a double way: either as close to the virtually static image of the symbolic-communicative system (see Chapter 1), or as a cultural asset to be defined on the basis of investigation. In spite of this differentiating effort, *turath* is still conceived as a tangible, objective corpus (Khalafallah, 1981, p. 137). He pleads for transcending the backward-looking orientation of the first, static type of heritage, as this is demanded by the imperative of "progress". It is our right, he argues, to elaborate the values of *turath*, just as our reputable ancestors also did on the basis of the requirements and experiences of their age (p. 138). However, the resulting use of the concept of *turath* by Khalafallah lacks, in the final analysis, any theoretical autonomy, dependent as it is on the plain need to overcome the staticity of "tradition" and to counter the ensuing – as he sees it – short-cut to solutionist Islamism.

Khalafallah's "progressive" appeal to *turath* is developed in a much more cogent way – on both a methodological level and in terms of social engagement – by some authors that I locate in the fifth circle, and for whom the hermeneutics of the cultural heritage occupies a central position. It may seem paradoxical that these endeavours (that are the most significant for the task of resuming the construction of a viable Arab–Islamic framework of reference during the "post-crisis" era) were bolstered not by a key category expressing confident overture, such as *nahda* (see Chapter 5), but by one stressing the importance of the roots, and thereby resulting in an effort to (re)construct "tradition", such as *turath*. References to *turath* in Arab–Islamic discourses go back to the formative period of *islah* at the end of last century, and have been interpreted as a pathological feature of the backward-looking attitude of modern Arab thought (see Tarabishi, 1991). This judgement is not based on an accurate historical analysis of the shifts in the use and meaning of this keyword, as well as of its association with other categories of intellectual discourses. It is true that we lack precise quantitative and qualitative data about such development, and it is also uncertain when the use of *turath* as opposed to *taqlid* ("imitative tradition", the canonically defined imitation of the interpretive solutions provided by previous scholars) began to take shape (Schulze, 1990b, pp. 31–2). It is nonetheless clear that the use of *taqlid* with a negative connotation is a crucial mark in the genesis of the modern construction of an Arab–Islamic framework of reference (see Chapter 3). However, the definition of the "progressive" meaning of *turath* was a much longer process, only completed after this term began to be commonly used in intellectual discourse, in the period here analysed, in connection with *asala* ("authenticity"), another keyword in the argumentative model of the fifth circle.

A quantitative study of the frequency of the thematization of *asala* in Arab "popular", "intellectual" and "religious" periodicals published between 1945 and 1970, has shown "an increasing concern for authenticity . . . especially in the popular and intellectual reviews" (Donohue, 1983, pp. 50–1). This investigation did not address, however, the crucial period of the 1970s. Moreover, its usefulness for the purposes of the present work is limited, in so far as we are interested in the maturation of an explicit reference to *asala* as a specific keyword, and especially in its enhancement to a particular discursive function in connection with *turath*. It is nonetheless interesting to see how the concept of authenticity gained terrain parallel to an increased concern for Islamic symbols, and how this growth did not primarily affect the narrowly defined religious press, but rather the intellectual and "popular" media and genres of public communication.

It is likely that the spread of *asala*'s appeal was initially favoured by the pressure to reformulate the question of *turath* by taking into account the nativist-essentialist claim entailed in the slogan of *al-sahwa al-islamiyya* (see Chapter 10). The first clues for this use of *asala* as complementary to *turath* originate from the conference on "Authenticity and Renewal in Contemporary Arab Culture" held in Cairo in October 1971. This was the first, and most modest, of a series of similar scholarly meetings (Boullata, 1990, p. 13) that were increasingly inspired by a joint reference to the conceptual pair *turath/asala* ("heritage/authenticity"), which began to delimit a unitary thematic area. The combination of the two concepts was to serve the effort to resume, after the "end of *nahda*", the definition of the place of the Arab–Islamic Self within the political-intellectual universe of modernity.

A paper delivered at the 1971 Cairo conference by Shukri 'Ayyad, examining the use of *asala* in Arab literature, showed how this word began to be employed on a relatively wide basis after the mid-1950s for signifying "original creation" and "liberation from tradition". It is through such a meaning that *asala* has begun to fertilize *turath* and consolidate its forward-looking tension, in contrast to *taqlid* (cf. Schulze, 1987). The joint use of *turath* and *asala* was even more evident in the Kuwait symposium of 1974 on "The crisis of civilizational development in the Arab homeland" (Boullata, 1990, p. 16). Many papers delivered at that conference show, nevertheless, that the above-illustrated process of defining the meaning of *turath* as a central concept for the modern shaping of an Arab–Islamic framework of reference has been gradual and controversial. Many authors still used *turath* as "tradition" in a negative sense, almost the equivalent of "atavism" (Boullata, 1990, pp. 16–23).[1]

These intellectual meetings marked the beginning of a process whose outcome has been the use of the concept of authenticity for working out a method of rational authentication of the heritage. According to this logic, *asala* becomes a methodological tool for fertilizing the textual assets of the heritage by means of the innovative hermeneutic activity of the knowing subject. Within this process, the conceptualization of *turath* in dynamic terms and the upgrading of the concept of authenticity to a methodological instrument are intimately intertwined. Accordingly, the main task of the fifth circle that we are going to analyse can be formulated as a "de-reification" of *asala* from its use as a term for a static and ahistorical reference to a heritage considered as given – as in the case of the discourse of *sahwa* of the seventh circle – towards its reshaping as a method for reactualizing *turath* (see also Salvatore, 1995b).

Muhammad 'Abid al-Jabiri, the first of the two authors here considered for an outline of the fifth circle, is very outspoken in considering *al-sahwa al-islamiyya* a slogan without any correspondence in historical reality, within which the idea of Islam falling asleep is pure nonsense (al-Jabiri, 1992, p. 39). Although he seems eager to recognize that the movement for the implementation of *shari'a*, which largely corresponds to the trend which carries the banner of *sahwa*, reflects the modern impulse to search for the reasons of the crisis, as well as for socially viable solutions (al-Jabiri, 1991, p. 11), he is very firm in denouncing the inadequate symbolic apparatus and the discourse of the "awakening". This deficit is not only to be seen in the lack of historical viability of the image used, but also in the fact (which also explains this deficit) that it mirrors the image of a "return of Islam" fabricated by the Western press and extraneous to the traditional Islamic semantic (see Chapter 8). It is much more correct, al-Jabiri maintains, to employ the Islamically consolidated category of *tajdid* ("renewal"), which well represents the profundity of historical change, especially on its subjective, intentional side (al-Jabiri, 1992, p. 40).

Tajdid, however, points only to the long-term process of renewal which should legitimize the modern task of constructing a viable Arab–Islamic framework of reference, whereas the concept of *turath* immediately recalls which asset one must turn to in performing this critical task. Within this line of reasoning, a historically crucial, intermediate concept like *nahda* cannot be lightheartedly left aside on account of its alleged failure. This is why al-Jabiri attempts to reconstruct the mechanisms of the Arab *nahda* in order to show that behind this keyword, and its related "project-dream", there is an actual interrogation, and how the feeling of an unfolding *nahda* has lasted for as long as this question has been raised, while remaining largely unanswered. It is the question *"limadha ta'akhkhara al-muslimun wa taqaddama ghairuhum?"* ("Why did the Muslims fall behind while the others – the West in particular – advanced?")[2] that immediately prompts the further interrogation: *"kayfa nanhadu?"* ("How to stand up, catch up (with the others)?") (al-Jabiri, 1985, p. 35).

While the clearly "distinctional" (in the sense of expressing an "intellectual distinction": see Chapter 2) character of the category of *nahda* allows us to subsume it under a minimalist definition of intellectual modernity as projected towards the shaping of a framework of communal reference, it is clear, on the other hand, where the difference lies between this word and the markers of Western modernity: the will to change expressed by *nahda* does not originate only from the reference to a decadent or stagnant past, as usual in distinctional modern categories, but has to cope with the visible change largely influenced by colonial penetration. The intellectual endeavour of *nahda* rejoices at this change and wants to appropriate its direction, to give it an imprint in conformity with endogenous interests and values, but, given the power imbalance with the encroaching West, is regularly frustrated in its striving (al-Jabiri, 1985, p. 36).

In this first emergence of transcultural dynamics the chasm between a past of decadence and a present of change is not filled through the necessary historicization of the passage, after the distinction between the two has been established. In the era of *nahda*, Arab intellectuals have written history in an overly apologetic and segmentary way, because of the urgent need to legitimize the distinction and under the pressure of social conflicts multiplied by colonialism (al-Jabiri, 1985, p. 51). This phenomenon, which cannot be imputed to a deficient endogenous intellectual impulse, marks a major difference towards Western paths of modern distinction. The paradox of *nahda* can also help to understand how the standard "reactivist" reading of the rise of intellectual modernity in the Arab–Islamic world, which refuses to take into account the original character of the markers of critical modernity within it, is no mere Western misreading, but is the mirror image of *nahda*, the exact reflection of the embeddedness of the work of defining an Arab–Islamic framework of reference within the transcultural space between the "West" and "Islam".[3]

The *nahda* desperately seeks an answer to the original question: pending this impossible, "final" answer, since only partial solutions can be provided, the Arab "renaissance" reproduces itself as an ongoing question: How to stand up? On the one hand, the idea of *nahda* embodies a clear will to carry out a modern turn. On the other, however, the "challenge of the West", while marking the urgency of this task and contributing to fulfilling the conditions for shaping an arena of political discourse guided by the principle of a "consensus of communication" (see Chapter 3), renders this will inadequate for the scope of the task. Even worse, it hampers the need to distinguish between the forces of *tajdid* and the forces of *taqlid* (al-Jabiri, 1985, pp. 41–2). The final consequence is that the Arab *nahda* cannot even define the aspiration it contains (p. 47). Its distinctional value is intrinsically weak, so that its dependence on the idea of a previous decadence, referring in particular to the eighteenth century (Schulze, 1987, p. 191), becomes totalizing and hinders historicization. The most enduring consequence is that the historical genesis of the Arab–Islamic framework of reference is no longer relevant (see Chapter 3). The intellectual discourse tends to be motivated by political urgency more than by a normatively crafted reappropriation of history.

This fundamental deficit of the Arab *nahda* has hindered the successful tackling of the problematic relationship between *al-asala wa-l-mu'asara*, "authenticity" and "modernity". The work of construction of an Arab–Islamic framework of reference has thereby resulted in a too early polarization of these terms into a binary opposition between two unrealistic "models" or void frameworks (*namadhij*, sing. *namudhaj*), the one being the "traditional Islamic" one of the *salafiyya*, the other looking at European modernity as a model to imitate (al-Jabiri, 1982, p. 59). Neither of the two models has evidently succeeded in claiming a universal value within the Arab–Islamic nation.

The 1984 Cairo conference on *al-turath wa-tahaddiyat al-'asr fi-l-watan al-'arabi. al-asala wa-l-mu'asara* ("The heritage and the challenges of the modern age in the Arab nation: authenticity and modernity") marked the highest point in the collective Arab intellectual endeavour to invest the conceptual pair "heritage/authenticity" in a conscious project of reconstruction of a framework of communal reference. Despite the still wide range of definitions of *turath*, the meeting consecrated this as a shared, communicatively effective term of political-intellectual discourse. This was mainly due to a use of *turath* for referring to selective impulses (see Hoffmann, 1990, pp. 50–1 and Roussillon, 1985, p. 7), made possible by the parallel adoption of *asala* as the principle of creative activation of an original interpretive power. Compared with the contrasts and ambiguities of the Kuwait symposium, a clear differentiation between the use of *taqlid* as a principle of imitation, and of *turath* as a principle of selective accumulation (hence, respectively, as the "conservative", backward-looking vs. the "progressive", modernity-engendering sides of "tradition") imposed itself as the object of virtually unanimous consensus. Furthermore, the concept of *turath*, by virtue of its close association with *asala*, began, especially through the central contribution of al-Jabiri that I am going to examine, to emancipate itself from a generic and eclectic use, and could thereby be analysed in its relationship to "modernity".

The importance of al-Jabiri's intervention should be evaluated by considering that, if one aims at defining an original Arab–Islamic framework of reference, the Western category of modernity does not provide a suitable key. If it is true that the word "modernity", or other similar terms in Western languages, embody a concern with the centrality of the knowing and acting subject and the resulting urge towards a qualitative distinction (see Chapter 2), one should admit that Arab intellectuals, especially when writing in their own language, are not able to capture this meaning in the most plausible and widespread translation of the word, *al-mu'asara*. This quite new term, which literally translated means something like the "contemporary age", seems rather to indicate the "globalizing and globalized" dimension of modernity.

One could object that there is another term in Arabic that, in its strictest meaning, is closer to "modernity" than *al-mu'asara*: it is the word *al-hadatha* (see Hoffmann, 1990, p. 51 and Schulze, 1993, p. 198). It is significant that in al-Jabiri the two terms are sometimes used jointly (*al-mu'asara wa-l-hadatha*) to designate what one usually calls, in Western languages, modernity. This does not happen by chance since from an Arab–Islamic point of view modernity entails the double dimension of a subject which is transculturally embedded in a Western-centred age, i. e. contemporary to it (*al-mu'asara*), but also involved in a potentially universal, although still Western-based, process of qualitative search for the new (*al-hadatha*). The former is taken for granted, even more so in a globalized environment, so that it is the latter which poses problems to the intellectual discourse engaged in defining an Arab–Islamic framework of reference.

Arab modernity cannot consist either of an impossible joining in *al-hadatha*, nor in a wholesale opposition to it. At first, it seems that there will always be a residual tension between *al-turath* and *al-hadatha* (al-Jabiri, 1982, p. 59). The picture changes if one accepts that the modern way of posing the problem of *turath* implies a question of method: "*kayfa nata'amalu ma'a-l-turath?*" ("How should *we* deal with the heritage?"). In this sense, *hadatha* is not the negation of *turath*, but precisely the historical force which defines the latter from a position of concern for the present, thereby producing and reproducing *al-mu'asara*, the modern, contemporary situation. The only access to it with a full right of citizenship is by activating the force of *hadatha* from within Arab culture, and this happens through posing the problem of the heritage and dealing with it methodically (al-Jabiri, 1991, pp. 7–10).

Al-hadatha has finally to be understood as a method of inspection which includes its goal in itself. As a result of its impulses, *al-turath*, this cumbersome entity which seems to overoccupy the Arab–Islamic consciousness, is de-absolutized and dynamized, thereby no longer representing an obstacle on the trail of modernity, or rather being indispensable to it. Any Arab attempt to adopt *hadatha* in its Western shape without this work on *turath* is doomed to failure. *Al-hadatha* is no Western monopoly but a universal and plural potentiality, and the Arab–Islamic modern intellectual venture can only be based on this force of innovation, which allows a methodical approach to *turath* (al-Jabiri, 1991, pp. 15–16).

This original dealing with the concept of *turath* in Arab intellectual discourse is paralleled, al-Jabiri observes, by the unique character of the intrinsic meaning of the word, which it is in fact impossible to translate into other languages. Al-Jabiri is eager to stress how no comparable use of *turath* or of an equivalent word belonging to the same root is documented in Arabic for periods prior to the Arab "renaissance". *Turath* is a term capable of conveying a complex signification which can be fully elicited only through an analysis of its relationship with other concepts. In its present meaning it is still a strongly reified term which denotes the feeling of commonality and totality of Arab culture, hinting at all its unrealized potentialities (al-Jabiri, 1991, pp. 21–5). Al-Jabiri's semantic reconstruction of the term *turath* points to the function of a pivotal catchcategory which serves the need to demarcate a consensus of communication within a framework of communal reference.

In more recent years al-Jabiri has tended to lay emphasis on the constructive aspects of the original features of modern Arab discourse, but on earlier occasions he focused on its pathological dimension, as rooted in inherent deficits of the "Arab mind" or "Arab reason" (*al-ʿaql al-ʿarabi*). In his first famous book, *Nahnu wa-l-turath* (1980), he offered concrete examples of how to cope analytically with prominent texts belonging to the Arab–Islamic cultural heritage like classical philosophical works, with the purpose of reactualizing its rational elements. But during the early 1980s he turned to a critique of *al-ʿaql al-ʿarabi* ("the Arab mind" or "reason") in two books (1984, 1986) which problematized the negative characteristics of *turath* as a burden for modern Arab thought (a third critique published in 1990 completed the trilogy). These works were introduced by a critical essay on *al-Khitab al-ʿarabi al-muʿasir* which sought to recapitulate the reasons for the methodological weakness of the historical construction of an Arab–Islamic framework of reference (1982). Following this line of investigation, al-Jabiri bracketed the historically convincing diagnosis of the shortcomings of *nahda* and ventured to denounce the impulse to refer everything supposedly new to a (past)-model (*namudhaj*) as a constitutive vice of the Arab mind (see Chapter 2).

Al-Jabiri's reconstruction of the reasons for the fragility and circularity of *nahda* connected with the discursive function of *turath* has provided a convincing way out of an obsession with inherent factors of the Arab–Islamic intellectual "syndrome", as well as the beginning of a path leading to recognizing the universal as well as the transcultural conditions for the making of an Arab–Islamic framework of reference. In the paper presented to the 1984 Cairo conference, al-Jabiri firstly makes it clear that intrinsic in the mechanisms of each kind of *nahda*, i.e. of "renaissance", is the appeal to a "heritage", taking the form of a return to the *usul* – the authentic "fundaments" – seen as embodied in a remote but easily identifiable past, whose evocation fulfils the function of marking a distinction from a closer past. This is perceived as the period whose decadence, in the sense of corruption of the fundaments, is responsible for the present disarray, and justifies a swift projection into the future. After reconstructing the general historical-cultural type of the phenomenon of "renaissance", al-Jabiri recognizes that these mechanisms were operating in the Arab *nahda* (al-Jabiri, 1985, p. 36). Based on this reconstruction of the univeral features of the phenomenon as given by a selective reappropriation of the past in order to forge the path to the future – whilst preserving a sense of historical concatenations – he attempts to rescue the innovative impulse that animated the Arab *nahda*, in spite of its desperately circular unfolding.

Al-Jabiri's following step, however, is a shift from the preliminary recognition of the universal affiliation of the progressive impetus of *nahda*, towards a complaint about the extent to which this was incapable of keeping faith with its promises and being consistent with its original impulse to dare a leap into the future. The resulting degradation of the immanent scope of *nahda* into a mere justification of the present was certainly influenced by the "external challenges". Of primary importance for al-Jabiri is, nonetheless, to show the hindrance that made the Arab renaissance stumble and fail: the lack of capacity to concentrate on a creative and selective elaboration of *turath* (al-Jabiri, 1985, p. 40). This is different from the mere *irth*, i.e. "inheritance", the plain transmission of an unchangeable asset through subsequent generations. *Turath* is instead a "pretended", constructed whole, that selectively draws on the cultural legacy, but is in the end more than the sum of its selected components (p. 46).

Al-Jabiri sees the concept of *turath* as suffering from an uncertain actualization of its innovative potentialities due to a too strong reification, which is largely the reflection of the Orientalist viewpoint grounded on an objectifying perspective (see Chapter 4). The adoption of a Marxist approach by some Arab intellectuals has only reiterated this dependence on an "externalist", reifying notion of *turath* (al-Jabiri, 1991, p. 29). The deficit of dynamic properties in the construction of the heritage lies, in the final analysis, in the absence of an adequately rational method for coping with *turath*, i.e. for authenticating it. The construction of a dynamic *turath* is definitively presented as a question of method, and it is not surprising that al-Jabiri's diagnostical investigation culminates in the exposition of a correct methodology for dealing with the heritage.

Apart from more technical suggestions concerning a discourse-analytic deconstruction of texts belonging to the Arab–Islamic *turath* – to be based on a network analysis of concepts and keywords – al-Jabiri prescribes a search for the ideological function of works belonging to the cultural heritage via a joint consideration of their actual discourse and the historical conditions which allowed their production. The method of analysis he suggests ends up in a double operation: a step consisting in taking distance from the text examined (*infisal*), after which the interpreter-authenticator proceeds to reappropriate its meaning by establishing a line of continuity with it (*ittisal*), while paying particular attention to the critical-rational potentialities of the work object of analysis (al-Jabiri, 1991, p. 33). Criticism is the method and the goal of coping with *turath*. The methodological hub of this critical attitude is the principle of authenticity (*asala*), which is a sort of functional quintessence of modernity as the qualitative search for the new (*hadatha*).

What distinguished al-Jabiri from most other speakers at the Cairo conference is that in his argumentation there is no trace of an apologetic attitude towards *asala* as a method and *turath* as the object of analysis. On the other hand, the crucial enterprise of disentangling the relationship between *al-asala wa-l-mu'asara*, between authenticity and "globalized" modernity, cannot be performed – he maintains – through class analysis alone: this would lead to a banalized partition of Arab societies into "modern" and "traditional" camps. Al-Jabiri clearly asserts that the question is of a genuinely cultural-intellectual nature (al-Jabiri, 1985, p. 45). The crux of the problem is that a deep abyss separates the intellectual task of reactualizing *turath* on the one hand, and the globalized modernity as defined by the "challenge of the modern-contemporary age" (*tahaddiyyat al-'asr*) on the other. Al-Jabiri maintains that the formula *al-turath wa tahaddiyyat al-'asr*, which is also the title of the 1984 conference, would lose its suggestive significance if translated into another language. This juxtaposition is highly significant in that it reflects the intellectual abyss within which Arab intellectuals have to construct a framework of communal reference (p. 47), squeezed as they are between the recognition of being part of a potentially modernity-engendering cultural tradition (i.e. compatible with the abstractly universal scope of modernity) and the historical road of universalization of the particular, "winning" model of modernity irradiating from the West, that is perceived as a "challenge" (p. 49).

How can one define the relationship between the original character of the Arab–Islamic heritage, and the allegedly universal requirements of political-intellectual modernity? Al-Jabiri sketches one concrete path, which consists in rewriting history as a way to reconstruct rationally, without the pressure of immediate political conflicts, the relationship between the unfolding of consciousness in the past and in the present – thereby with a sense for historical concatenations and selectivity – in order to be prepared to shape the future. Such a task should be fulfilled by taking full account of the crux represented by the relationship between the original heritage-oriented trail and the Western-centred unfolding of universal modern thought, but the analysis should always adopt an Arab–Islamic perspective (al-Jabiri, 1985, pp. 50 and 58). This method would also allow for a critical confrontation with the "exemplary", Western version of modernity, which claims universal validity (p. 55). This is the point where the explicit self-critique of the Arab intellectual in the style of Abdallah Laroui ([1973] 1974) and the largely implicit critique of Orientalism are moulded together to indicate a path deemed capable of grounding the Arab–Islamic discourse of modernity on original foundations. The critique of the Self and his "reason" (*'aql*) should be built on the critique of the Other as known and experienced by the Self (al-Jabiri, 1991, p. 11).

This is also the point where the search for such foundations is emancipated from the perspective, however fictitious, of having to seek inspiration in already given "fundaments" (*usul*), and is instead grounded anew on the application of the principle of authenticity (*asala*)[4] as the tool for creatively shaping one's own *turath*, for historically authenticating one's own past as an original way of access to modernity. Put slightly differently, the actual task of the Arab intellectual is to invent a new foundation of the fundaments, *i'ada ta'sil al-usul* (al-Jabiri, 1992, p. 50). This should be the basis of a collective intellectual venture, inaugurating a new "age of recording" comparable to the formative era of Islamic civilization, and therefore capable of formulating adequate cultural solutions to the demands of actual social developments (al-Jabiri, 1991, pp. 10–12).

In spite of sketching a voluntaristic programme and the scenario of a new age of intellectual endeavour, al-Jabiri's main contribution to a successful resuming of the construction of an Arab–Islamic framework of reference is limited to a basically deconstructionist clarification. The position of the Cairene thinker Hasan Hanafi is particularly interesting for proposing a more encompassing attempt to sketch a socially constructive path of authentication of *turath*, while seeking inspiration in a dynamic, "developmental" hermeneutic perspective comparable to that of al-Jabiri.[5] A conscious investment of the hermeneutics of the Arab–Islamic *turath* in a new type of public discourse is provided by a few Egyptian authors engaged in transcending the polarization between solutionism and neutralism. However, most of their efforts reach a level of theoretical elaboration which is insufficient to cope with all implications of the problematic tackled by an author like al-Jabiri, and are more immediately concerned with recycling the older, more generic attitude of affirming a "cultural Islamism" (as propagated by Anwar Abdel-Malek). We can cite several authors representing this tendency in post-crisis Egypt (such as the "leftist neo-Islamists" Jalal Amin, Tariq al-Bishri and 'Adil Husayn: Ayubi, 1991, p. 213), but prevalent in them is the impulse of "going Islamic" that pays tribute to the shift in the symbolic focus within the public arena.

The goal of overcoming the temptation rapidly to "close the circle" through an overly narrow and pragmatic circularity, and engaging, instead, in a reproblematization of the intellectual potentials of an Arab–Islamic framework of reference in the post-crisis era, has been at the core of Hasan Hanafi's efforts since the late 1970s. He distinguishes himself in both his purpose of sketching a civilizational project stretching beyond the contingencies of the struggles on the political stage, and in consciously trying to address the transcultural space as a whole (in this sense really operating in the wake of Abdel-Malek), thereby giving the fifth circle the desired "more-than-native" dimension without which it is impossible to cope seriously with the challenge of commensurableness with Western-centred modernity.

The "search for a fifth circle", as a public-intellectual enterprise, is at least partly dependent on the publicity it gets through the attention of authors based in the West, in particular those orbiting around the fourth circle. Hanafi, as a particular case of the "intercultural competence" characterizing several Arab intellectuals, tries to use this skill to give the fifth circle the necessary transcultural notoriety. While in general interculturally competent Arab authors are not able or willing to join any definite circle because they are too suspended between both sides of the transcultural space (as in the case of Abdallah Laroui) or are engaged in the difficult task of constructing a new interpretive model that radically questions the epistemological fundaments of virtually all of the indigenous field of intellectual production (this is the case of Mohammed Arkoun: see Chapter 12), Hanafi consciously attempts to argue with transcultural efficacy, while maintaining (or hoping to maintain) some degree of rootedness within the Egyptian and Arab-Islamic public arena.

It is indeed symptomatic that Hanafi differently from al-Jabiri, who only publishes in Arabic – wrote during the 1980s two monumental, largely redundant works in Arabic and a series of much more concise essays in Western languages, that mostly constitute abridged versions of his larger publications. The first major work, *al-din wa-l-thawra fi-misr* ("Religion and Revolution in Egypt, 1952–1981"), in eight volumes, aims at reconstructing the continuity in the function of Islam in Egyptian political contests from the "Free Officers' revolution" of 1952 to the assassination of Sadat in 1981. The second, more markedly theoretical work, consisting of five volumes, is entitled *min al-'aqida ila l-thawra* ("From doctrine to revolution") and is intended as the first section of an even larger project on *al-turath wa l-tajdid*. *mawqifuna min al-turath al-qadim* ("Heritage and renewal: our attitude towards the ancient heritage"): for a synopsis of the whole project see Hanafi, 1991, p. 10), whose general introduction has been published in a separate book (Hanafi, 1980), where *turath* is approached as inherently transcending itself, through the work of the authorized interpreter, for the sake of renewal.

In spite of the greater complexity of these larger projects, it seems that the essays published in Western languages provide the major terrain of proof of Hanafi's ability to consolidate a new argumentative model or circle, since freeing the making of an Arab–Islamic framework from the hegemonic pretensions of the Western culture at large is a crucial intermediate goal that he deems dependent on a skilled strategy of intervention in the Western side of the transcultural space. For these reasons, and unlike all other authors examined here, there will be no central text of reference in the case of Hanafi. The reconstruction of his argumentative model will be based on a targeted mix of elements drawn from his writings in both Western languages and in Arabic. Among these, I will mainly refer to two contributions published by Hanafi in a delicate phase of the formation of the interpretive field of "political Islam", between the end of the 1970s and the beginning of the 1980s.

Both such works were addressed to a broader public than usual for the writings of Hanafi. They are the Introduction to Khomeini's major ideological work (Hanafi, 1979), whose publication in Arabic the Cairene philosopher was more rapid to sponsor than any seventh circle's solutionist, and the essay presenting his "Islamic left" (Hanafi, 1981), which was and still is the name he has given to his own intellectual enterprise. It is evident that in Hanafi's case my criteria for selecting texts have been almost the opposite of those applied to all other authors examined, where I felt obliged to choose contributions less charged by the need for immediate publicity. The reason for this discrepancy is that, differently from the other cases, Hanafi's own model is new and consequently suffers from a lack of notoriety, so that the open search for public resonance is particularly valuable in order not to confine the analysis to a sterile, uninfluential scholarly domain. The preferred focus on material tailored to broader aims of public communication (this is also the case with virtually all contributions in Western languages, whose intended targets are Western intellectuals) is however balanced by selective references to some crucial passages of his main theoretical works.

Hanafi's scholarly competence embraces both the discursive formation of *'ilm*, in particular the spheres of *usul al-din* and *usul al-fiqh* (what we could call non-speculative theology and legal theory) and philosophy in its Western (especially German) shape, and more in particular in its phenomenological branch. We will see how on the basis of a largely original cocktail between these two different scholarly traditions he attempts to mould the fifth circle in the form of a sort of "neo-*fiqh*" that is able to speak a transculturally compatible modern-intellectual language, and to transcend the polarization between conflationism and deconflationism. Hanafi's enterprise is in this sense much more directly tied to the two different, but complementary, innovative interventions by 'Abd al-Raziq and Qutb (see Chapter 10), than to the two consolidated local circles, the seventh and the sixth, to the extent that he has spontaneously, and seldom explicitly, to rely on any anchorage, however idiosyncratic (as both 'Abd al-Raziq and Qutb are), which facilitates an emancipation from a too strictly conceived *fiqh*.

The enterprise of "closing a circle" on the basis of such an innovative perspective is arduous enough, and a cursory look at Hanafi's writings would give the impression that his argumentative paths are multiple, or even inconsistent on a number of points, especially in specifying what a socially viable "true Islam" should consist of. In my opinion there is a lowest common denominator in Hanafi's positions that is coherent enough and has the merit of unfolding according to a rationale that is crucial to any effort to close the fifth circle: it consists of conceiving the necessary revitalization of *turath* as being consciously guided by the principle of taking up the rational and revolutionary aspects of all traditional Islamic sciences (Hanafi, 1981).

However, his own path of rational authentication of the cultural heritage is not preliminarily theorized as a methodological attitude essential to reconstruct an Arab–Islamic framework of reference, as in the case of al-Jabiri, but results quite directly from considering the factuality of revelation, as recorded in the Koran, and the factuality of the actual social situation in Arab–Islamic societies, as experienced by individuals today. Hanafi dares to see a single process at the confluence of both, as he states that "the basis of revelation is the social reality" (Hanafi, 1982, p. 94). This is the platform for constructing a phenomenological theory of man (as Muslim) in history, with respect to which authentication is not a methodological a priori, but rather the result of the reciprocal fertilization and the final identification between being a Muslim and being a socially concerned citizen. This procedure is transculturally legitimized by a consideration of Western-centred modernity that tries to go beyond a generically "critical" attitude and bears, instead, upon the consciousness of an epistemic break – a "crisis" – in it. This is elaborated by Hanafi in discursively more cogent terms than by al-Jabiri.

This position is attained through a critical consideration of the work of Sayyid Qutb, whose basically unorthodox thought had a considerable impact on the formation of Hanafi's original synthesis (see Schulze, 1992b, pp. 75–6). After paying tribute to Qutb as a martyr, he praises his free, not Islamist-bound, intellectual endeavour performed during the 1930s, the 1940s and the early 1950s, during what Hanafi classifies as the longer "literary" (1930-50) and the shorter "social" phases (1951–3) in Qutb's thought, which preceded his final metaphysical involution (Hanafi, 1988–1989, v, pp. 167–91). Hanafi is eager to highlight how the origin of Qutb's intellectual venture was not in a hermeneutics of the text but in the emphasis on the subject's own creativity (p. 192). Through this path Qutb attained the reformulation of the theological notion of *tawhid* (God's "unity") as a principle of social revolution, an idea that has become central, as we will see, in Hanafi's own framing model (p. 196).

Hanafi is very outspoken, however, in denouncing the progressive degeneration of Qutb's work into a "prison's psychopathology" during the mid-1950s (Hanafi, 1982, p. 60). The concept of *hakimiyya* (God's "sovereignty"), central to Qutb's production during this phase, is rejected as the outcome of a mere overreaction to secular currents (p. 85), a notion devoid of any significance from the point of view of the necessary reformation of the Islamic community (Hanafi, 1979, pp. 28–9). "The question is: Sovereignty of God for whom? For the rich or for the poor? For the oppressor or for the oppressed?" (Hanafi, 1982, p. 73).

The theoretical goal of Hanafi is to construct a sort of neo-*fiqh* capable of grounding interpretive authority on both the historical factuality of Islam and on the need to cope with the demands of the actual social situation. Before beginning to work on building an integrated theoretical framework on the basis of the project on "heritage and renewal", he was ready, after the Iranian revolution, to appropriate the Khomeinian norm of the authority of the *faqih*. Hanafi attempted to speak as a *faqih* interested in applying *ijtihad* ("free reasoning") to the organization of social life in all its aspects. In Hanafi's own reading of the main ideological writing of Khomeini, illustrated in the introduction to the Arabic translation of the work (Hanafi, 1979), he attempts, however, to turn Khomeini's theory "on its head", in the sense that he claims that change in government and in the structure of domination cannot be theorized independently of an analysis of social change. This is an occasion for Hanafi to criticize a long tradition, spanning from al-Afghani to Qutb, of invoking an Islamic revolution, or something equivalent, to mask a mere takeover of power (p. 27).

Along similar lines, in the course of the 1980s Hanafi has been very outspoken in his critique of mainstream Islamism as solutionism, that he does not hesitate to accuse of lack of sense of history, and, as a consequence of this deficit, of ignoring the real spirit of *shari'a* (Hanafi, 1990, p. 36). Hanafi's own definition of this concept is certainly indebted to Qutb's monistic vision. The Cairene philosopher tries to specify his view through an elaborate argumentation which is even more dependent on the concept of *tawhid*. This is seen as the engine of a revolutionary endeavour, since it does not exhaust itself in the dogma of the unity of God, but epitomizes the striving of each Muslim towards unification with Him by virtue of the symbolic strength of the *shahada*, the Islamic profession of faith. This cannot stiffen, as Hanafi maintains, into socially irrelevant mystical exercises, but must provide the initial impulse for the construction of a perfect community of believers-citizens.

It almost seems that Hanafi establishes *shari'a* as the systemic force stemming from this hermeneutic and practical process rooted in the consciousness of every Muslim. He seems to go a full step further than Qutb as he states that the meaning of the end of Prophecy with Muhammad was to set man free to move consciously and autonomously in history, towards progress. This consists first and foremost, according to the concrete definition of the goals of the "Islamic left", in social justice, as rooted in the Koran (Hanafi, 1981). Moreover, Hanafi's understanding of *shari'a* contributes to the view that each Muslim is a potential *faqih*. This assessment opens up a clear conflict with the vision supported by the Islamists-solutionists, which Hanafi is eager to attack, by highlighting how their call for the implementation of *shari'a* is devoid of a socially viable theory of the relationship between the individual Muslim and *shari'a* itself, and therefore degenerates into a claim for restoring traditional authority to the clerics.

It is not hard to see that this reformulation of *shari'a* is the theoretical platform for a coherent "fundamentalist" view, as it helps to theorize the right of every *faqih* – hence, at least potentially, of every Muslim – to a direct, unmediated access to the fundaments of truth. It comes as no surprise that the Arab equivalent of "fundamentalism" (*usuliyya*) is reappropriated by Hanafi and employed as an analytically useful term for designating Islam's new movement of the last two decades, that labels like *sahwa* or "resurgence" are unsuitable to account for. This is possible by reference to the term *usul*, "fundaments", a well-known keyword of Islamic sciences, in particular with regard to the *'ilm al-usul* that constitutes the sciences of *usul al-din* and of *usul al-fiqh*.

In this sense, it matters little if the word "fundamentalism" (see Chapters 3 and 8) was first introduced in the West, and that the Western use is largely mistaken in its implicit assumption of an opposition between fundamentalism and modernity. Hanafi briefly analyses these two terms and finds that they come very close to each other, if we accept that modernity is basically a selective search for fundaments, the authentication of a tradition (cf. this view with the one of Zubaida and the fourth circle: see Chapter 9). Due to the traditional rooting of a science of fundaments in Islam, as embodying the impulse to search methodically for a solid hermeneutic footing (cf. Hallaq, 1993, p. 589), it is possible to say, concludes Hanafi, that Islamic fundamentalism is a suitable definition for the modern phase in the unfolding of Islamic civilization, consisting in a selective reconstruction of the cultural heritage that is preserved in the consciousness of the masses (Hanafi, 1990, p. 34).

Hanafi's integration of al-Jabiri's criticism is in his firm leaning on phenomenological premises, when stating that the criteria of selectivity are given by the subject (Hanafi, 1992, p. 91). What qualifies *turath* is neither the attribute Arab nor Islamic, but simply its being *turathuna*, "our" heritage, where the "we" becomes an autonomous, self-qualified, marker of the legitimacy of the authentication performed by the knowing subject.[6] In Hanafi's main theoretical work to date (Hanafi, 1988), he invests his view of *turath* in working out a revolutionary dimension out of the Islamic doctrine, as incorporated in the central *'ilm* of *usul al-din*. The philosophical foundation of this enterprise, that still makes a prevalent use of terms of discourse of Islamic sciences, is a phenomenological anchoring of the knowing and acting subject in the "lifeworld", which Hanafi deems essential to transcend the dualism between theory and praxis (cf. Campanini, 1990, pp. 245–6).

Hanafi is firm in claiming that no determination of the criteria of truthfulness is possible outside of the mind (*'aql*) of the knowing subject (Hanafi, 1988, I, p. 8). In its path to truth, however, the individual consciousness has to be activated by virtue of mass mobilization, whose end is revolution. The indispensable engine of this process is the intellectual vanguard, which shapes a collective consciousness through impinging upon individual consciences (p. 9). The validity of knowledge as well as its comprehensiveness are thereby rooted in the intellectual's own life experience and cannot be separated from it (p. 48).

One can interpret this statement as a rejection of any form of reification of knowledge (Campanini, 1990, p. 246). With regard to the task of rationally authenticating *turath*, the term *usuliyya* becomes a crucial keyword in opposing the neo-*faqih* acting on behalf of the Muslim, i.e. the believer-citizen, to the reified and dualized horizon of knowledge of most of the practitioners of traditional Islamic sciences. The *faqih* is here conceived as the interpreter of the living *turath* who is empowered to intervene on social reality for the sake of the central norm of justice. The divergence with the *salafiyya*'s apologetic, non-analytic attitude towards *turath*, largely reflected in the writings of al-Qaradawi, is here dramatic. From Hanafi's point of view, the *sahwa* Islamists are no fundamentalists but simply backward-looking conservatives whose view depends on the myth of a golden age, which only produces theoretical aberrations in the form of dualisms, like the one (here Qutb is implicitly called into question) between *islam* and *jahiliyya* (Hanafi, 1988, V, p. 393).

Hanafi's extensive and innovative interpretation of the concept of *tawhid* as the theoretical pivot of the science of *usul al-din* represents the crucial passage in his monistic-revolutionary hermeneutics. After specifying that *tawhid* is not a simple concept or quality or attribute, he makes explicit its being first and foremost a "process" (*'amaliyya*), the process of unification, the principle itself of social cohesion, in its horizontal dimension: a principle, moreover, which, if rightly interpreted, makes obsolete any dualism between theory and praxis, between knowledge and social implementation. Against the dualism that still hampers contemporary Islamism, he states that *tawhid* is not merely "vision", *tasawwur*, but also "system", *nizam* (Hanafi, 1988, II, pp. 324–5). While in al-Jabiri the tension between the traditional hermeneutics of the text and the methodological potential of modernity (*hadatha*) as rooted in the knowing subject is never completely overcome, Hanafi attempts to outline a path for deriving the latter from the former. Moreover, he conceives this venture as no mere intellectual task, but as one cognitively rooted in social praxis. Any intellectual attempt to represent the interests of the masses and thereby to suppress the dualism between theory and praxis is necessarily sustained by a high degree of unrealistic optimism, and the position of the Cairene philosopher certainly reflects this attitude in an almost prototypical form. It is nonetheless evident that Hanafi's tentative monistic theory is much more coherent than al-Jabiri's position, if evaluated in terms of the aspiration entailed by any discursive model grounded on an impulse of "intellectual distinction" (see Chapter 2).

The theory of the *imama* ("Imamate") as the Islamic embodiment of the authority principle represents the culmination of Hanafi's new foundation of *usul al-din*. He consciously stresses how this dealing with the question of authority cannot be the object of a separate science of the political domain, but is the ultimate result and goal of a science of the fundaments grounded on *tawhid*, and therefore represents a truly fundamentalist achievement (Hanafi, 1988, v, pp. 163–4). Hanafi proceeds from here through a specification that is common to the "extremist" version of solutionist Islamism, and according to which if the *imam* does not observe the fundamental Islamic injunction of "commanding good and prohibiting evil" in his leadership over the *umma*, every Muslim is entitled to refuse obedience to him (p. 313; also quoted in Campanini, 1990, pp. 247–8). In this way Hanafi's theory of the Imamate almost takes the form of a negative theory of power on the one hand, and of a positive theory of the transformation of the existing configuration of power, hence of *thawra* ("revolution"), on the other. Hanafi's argumentation finally leads to a theory of the democratic limitations of power and of the right to rebel against his possessor (see also Hanafi, 1984, p. 52). Combined with his specification of the *tawhid* principle (see above), this constitutes a theory of social revolution in Islamic terms whose aim cannot merely be – as for the seventh circle – the formation of an Islamic state, but rather the accomplishment of Islam in history through the realization of social justice (pp. 52–3).

The most interesting aspect of Hanafi's theorizing is the extent to which this delimitation of the legitimacy of political authority through a theory of social revolution is dependent on a hermeneutics of the subject (Schulze, 1992b, pp. 75 and 80) constructed through a qualitative enhancing, and not a rejection, of the traditional Islamic hermeneutics of the text. Hanafi tries to reactualize those rational elements of the Islamic *turath* that were already grounded – as he maintains – on this type of hermeneutics (Hanafi, 1982, p. 58), beyond the surface of textual boundedness. The explicitation of *turath*'s selectivity (close to the application of authenticity as a criterion) that results from this actualization provides the basis for a reassessment of interpretive competences: the methodological fault of the hermeneutics of the text in its static nature is recognized in the breaking up of its object, which manifests the incapacity of the interpreting subject to read through it in order to attain a selection of topics or dimensions that conform to the needs of the social actor and his epoch (Hanafi, 1992, p. 95).

The ultimate goal is to redress the hermeneutic relationship between the subject and the text, whilst relying on the awareness that there are inescapable conditions, based on the "recognition" of reality, for shaping a socially creative discourse (Hanafi, 1992, p. 104). In this way Hanafi attempts to provide a solution to the dilemma of the "hegemony of the text" that has so often induced al-Jabiri to fall into the theorization of an Arab mind. Hanafi attains this result through merging his theoretical affiliation to phenomenology in philosophy with his political-intellectual identity as a revolutionary *faqih*.

This approach leads Hanafi to give a fully transcultural value to his hermeneutics of authenticity: an authentic source (or fundament = *asl*) can be also detected through Western history, sometimes seen as inherited from Islam, sometimes, in a less apologetic mood, referred to the cross-fertilizing dimension of the transcultural exchange (otherwise dominated by the game of opposing essentialisms). He fully recognizes the constraints acting upon the Arab intellectual as through "a discourse between the Self and the Other", up to the point where he admits that the selectivity in authenticating *turath* can or must also apply to the heritage of the Other (Hanafi, 1992, p. 99). On this and other points, Hanafi's discourse is more daring, albeit methodologically less sophisticated, than al-Jabiri's. The Western heritage is a powerful influence which has not to be rejected, but cognitively domesticated. In order to complement his study of the Arab–Islamic *turath* with an investigation of the Western cultural heritage, Hanafi has initiated a project whose purpose is to counter Orientalism, as indicted by Said, through a new Islamic social science called *istighrab*, "Occidentalism", targeted at the study of Western civilization from an Islamic point of view, and thereby obtaining the same domesticating effect engendered by Orientalism in its dealing with the Islamic world (Hanafi, 1991).

This might appear, and indeed be, a too bluntly provocative undertaking without serious social-scientific or historical foundations, yet Hanafi has proved not naive, but consciously daring, in his dealing with transcultural problematics affecting the relationship between the "West" and "Islam". An important corollary of Hanafi's shift of interpretive perspective is that the dimension of crisis – consisting of the impossibility of being satisfied by a consolidated paradigm made up by correlated truths in a series which culminates in the construction of a framework of communal reference – is according to him primarily located in the universal modern mind, and not in an inescapable syndrome of the "Arab mind". Based on this conscious elaboration of the epistemic break, which includes a recognition of the transcultural "short-circuit" that engenders the image of an "Islam in movement", and in the related concept of "political Islam", Hanafi agrees to situate his own claims within the visionary landscape that grounds the hermeneutic field of political Islam. He has been the first author to use the formula *al-islam al-siyasi* in Arabic, and to justify the use of the term *usuliyya*, the equivalent of "fundamentalism", with reference to contemporary Islam. His strategy is to turn such operations to the advantage of the option he pursues, in the sense of making his own argumentative model palatable to both Western scholars and formerly "secularly committed" Arab thinkers. His enterprise of launching an "Orientalism in reverse" is probably an excellent example of both the historical urgency and the hermeneutic limitations of the challenge that the fifth circle has posed to the whole interpretive field of political Islam, as well as of the consequent, ambitious but arduous project of constructing a political discourse of modernity in Islamic terms.

NOTES

1   It is highly symptomatic that two authors like Tayyib Tizini and Husayn Muruwwa, who as Marxists belong to a category of Arab intellectuals which considered itself the vanguard of the efforts to liberate Arab thought from its dependence on obsolete models, have been the most rapid in providing ambitious, systematic and historically grounded conceptualizations of the cultural "heritage". With Muruwwa in particular we come close to a combined dealing with *turath* and *asala* that makes the first the tool for defining a sort of "objective" set of inherited sociocultural conditions, and the second the instrument for interpreting these conditions creatively and selectively, in order to reshape the heritage itself (Boullata, 1990 pp. 31–6).

2   This is also the title of a famous book written by the Islamic reformer and political agitator Shakib Arslan (1930), but al-Jabiri maintains that this is precisely the question that had haunted the Arab *nahda* since its inception.

3   Scholars of Arab origin working in the West have decisively contributed to consolidate transculturally, during the era of hegemony of modernization theory, the ambiguities of the "reactivist" construction of *nahda*. "The theme of Western-inspired renaissance, central to the work of Albert Hourani . . . and Hisham Sharabi, was so entrenched until recently as to go virtually unexamined." (Tucker, 1990, p. 211.) We have to recognize that the idea of *nahda* is present even when not overtly used. Hourani does not employ it in his famous work *Arabic Thought in the Liberal Age* (Hourani, [1962] 1983), but it is symptomatic that its Arabic translation (*al-fikr al-ʿarabi fi-ʿasr al-nahda*) renders "liberal age" through *nahda*.

4   *usul* (singular *asl*) and *asala* are drawn from the same root.

5   It is worth mentioning that an intermediate step between deconstruction and reconstruction is provided by the ambitious theorizing of the Syrian Marxist Tayyib Tizini, mediated by what he calls "historical heritagial dialectics" (*al-jadaliyya al-tarikhiyya al-turathiyya*), based on the principle of "heritagial selectivity", and aiming at engendering a "heritagial revolution" (see Boullata, 1990, pp. 32–4 and von Kügelgen, 1994, pp. 241–50). Tizini has certainly been one major influence on both Hanafi and al-Jabiri. The particular interest of the framing models of the two thinkers here examined lies, however, in their ability to depart substantially from a Marxist perspective and take seriously into account the Islamist challenge, whilst remaining faithful to values of social justice. An attempt to find common terrain between the distance-taking attitude of al-Jabiri and the "creationist" approach of Hanafi is in their *hiwar* ("dialogue") on issues of foremost importance for the definition of an Arab–Islamic framework of reference, carried out from the columns of the weekly *al-yawm al-sabiʿ* (Paris) in 1989 (collected and reprinted in Hanafi and al-Jabiri, 1990). As a search for a hermeneutic key capable of making the two perspectives complementary, this dialogue deserves a separate study.

6   My talk with Hanafi, 1 October 1992.

CONCLUSION

Thinking Islam

We have seen how within the hermeneutic field of "political Islam" there is a permanent, self-reproducing tension between an impulse towards an open problem-raising and its closure in the form of a rapid interpretive problem-solving finalized to prevail in the contention. In this sense, the emergence and functioning of the interpretive field is not only a power game resulting in discursive rigidities, but also acts as a catalyst for new patterns of problematization. The emergence of the field through the staging of the transcultural crisis in late 1973 contained the seeds of the process through which the discursive limitations immanent in the dynamics of the field itself could be transcended. Its rise, and the underlying metamorphosis of the transcultural space, signified more than a mere amplification – within a horizon of pervasive communication dominated by new, powerful mass media – of inherited Orientalist models for cognitively domesticating Islam (see Chapter 8).

At the origin of the transcultural transformation there was the gradual crisis of "Weberism" (see Chapter 6), through which the Western model of essentialization (which was "strong" because based on a "sharp", grandiose intellectual distinction and was discursively powerful by virtue of the political pre-eminence of the West: see Chapters 2 and 3) was weakened. At the same time the Arab–Islamic model of essentialization (which was "weak" since grounded on a "smooth", less spectacular intellectual distinction, and suffered additionally from a feebler position within the transcultural game of opposing essentialisms) was strengthened. I also looked at the impact of some thinkers of Arab origin – like Abdel-Malek, Hourani and Said – on the critique of Weberism. In this sense, the metamorphosis of the transcultural space was also catalyzed by the repositioning of several Arab authors as the result of a gradual brain drain to the West. And it is well-known that this process was the consequence of the historical imbalance in terms of "power-knowledge" within the transcultural space, since valid knowledge about Islam could be legitimized only by a varying degree of association with the Western academic establishment.[1]

The metamorphosis of the transcultural space did not merely result in the mass-media theorem which laid, with the support of Bernard Lewis's warning of *The Return of Islam*, the foundations of the image of an Islam in movement, but swiftly permitted the making of a counter-theorem (see Chapter 8). This self-proclaimed "critical" undertaking was in itself no challenge to the stability of the hermeneutic field, as shown by the fourth circle (see Chapter 9), which to some extent translated the Saidian counter-theorem into the terms which are specific to the vision of political Islam. However, this critical attitude has been appropriated by a "local" circle, the fifth one (see Chapter 12), in its impulse to reformulate the suppressed problematic embodied by the concept of political Islam according to the rationale of articulating a political discourse of modernity in original "Arab–Islamic" terms.

The main limit of the allegedly critical, anti-essentialist attitude was that, in as far as it succeeded in formulating a clear goal, it tended to deny that there is a problem behind the image of "political Islam", and to assert that any hermeneutics of Islam has no autonomy of its own and merely depends on socio-political variables. This claim inhibits questions on the extent to which "Islam" is constituted, and acquires a high degree of autonomy as a framework of communal reference, through a political discourse of modernity grounded on the politics of "intellectual distinction" (see Chapter 2).

The emancipation from the fallacy of political Islam is not purely a matter of goodwill. There are some specific loci of intellectual endeavour, some particular junctures or gulfs within the transcultural space – both at the heart of the interpretive field of political Islam and at its margins – which favour this process. The hermeneutics of authenticity of the fifth circle adds to this process, by transcending the transcultural game of interpreting "Islam in movement" through engaging a basically intracultural game – inevitably constrained by transcultural standards, but not succumbing to them – which entails "moving Islam through defining it", in the form of both a reified framework of universal reference and a pathway to the reshaping of subjectivity in history.

As a result, the fifth circle shows an impetus to overcome both patterns of polarization between conflationism and deconflationism – the one between the third and the fourth, and the other between the seventh and the sixth circles – which are equally unsuitable to tackle the crucial question of the commensurableness between global, Western-centred modernity, and the "local", Arab–Islamic one. This impulse is inevitably accompanied by a hybrid methodological attitude, which cannot be reduced either to the "externalist" perspective of Western-based authors (see Chapter 9) or to the "internalist" viewpoint which governs the dispute between "solutionists" and "neutralists" in the Middle East (see Chapter 4). The path of problematization common to some Arab authors, or to parts of their work (in what I have pictured as the fifth circle's effort to escape the attraction of the hermeneutic field of political Islam while capitalizing on the difference it has made in the evolution of the transcultural space) seems to discount a closed, sometimes desperate, self-referential character. The discourse of these *turathiyyun* ("heritage advocates") in general, and of Hasan Hanafi in particular (see Chapter 12), has been the object of uncompromising criticism (see Tarabishi, 1991, pp. 150–64), because it appears to degenerate into a merely autobiographical game. This critique ignores that in order to ease the rigidities of consolidated hermeneutic circles and fields (see Chapter 2), new research trails are needed where the personal investment of the author is the highest and most transparent, i.e. consciously used to prompt the questioning of schematizations which otherwise are taken for granted (cf. Szakolczai, 1993b). In this sense, the autobiographical approach of the *turathiyyun* is no retreat, but the only possible road to dissolving the dominant discursive encrustations within the transcultural environment.

This intellectual endeavour is, however, insufficient to neutralize the negative effects of the hermeneutic syndrome of political Islam on the efforts at defining a viable Arab–Islamic framework of reference as a fully-fledged medium for political-intellectual modernity. We have seen how the transcultural space between the "West" and "Islam" constitutes itself primarily through the Western impulse to define an original and prototypical model of modernity, and how this process poses an acute hindrance to the Other's definition of its own modernity. I have attempted to show how the Weberian heritage – which produced a social-scientificization of essentialism (see Chapter 6), and was distorted and trivialized until very recently in the guise of Weberism – has been largely responsible for setting the basic features of the interdiscursive game within the transcultural space. Weber's reconstruction of the distinctiveness of Western rationality, compared with other such patterns, helped to prompt the question: can the evolution of non-Western models of rationality (in our case the "Arab–Islamic" one) be reconstructed, within a comparative framework, by redirecting the inevitable essentialist constraint? This reformulation should contribute to make essentialism no longer dependent on the need to consolidate the Western distinction, but to lighten the burden of the uncontested centrality of the West in global modernity, which inhibits a formulation of "regional" paths of intellectual distinction based on "inherited" models of rationality. In other words: is the heuristic Eurocentrism acknowledged by Weber worthy of being "regionalized" by contemporary Western scholars in order to adapt their work to the spirit of the time, which demands an engagement with "multiculturalism" and a compliance with its ever-present hermeneutic constraints?

This task would imply going beyond a mere critique of Weberism, and rediscovering and fertilizing the potentialities of a neo-Weberian path of investigation that recognizes, as Weber could not, that there may be more than one way to uncover patterns of rationalization and universalization. The fourth circle has unfortunately posed an end to the critique of Weberism by seeking an ecumenical refuge in the globalizing dimension of modernity as the only matrix of universal value in the contemporary world (see Chapter 9). Commenting rather incidentally on Weber's Foreword to RS, Zubaida insists on the possibility of a non-essentialist path of historical analysis, however likely that might slip into essentialist procedures, a case that he sees epitomized precisely in the famous introductory essay by the German sociologist (Zubaida, 1989c, pp. 129–30). By so doing, Zubaida neither falls into a wholesale simplification of Weber's approach, as did Rodinson, nor forces the interpretation of Weber's method towards establishing the primacy of structural-institutional factors, as in the case of Turner (see Chapter 8), but tries to maintain a truly Weberian equilibrium.

Although very conscious – as probably no student of Islam before him – of the potential value of the Weberian heritage in paying attention to questions of life conduct, Zubaida still seems much more preoccupied with Weberist degenerations. The consequence is that he neglects Weber's quasi-self-denunciation of essentialism at the beginning of the Foreword to RS, and indulges in sketching, rather obscurely, what a non-essentialist method should look like (p. 130), thereby reiterating the illusory alternative advanced in the mid-1970s by the *Review of Middle East Studies*, and elegantly avoided by Said (see Chapter 8). Zubaida's perspective, and indeed the whole discussion conducted on essentialism, suffers from a mono-dimensional concept of this cognitive phenomenon: it looks for essentialism only in its apparent unfolding, but not in the historically cultural-specific genesis of the method of knowledge applied by students of Islam or the "Middle East" (see Chapter 6).

This simplification goes along with a marked unwillingness to recognize the value of "regionalized" truth-claims, a deficit revealed by the way that Zubaida, as a representative of the fourth circle (see Chapter 8), addresses the area of the fifth circle by reviewing some essays written by 'Adil Husayn (see Chapter 12).[2] Zubaida specifies at the outset that he intends "to argue with a colleague" (Zubaida, 1988, p. 14), thereby implying that he shares with him a claim to serious knowledge, and also making clear that he does not intend to assume the position of the (neo)-Orientalist who possesses the exclusive competence to interpret Islam and related phenomena. Following the argumentative line of Zubaida's own commentary on Husayn would require a more detailed presentation of the latter author, and this would be of no use for our purposes. It is nonetheless interesting here to summarize the review's conclusion, in which Zubaida maintains that the Egyptian thinker fails to shape a discourse as coherent as that of pure Islamists (roughly corresponding to our seventh circle: see Chapter 11). This is plausible, if we consider the peculiar character of the fifth circle, i.e. its low degree of determination. This evaluation has nonetheless far-reaching implications, in so far as Zubaida appears to claim that, beyond the limits of the Western-based, social-scientifically grounded location of the fourth circle, which he represents and considers the only alternative to the neo-Orientalism of the third circle (see Chapter 9), there is no other enlightened and scientifically viable chance for an Arab intellectual to transcend the polarization between "solutionism" and "neutralism". In the best case, Zubaida argues, authors grouped around the fifth circle can "islamize" themes produced within the Western philosophical and social-scientific tradition. "This exercise may serve political or rhetorical functions, but does not bear close analytical scrutiny" (pp. 27–8).

All that the fourth circle is able to offer to "locally-based" Arab intellectuals, against the neo-Orientalist third circle, is an inclusivist concept of modernity, reshaped in the context of the homogenizing wave of "globalization": a concept unsuitable for re-examining the minimal regional conditions for autonomously grounding a universalizing intellectual path based on the authentication of endangered (or even broken) traditions, and finalized to define a viable, original framework of communal reference. It greatly matters in the evaluation of all crossculturally relevant phenomena if we adopt a concept that presupposes the singularity of universalization, or one more likely to allow heuristically the consideration of the modernising potentialities of non-Western intellectual traditions.

The work of the revisionist historians (see Chapter 3), who include locally-based Arab authors, is still hampered, to a large extent, by the absence of a clear formulation of an underlying concept of modernity. An attentive scrutiny of the theoretical profile of such works – which are not directly involved in the interpretive field of political Islam – would likely indicate that they are sustained by a pluralizing ethos, but are still caught up in the rhetoric of maximalist modernity and of the related anti-essentialist campaign. What is difficult for everybody, including revisionist historians, is to demonstrate that Islamic modernity unfolds as a "project", according to a vision of modernity central to the contemporary work of Habermas, and which Bassam Tibi has adopted in order to theorize Islam's lack of propensity to a modern transformation (see Chapter 9).

We should be able, however, to recognize that the "project" metaphor results from the need to reassert the values of Enlightenment in an era of threatening, fashionable "post-modern" theorizing, and for these reasons also appeals to those scholars engaged in countering the enduring stereotypes of a stagnant Orient redeemed by the Western irradiation of modernity worldwide. The paradox is that in this way a tentatively anti-Eurocentric undertaking reproposes the hard shell of Hegelism as a constant feature of the self-understanding of the Enlightenment's dialectic (see Chapters 4 and 6). I have deemed it more useful and more honest, in a crosscultural perspective, to reconstruct intellectual modernity not as a project, but as the impulse to affirm a distinction within a framework of universal projection and of communal reference, with no preordained path of access to the formulation of this distinction (see Chapters 1, 2 and 3).

It is obvious that around and beyond the hermeneutic chain of political Islam that I have attempted to reconstruct there are several other models for defining the relationship between "Islam" and the "political" worthy of analysis. I opted for the most focused ones from the viewpoint of the consistency in constructing (or deconstructing) the concept of political Islam. These were also the positions which most clearly showed a coherence between the hermeneutic location, within the transcultural space, of the authors examined and their argumentative paths. The various models or circles have been ordered in such a way as to show how they – sometimes chronologically, always logically – derive from each other. The trajectory shown leads to the unmaking of the category of "political Islam" and to emphasizing the efforts to situate Arab–Islamic discourses within political-intellectual modernity, i.e. to construct them as manifestations of a specifically "Arab–Islamic" political discourse of modernity.

In this sense, the trajectory is far from finished. The deconstruction of "political Islam" and the reconciliation of the hermeneutics of Islam with the political discourse of modernity is an intellectual goal demanding a tough interpretive struggle and a long-term commitment to an integrated (both historiographic and social-scientific) research project: the latter condition is lacking within virtually all of the hermeneutic chain of "political Islam". The innovative fifth circle is only a partial exception to this rule (see Chapter 12).

A prominent example of a commitment of this sort, and as such of a research programme located outside the chain sketched in the present study, is in the work of the Algerian-born Sorbonne professor, Mohammed Arkoun. He has been a pioneer in grounding anew the possibility of a hermeneutics of Islam "as such", according to a rationale liberated from Western Orientalism as much as from Islamic, however reformed, *fiqh*: two discursive traditions that tightly share the criteria for classifying what is science in Islamic terms (Arkoun, 1984a, p. 10; see also Chapter 4). The hub of such an endeavour is in the ability to acknowledge the primacy of method, whilst keeping faith with the goal of defining and interpreting Islam as a coherent, albeit plural, cultural system fostering an original tradition of knowledge. This primacy entails a commitment both to epistemological transparency and to a truly historical perspective. Arkoun's claim is that Islam has to be historically reconstructed beyond its political-ideological use and misuse through different authors and schools. In order to reach this goal one should recognize that any interpreter is authorized to elicit the meaning of Scripture and tradition, but on the condition that the method of interpretation accords with the most current methods of those branches of the literary, linguistic and social sciences that are concerned with the analysis of texts and their rules of production.

As a result, Arkoun has conceived and propagated, especially since the emergence of the hermeneutic field of political Islam – and in a polemic attitude with both Western and Arab–Islamic views – a project of "rethinking", or simply "thinking" Islam. This should allow it to transcend the limits of what today is still unthinkable, due to the inhibitions institutionalized in both the academic and political landscapes. Thinking Islam is an operation of interpreting and reconstructing the *turath* (an attitude which Arkoun shares with the indigenous side of the interpretive field and in particular with the fifth circle), but this activity has to adopt a sufficiently "external", social-scientifically grounded perspective (a principle rooted within the Western side). Arkoun pleads for a figure of "historian-thinker" (p. 7), who is able to merge the analytic with the normative dimension of the hermeneutics of Islam.

The importance of this programmatic undertaking is due to the fact that both the autochthonous project of reshaping an Arab–Islamic political discourse of modernity and the Western effort to look at Islam in a social-scientific, but non-Weberist fashion, are at least implicitly dependent on the task of reformulating the epistemological conditions of thinking Islam. It could be objected that the Arkounian path is not autonomous, but cumulates these two domains of innovative hermeneutic work without giving them a common denominator. He himself is inclined to admit that his effort is at the crossroads between reproblematizing the basis of an Arab–Islamic framework of reference and pursuing a sort of neo-Weberian, comparative ethical anthropology:

> The project of *thinking* Islam is basically a response to two major needs: 1) the particular need of Muslim societies to think, for the first time, about their own problems, which had been made unthinkable by the triumph of orthodox scholastic thought; and 2) the need of contemporary thought in general to open new fields and discover new horizons of knowledge, through a systematic cross-cultural approach to the fundamental problems of human existence (Arkoun, 1987, p. 13).

Apart from the fact that Arkoun tends to make the alleged prevalence of scholasticism in Muslim societies, more than the transcultural short-circuits, responsible for the missing capacity to reproblematize Islam, and tends to deny any autochthonous modern quality to the thought of *islah* (see Chapter 5), his approach and the fifth circle share a clear awareness both of the strategic value of an autobiographical rooting for any innovative research undertaking (Arkoun, 1984a, p. 7), and of the tension existing between the making of an Arab–Islamic framework of reference and the dynamics of global, Western-centred modernity. This common motivational and problematizing background notwithstanding, Arkoun has had trouble entering a cross-fertilizing exchange with the "locally-based" *turathiyyun* of the fifth circle. Invited to the most important Arab conference on *turath* to date (the Cairo Symposium of 1984: see Chapter 12), he sent a paper which aroused widespread hostility from the participants, who accused him of speaking a language too patently imitative of the analytic sophistications of Western social sciences, thereby jeopardizing the efforts to attain a synthetically viable definition of *turath* suiting the requirements of their search for identity in the modern world (see Roussillon, 1985, pp. 6 and 18). From the viewpoint of the present work, we have to appreciate the fact that the hybrid, non-local position of Arkoun has aided his task of purging the residual apologetic tones in the hermeneutics of authenticity within the area of the fifth circle (and especially at its periphery, among its theoretically less solid contributions) from the definition of *turath*.[3] Arkoun distinguishes in particular between the *imaginaire social* and the *mémoire-tradition*, which corresponds to the *turath* proper (Arkoun, 1981). This distinction allows him to argue, the former represents the images and values preserved by the latter; but when ruptures, either gradual or abrupt . . . , occur within the *mémoire-tradition*, the *imaginaire social* nurtures itself with improvised contributions and is susceptible to being mobilized by actions that cannot be integrated within the deep history of the group (Arkoun, 1984a, p. 31).

Arkoun began to approach the question of *turath* in methodological terms before, and in a more cogent way than al-Jabiri did, while not feeling bound by an all-encompassing standard such as "authenticity". He maintains that approaching *turath* presupposes a total, uncontradictory embrace of modernity; on the other hand, the elaboration of modernity presupposes a firm option in favour of the historical, vs. the "mythological", *turath* (Arkoun [1976] 1984a, p. 57). In this way Arkoun attempts to isolate the definition of *turath* from the contingencies of the political competition, and this is the basis for justifying an uncompromising attitude (much more vehement than in the case of the *turathiyyun*) against the "unauthentic" and instrumental character of Islamist-solutionist discourse. He recognizes the modern functional strength of this type of discourse in terms of social mobilization and integration (Arkoun, 1984a, p. 30), but denounces its distance from reflecting the historical *turath*:

> The function of psychological, moral and social integration of the *mémoire-tradition* is only partly fulfilled through the insistent appeal to Islam and the restoration of its Law; . . . it is the case of an ideological manipulation more than of a movement of thought committed to a spiritual and intellectual heritage (p. 32).

Arkoun conceives this manipulation as an undue conversion of authority into power. While authority is only grounded on *din* and prophetic charisma, power is an exclusively mundane matter with which the *'ulama'* have historically had to cope. The result has been a contamination between the two spheres that is justifiable not through doctrinal arguments but in pragmatic terms alone, by invoking the need to protect the *umma*'s cohesion (Arkoun, [1981] 1984c, p. 156–75).[4] Contemporary Islamism, as in the Iranian revolution, is the modern reactualization of the same phenomenon, hostile to the necessary task of *thinking* Islam using up-to-date social-scientific knowledge and methods (p. 180). Arkoun's critique implies an outright rejection of the mechanisms of reduction and simplification that have been used for constructing an Arabic-Islamic framework of reference (see Chapter

3), and a plea for thinking Islam historically. Older *'ulama'* and new intellectuals have in fact eluded a wide domain of unthinkability that marks the unthought-of-Islam, thereby sanctioning the impossibility of tackling its historical construction as an open question. This task is necessary not merely for the sake of science and knowledge, but as the only way to erode the surreptitious assimilation of power to authority: or, in other words, in order to jettison the vision of an inevitable politicization of Islam (p. 187).

Arkoun represents the most interesting example of a contemporary Arab intellectual engaged in turning the re-essentialization constraints entailed by the "post-crisis" transcultural dynamics into a methodologizing option. My preliminary placement of the hermeneutics of Islam in a historical perspective in Part I of the present work also resulted from a similar commitment. In particular, reading Arkoun is helpful to situate the modern construction of Islam at the crossroads between processes of subjectification-interiorization, which are the complex and creative sources of any social distinction, and of objectification-reification, which employ models of distinction while taking them for granted (see Chapter 3). Yet the latter immediate influence the shaping of frameworks of communal reference. This phenomenon of discursive reduction and systematization of underlying shifts in codes of life conduct and lifestyle is at the root of the modern "intellectual distinction" (see Chapter 2). The truth-games taking place within the hermeneutic field of political Islam are tightly caged in this horizon of reification, so that their bracketing of subjectification processes causes radical alienation from actual social reality.

We should not forget, however, that disposition-building processes are the sources for authorizing discourses as well as the substratum of the institutions that control social behaviour. Put more simply: social action is at the origin of communicative innovations, of "new meaning". Any such novelty is given by the possibility of picking up, reassembling and transforming elements of signification, symbolic assets and discursive traditions with a long history of their own. This is a typically intellectual task, an act of turning social agency into political subjectivity. But this is also a highly problematic operation, which is made possible only by a high degree of reification of – and alienation from – social action. The mismatch between social agency and political subjectivity is inherent in intellectual discourse and is no specific illness of the "Arab mind" (see Chapter 2). However, in the case of "Arab–Islamic" intellectual discourse the mismatch is made more dramatic by its inescapably transcultural constraints, which entail the superimposition of a sharp (Western) intellectual distinction on a soft (endogenous) one (see Chapter 3), as well as by the authoritarian character of most Arab polities which is itself partly due to colonialism, neo-colonialism and the present post-colonial dependencies. This happens at the same time as the transcultural dynamics continue to be used to attenuate the West's own mismatch between social agency and political subjectivity (see Chapter 2), by way of an artificial stress on the "normality" of the Western path of historical development, an effect engendered by the discourse of dissonance about "Islam" (see Chapters 4 and 6).

As a result, the discursive artifact of "political Islam" is trapped within a chasm between social agency and political subjectivity made even more unbridgeable by transcultural dynamics. The related hermeneutic field is barely permeable to the creative influence of grass roots communicative action, although the genealogical account I have attempted to offer here lays stress (see Chapter 12) on developments within the area of the fifth circle which may help to create a more symbiotic dynamics between patterns of intellectual distinction and the symbolic and discursive material produced via innovative social action. In a certain sense, this is also the inevitably interventionist outcome of the present work: to demystify the historical weight of the transcultural "hermeneutic syndrome" pivoting on the category of "political Islam", to detect its roots and lines of development, and finally to highlight some current modalities through which this syndrome may be cured and transcended.

NOTES

1 This "repositioning effect" has been described as follows: "When we came to Western universities to study 'ourselves', it was not just because these universities had better libraries and research facilities, or even better qualified teachers . . . It was . . . in recognition of the fact that Western scholarship has become the perceived apex of human endeavor in most fields, and it is within it that one must prove himself." (El-Affendi, 1991, p. 85).

2 Husayn's degree of hermeneutic elaboration is probably less profound than in the case of the authors examined in Chapter 12, but he certainly enjoys a higher notoriety in Egypt as the editor of the opposition newspaper *al-sha'b*.

3 In this respect, Arkoun criticizes Hanafi when the latter, in spite of his denunciation of the dangers of solutionist visions *à la Khomeini* that centre the theory of authority on the top and not on the base (see Chapter 12), is all too eager, like other representatives of the fifth circle, to trace back to Islam acknowledged Western values (Arkoun, [1981] 1984c, p. 184), a procedure common to the seventh circle as well.

4 Through this critique, Arkoun places himself within the same tradition of the founders and reshapers of discursivity in Islamic terms where I have located 'Abduh, 'Abd al-Raziq and Qutb (see Chapters 5 and 10). It is symptomatic that after the thorough metamorphosis of the transcultural space occurred in the 1970s, the continuation of this tradition is only possible from a hybrid hermeneutic location like the one occupied by Arkoun.

ABAZA, MONA and STAUTH, GEORG. [1988] 1990. "Occidental reason, Orientalism, Islamic fundamentalism: a critique". *Globalization, Knowledge and Society*, ed. Martin Albrow and Elizabeth King. London: SAGE.

'ABD AL-RAZIQ, ALI. 1925. *Al-islam wa usul al-hukm*. Cairo: Matba'a Misr.

ABDEL-MALEK, ANOUAR. 1963. "L'Orientalisme en crise". *Diogène*, 44:109–42.
—1979. "El Islam político". *Revista mexicana de sociología*, 41:900–23.

EL-AFFENDI, ABDELWAHAB. 1991. "Studying my movement: social science without cynicism". *International Journal of Middle East Studies*, 23:83–94.

AKSAN, VIRGINIA. 1993. "Ottoman political writing, 1768–1808". *International Journal of Middle East Studies*, 25:53–69.

ARKOUN, MOHAMMED. 1964. "L'Islam moderne vu par le professeur G. E. von Grunebaum". *Arabica*, 11:113–24.
—1981. "Al–turath wa-l-mawqif al-naqdi al-tasa'uli". *Mawaqif*, 40:40–57.
—1984a. "Introduction: comment étudier la pensée islamique?" *Pour une critique de la raison islamique*. Paris: Maisonneuve et Larose.
—[1976] 1984b. "Pour une islamologie appliquée". *Pour une critique de la raison islamique*. Paris: Maisonneuve et Larose.
—[1981] 1984c. "Autorité et pouvoirs en Islam". *Pour une critique de la raison islamique*. Paris: Maisonneuve et Larose.
—1987. *Rethinking Islam*. Washington, D.C.: Center for Contemporary Arab Studies.

ASAD, TALAL. 1993. *Genealogies of Religion: Discipline and Reasons of Power in Christianity and Islam*. Baltimore and London: The Johns Hopkins University Press.

ASAD, TALAL and OWEN, ROGER. 1975. "Introduction". *Review of Middle East Studies*, 1.

AL-ASHMAWY, SAID. 1986. "Islamic Government". *Middle East Review*, 18:7–13.
—1987. *Al-islam al-siyasi*. Cairo: Sina.

AYUBI, NAZIH N. 1991. *Political Islam: Religion and Politics in the Arab World*. London and New York: Routledge.

AL-AZMEH, AZIZ. 1993. *Islams and Modernities*. London and New York: Verso.

BAUMAN, ZYGMUNT. 1987. *Interpreters and Legislators*. Oxford: Polity Press.

BELLAH, ROBERT N. 1970. *Beyond Belief: Essays on Religion in a Post-Traditional World*. New York: Harper and Row.

BEN-NÉFISSA PARIS, SARAH. 1992. "Le Mouvement associatif égyptien et l'Islam. Eléments d'une problématique". *Monde arabe – Maghreb-Machrek*, janvier-février-mars, 19–36.

BERGER, PETER L. 1969. *A Rumour of Angels*. New York: Doubleday.

BINDER, LEONARD, ed. 1971. *Crises and Sequences in Political Development*. Princeton: Princeton University Press.
—1976. "Area studies: a critical reassessment". *The Study of the Middle East: Research and Scholarship in the Humanities and the Social Sciences*, ed. Leonard Binder. New York: John Wiley and Sons.
—1988. *Islamic Liberalism: A Critique of Development Ideologies*. Chicago and London: The University of Chicago Press.

BOULLATA, ISSA J. 1990. *Trends and Issues in Contemporary Arab Thought*. Albany, NY: State University of New York Press.

BOURRICAUD, FRANÇOIS. 1987. "Modernity, 'Universal Reference' and the process of modernization". *Patterns of Modernity*, ed. Samuel Noah Eisenstadt. London: Pinter.

BRUNS, GERALD. 1987. "On the weakness of language in the social sciences". *The Rhetoric of the Human Sciences*, ed. John N. Nelson *et al*. Madison: University of Wisconsin Press.

BÜTTNER, FRIEDEMANN. 1991. "Zwischen Politisierung und Säkularisierung". *Religion und Politik in einer säkularisierten Welt*, ed. Erhard Forndran. Baden-Baden: Nomos.

BURKE, EDMUND III. 1988. "Islam and social movements: methodological reflections". *Islam, Politics and Social Movements*, ed. Edmund Burke III and Ira M. Lapidus. Berkeley: University of California Press.

BURKE, KENNETH. [1961] 1970. *The Rhetoric of Religion: Studies in Logology*. Berkeley: University of California Press.

CALHOUN, CRAIG. 1992. "Introduction: Habermas and the public sphere". *Habermas and the Public Sphere*, ed. Craig Calhoun. Cambridge, Mass.: The MIT Press.

CAMPANINI, MASSIMO. 1990. "Islam e rivoluzione in un'opera recente di Hasan Hanafi". *Islam. Storia e Civiltà*, 9:243–51.

CARRÉ, OLIVIER. 1993. *L'Islam laïque ou le retour à la Grande Tradition*. Paris: Armand Colin.

CASANOVA, JOSÉ. 1992. "Private and public religions". *Social Research*, 59: 28–57.
—1994. *Public Religions in the Modern World*. Chicago: University of Chicago Press.

CLÉMENT, JEAN FRANÇOIS. 1983. "Journalistes et chercheurs des sciences sociales face aux mouvements Islamistes". *Archives des Sciences Sociales des Religions*, 55:85–104.

COSER, L. A. 1970. *Men of Ideas: A Sociologist's View*. New York and London: Free Press.

DAVIS, ERIC. 1987. "The concept of revival and the study of Islam and politics". *The Islamic Impulse*, ed. Barbara Stowasser. London and Sidney: Croom Helm.

DONATI, PAOLO R. 1991. "Political discourse analysis". *Studying Collective Action*, ed. Mario Diani and Ron Eyerman. London: SAGE.

DONOHUE, JOHN J. 1983. "Islam and the search for identity in the Arab world". *Voices of Resurgent Islam*, ed. John Esposito. New York and Oxford: Oxford University Press.

DREYFUS, HUBERT L. and RABINOW, PAUL. 1982. *Michel Foucault. Beyond Structuralism and Hermeneutics*. Brighton: The Harvester.

ECCEL, CHRIS. 1988. " 'Alim and mujahid in Egypt: orthodoxy versus subculture or division of labor?" *The Muslim World*, 78:189–208.

EDER, KLAUS. [1985] 1991. *Geschichte als Lernprozeß? Zur Pathogenese politischer Modernität in Deutschland*. Frankfurt: Suhrkamp.
—1993. *The New Politics of Class: Social Movements and Cultural Dynamics in Advanced Societies*. London: SAGE.

EICKELMAN, DALE F. 1981. *The Middle East: An Anthropological Approach*. Englewood Cliffs, N.J.: Prentice-Hall.
—1992. "The re-imagination of the Middle East: political and academic frontiers". (Presidential Address – MESA 1991.) *MESA Bulletin*, 26:3–12.

EISENSTADT, SHMUEL N. 1986. "Introduction: the Axial Age breakthroughs – their characteristics and origins". *The Origins and Diversity of Axial Age Civilizations*, ed. Shmuel N. Eisenstadt. Albany, NY: State University of New York Press.

ERIBON, DIDIER. 1989. *Michel Foucault: 1926–1984*. Paris: Flammarion.

ERIKSSON, BJÖRN. 1993. "The first formulation of sociology: a discursive innovation of the 18th century". *Archives européennes de sociologie*, 34:251–76.

ESPOSITO, JOHN L. 1990. "The study of Islam: challenges and prospects". (Presidential Address – MESA 1989.) *MESA Bulletin*, 24:1–11.

FAIRCLOUGH, NORMAN. 1992. *Discourse and Social Change*. Cambridge: Polity Press.

FEATHERSTONE, MIKE. 1990. "Global culture: an introduction". *Theory, Culture and Society*, 7:1–14.

FISH, STANLEY. 1980. *Is There a Text in This Class? The Authority of*

Interpretive Communities. Cambridge, Mass.: Harvard University Press.
—1989. *Doing What Comes Naturally: Change, Rhetoric and the Practice of Theory in Literary and Legal Studies*. Oxford: Clarendon Press.

FLORES, ALEXANDER. 1993. "Secularism, integralism and political Islam: the Egyptian debate". *Middle East Report*, July–August, 32–38.

FOUCAULT, MICHEL. 1966. *Les Mots et les choses: une archéologie des sciences humaines*. Paris: Gallimard.
—1969. *L'Archéologie du savoir*. Paris: Gallimard.
—[1969] 1972. *The Archeology of Knowledge*. New York: Harper Colophon.
—1978a. "A quoi rêvent les iraniens?" *Le Nouvel Observateur*, 9 October: 48–9.
—1978b. "Réponse à une lectrice iranienne". *Le Nouvel Observateur*, 13 November: 26.
—1979a. "Pour une morale de l'inconfort". *Le Nouvel Observateur*, 23 April: 82–3.
—1979b. "Inutile de se soulever?" *Le Monde*, 11 May: 1–2.
—1984a. "Polemics, politics and problemizations". *The Foucault Reader*, ed. Paul Rabinov. New York: Pantheon.
—[1969] 1984b. "What is an author?" *The Foucault Reader*, ed. Paul Rabinow. New York: Pantheon.
—1984c. "What is Enlightenment?" *The Foucault Reader*, ed. Paul Rabinow. New York: Pantheon.
—[1971] 1984d. "Nietzsche, genealogy, history". *The Foucault Reader*, ed. Paul Rabinow. New York: Pantheon.
—[1983] 1986. "Kant on Enlightenment and revolution". *Economy and Society*, 15:88–94.
—[1979] 1988. "Iran: the spirit of a world without spirit". *Politics, Philosophy, Culture*, ed. Lawrence D. Kritzman. London: Routledge.
—[1968] 1991. "Politics and the study of discourse". *The Foucault Effect. Studies in Governmentality*, ed. Graham Burchell *et al*. Hemel Hempstead, Hertfordshire: Harvester Wheatsheaf.

FRASER, NANCY. 1992. "Rethinking the public sphere: a contribution to the critique of actually existing democracy". *Habermas and the Public Sphere*, ed. Craig Calhoun. Cambridge, Mass.: The MIT Press.

FÜCK, JOHAN W. 1955. *Die arabischen Studien in Europa bis in den*

Anfang des 20. Jahrhunderts. Leipzig: Otto Harrassowitz.

GABRIELI, FRANCESCO. 1965. "Apology of Orientalism". *Diogène*, 50:128–36.

GALLAGHER, NANCY. 1989. "Islam v. secularism in Cairo: an account of the Dar al-Hikma debate". *Middle Eastern Studies*, 25:208–15.

GARDET, LOUIS. 1978. "Islam". *The Encyclopaedia of Islam*, New Edition, vol. IV. Leiden: Brill.

GELLNER, ERNEST. 1981. "Flux and reflux in the faith of men". *Muslim Societies*, Cambridge: Cambridge University Press.
—1983. *Nations and Nationalism*. Ithaca, NY: Cornell University Press.
—1992. *Postmodernism, Reason and Religion*. London: Routledge.

GERHARD, UTE and LINK, JÜRGEN. 1992. "Der Orient im Mediendiskurs – aktuelle Feindbilder und Kollektivsymbolik". *Der Islam im Aufbruch? Perspektiven der arabischen Welt*, ed. Michael Lüders. München: Piper.

GILSENAN, MICHAEL. [1982] 1990. *Recognizing Islam: Religion and Society in the Modern Middle East*. London and New York: I. B. Tauris.

GONZALEZ-QUIJANO, YVES. 1991. "Les Livres islamiques: histoires ou mythes?" *Peuples méditerranéens*, no. 56–7, 283–92.

GORDON, COLIN. 1987. "The soul of the citizen: Max Weber and Michel Foucault on rationality and government". *Max Weber, Rationality and Modernity*, ed. Scott Lash and Sam Whimster. London: Allen and Unwin.

GOULDNER, ALVIN W. 1979. *The Future of the Intellectuals and the Rise of the New Class*. New York: The Seabury Press.

GRAN, PETER. 1979. *Islamic Roots of Capitalism: Egypt, 1760–1840*. Austin and London: University of Texas Press.

HABERMAS, JÜRGEN. 1981. *Theorie des kommunikativen Handelns*, 2 vols. Frankfurt: Suhrkamp.
—[1984] 1986. "Taking aim at the heart of the present". *Foucault: A*

Critical Reader, ed. D. C. Hoy. Oxford: Basil Blackwell.
—1992a. "Further reflections on the public sphere". *Habermas and the Public Sphere*, ed. Craig Calhoun. Cambridge, Mass.: MIT Press.
—1992b. *Die Moderne – Ein unvollendetes Projekt*. Leipzig: Reclam.

HADDAD, YVONNE Y. 1983. "Sayyid Qutb: ideologue of Islamic revival". *Voices of Resurgent Islam*, ed. John L. Esposito. New York and Oxford: Oxford University Press.
—1991a. "The revivalist literature and the literature on revival". *The Contemporary Islamic Revival. A Critical Survey and Bibliography*, ed. Yvonne Y. Haddad *et al*. New York: Greenwood.
—1991b. "Middle East studies: current concerns and future directions". (Presidential Address – MESA 1990.) *MESA Bulletin*, 25:1–12.

HALL, JOHN A. 1995. "In search of civil society". *Civil Society – Theory, History, Comparison*, ed. John A. Hall. Cambridge: Polity Press.

HALLAQ, WAEL B. 1993. "Was al-Shafi' the master architect of Islamic jurisprudence?" *International Journal of Middle East Studies*, 25:587–605.

HALPERN, MANFRED. 1963. *The Politics of Social Change in the Middle East and North Africa*. Princeton: Princeton University Press.
—1977. "Four contrasting repertoires of human relations in Islam". *Psychological Dimensions of Near East Studies*, ed. Carl L. Brown and Norman Itzkowitz. Princeton: The Darwin Press.

HANAFI, HASAN. 1979. "Muqaddima". Introduction to Khomeini's *al-Hukuma al-islamiyya*. Cairo.
—1980. *Al-turath wa-l-tajdid*. Cairo: al-Markaz al-'Arabi li-l-Bahth wa-l-Nashr.
—1981. *Al-yasar al-islami*. Cairo: al-Markaz al-'Arabi li-l-Bahth wa-l-Nashr.
—1982. "The relevance of the Islamic alternative in Egypt". *Arab Studies Quarterly*, 4:54–74.
—1984. "L'Islam: sa fonction dans les processus revolutionnaires". *Cahiers de la Fondation Internationale Lelio Basso pour le droit et la libération des peuples*, Octobre, 47–53.
—1988. *Min al-'aqida ila al-thawra*. 5 vols. Cairo: Madbuli
—1988–1989. *Al-din wa-l-thawra fi-misr*. 8 vols. Cairo: Madbuli.
—1990. "Al-usuliyya wa-l-'asr". *Hiwar al-mashriq wa-l-maghrib*, Cairo: Madbuli.
—1991. *Muqaddima fi 'ilm al-istighrab*. Cairo: Dar al-Fanniyya.

—1992. "Die Aktualität eines 'linken Islam'". *Gesichter des Islam. 2. Orient–Tagung im Haus der Kulturen der Welt*, Berlin: Das Arabische Buch.

HANAFI, HASAN and MUHAMMAD 'ABID AL-JABIRI. 1990. *Hiwar al-mashriq wa-l-maghrib*. Cairo: Madbuli.

HARTMANN, RICHARD. 1943. "Islam und Politik". *Jahrbuch der Akademie der Wissenschaften in Göttingen, 1942/3*. Göttingen: Vandenhoeck and Ruprecht.

HEGLAND, MARY ELAINE. 1987. "Introduction". *Religious Resurgence*, ed. Richard T. Antoun and Mary Elaine Hegland. Syracuse, NY: Syracuse University Press.

HELLER, AGNES. [1988] 1990. "Sociology as the defetishisation of modernity". *Globalization, Knowledge and Society*, ed. Martin Albrow and Elizabeth King. London: SAGE.

HENNIS, WILHELM. 1987. *Max Webers Fragestellung: Studien zur Biographie des Werks*. Tübingen: Hans Mohr.

HOFFMANN, GERHARD. 1990. "'At-turath' und 'al-mu'asara' in der Diskussion arabischer Intellektuellen der Gegenwart". *Orientalische Philologie und arabische Linguistik*. Asien, Afrika, Lateinamerika, Sonderheft 2, ed. Wolfgang Reuschel. Berlin: Akademie-Verlag.

HOFHEINZ, ALBRECHT. 1993. "Der Scheich im Über-Ich oder Haben Muslime ein Gewissen? Zum Prozeß der Verinnerlichung schriftislamischer Normen in Suakin im frühen 19. Jahrhundert". *Wuquf*, 7–8:461–81.

HOURANI, ALBERT. [1967] 1980. "Islam and the philosophers of history". *Europe and the Middle East*. St Antony's/Macmillan Series. London: Macmillan.
—[1962] 1983. *Arabic Thought in the Liberal Age, 1798–1939*. Cambridge: Cambridge University Press.
—1991. *A History of the Arab Peoples*. London: Faber and Faber.

IZUTZU, TOSHIKIKO. 1965. *The Concept of Belief in Islamic Theology*. Tokyo: The Keio Institute of Cultural and Linguistic Studies.

AL-JABIRI, MUHAMMAD 'ABID. 1980. *Nahnu wa-l-turath*. Beirut: Dar al-Tali'a.
—1982. *Al-khitab al-'arabi al-mu'asir: dirasa tahliliyya naqdiyya*. Beirut: Dar al-Tali'a.
—1984. *Takwin al-'aql al-'arabi*. Beirut: Dar al-Tali'a.
—1985. "Ishkaliyyat al-asala wa-l-mu'asara fi-l-fikr al-'arabi al-hadith wa-l-mu'asir: sira' tabaqi am mushkil thaqafi?" *Al-turath wa tahaddiyat al-'asr fi-l-watan al-'arabi: al-asala wa-l-mu'asara*, ed. al-Sayyid Yasin. Beirut: Markaz Dirasat al-Wahda al-'Arabiyya.
—1986. *Bunyat al-'aql al-'arabi*. Beirut: Markaz Dirasat al-Wahda al-'Arabiyya.
—1990. *Al-'aql al-siyasi al-'arabi: muhaddadatuhu wa tajalliyyatuhu*. Beirut: Markaz Dirasat al-Wahda al-'Arabiyya.
—1991. *Al-turath wa-l-hadatha: dirasat . . . wa munaqashat*. Beirut: Markaz Dirasat al-Wahda al-'Arabiyya.
—1992. *Wijhat nazar nahwa i'ada bina' qadaya al-fikr al-'arabi al-mu'asir*. Beirut: Markaz Dirasat al-Wahda al-'Arabiyya

JACOB, MARGARET C. 1992. "Private beliefs in public temples: the new religiosity of the eighteenth century". *Social Research*, 59:59–84.

JANSEN, G. H. 1979. *Militant Islam*. London and Sidney: Pan Books.

JANSEN, JOHANNES J. 1986. *The Neglected Duty*. London: Macmillan.

JOHANSEN, BABER. 1990. "Politics and scholarship: the development of Islamic Studies in the Federal Republic of Germany". *Middle East Studies: International Perspectives on the State of the Art*, ed. Tareq Ismael. New York: Greenwood.

KEDDIE, NIKKI R. 1994. "The revolt of Islam, 1700 to 1993: comparative considerations and relations to imperialism". *Comparative Studies in Society and History*, 36:463–87.

KELLEY, DONALD R. 1990. "What is happening to the history of ideas?" *Journal of the History of Ideas*, 51:3–25.

KHALAFALLAH, MUHAMMAD AHMAD. 1967. *Al-Qur'an wa mushkilat hayatina al-mu'asira*. Cairo: al-Maktaba al-Anglo-Misriyya.
—1973. *Al-Qur'an wa-l-dawla*. Cairo: al-Maktaba al-Anglo-Misriyya.
—1981. "Al-turath wa-l-tajdi". *Al-Mustaqbal al-'Arabi*, no. 28, 137–41.

—1988. "Al-islam bayna wahda al-iman wa ta'addud al-qira'at wa al-mumarasat". *Al-sahwa al-islamiyya wa humum al-watan al-'arabi*, ed. Sa'd al-din Ibrahim. 'Amman: Muntada al-Fikr al-'Arabi.

KHURI, FUAD I. 1990. *Imams and Emirs: State, Religion and Sects in Islam*. London: Saqi Books.

KOSELLECK, REINHART. 1959. *Kritik und Krise: Eine Studie zur Pathogenese der bürgerlichen Welt*. Frankfurt: Suhrkamp.
—[1959] 1988. *Critique and Crisis: Enlightenment and the Pathogenesis of Modern Society*. Oxford: Berg.

KRÄMER, GUDRUN. 1992. "Staat und Zivilgesellschaft im Nahen und Mittleren Osten – Das Beispiel Ägyptens". *Zivilgesellschaft und Staat in der Dritten Welt*, ed. Erdmann Gormsen and Andreas Thimm. Mainz: Universität Mainz.

LAPIDUS, IRA. 1983. "Review of Ernest Gellner, *Muslim Society*". *International Journal of Middle East Studies*, 15:421–4.
—1988. *A History of Islamic Societies*. Cambridge: Cambridge University Press.

LAROUI, ABDALLAH. [1973] 1974. *La Crise des intellectuels arabes: traditionalisme ou historicisme?* Paris: Maspero.

LASH, SCOTT and FRIEDMAN, JONATHAN eds. 1992. *Modernity and Identity*. Oxford and Cambridge, Mass.: Blackwell

LAWRENCE, BRUCE B. 1987. "Muslim fundamentalist movements: reflections toward a new approach". *The Islamic Impulse*, ed. Barbara Stowasser. London and Sidney: Croom Helm.
—1989. *Defenders of God. The Fundamentalist Revolt Against the Modern Age*. New York: Harper.

LAWSON, E. THOMAS and McCAULEY, ROBERT N. 1990. *Rethinking Religion. Connecting Cognition and Culture*. Cambridge: Cambridge University Press.

LEACH, EDMUND. 1976. *Culture and Communication*. Cambridge: Cambridge University Press.

LERNER, DANIEL. [1958] 1964. *The Passing of Traditional Society. Modernizing the Middle East.* Glencoe: Collier–Macmillan.

LEWIS, BERNARD. 1976. "The return of Islam". *Commentary*, January, 39–49.

LUCKMANN, THOMAS. 1967. *The Invisible Religion: The Problem of Religion in Modern Society.* New York: Macmillan.

LÜCKE, HANNA. 1993. *"Islamischer Fundamentalismus". Rückfall ins Mittelalter oder Wegbereiter der Moderne? Die Stellungnahme der Forschung.* Berlin: Klaus Schwarz.

MACLEAR, J. F. 1992. "Isaac Watts and the idea of public religion". *Journal of the History of Ideas*, 53:25–42.

MAKDISI, GEORGE. 1979. "The Hanbali School and Sufism". *Boletín de la Asociación Española de Orientalistas*, 15: 115–26.

MARTY, MARTIN E. and R. SCOTT APPLEBY. 1992. *The Glory and the Power. The Fundamentalist Challenge to the Modern World.* Boston: Beacon Press.

MATTHES, JOACHIM. 1993. "Was ist anders an anderen Religionen?" *Religion und Kultur*, ed. Jörg Bergmann *et al.* Opladen: Westdeutscher Verlag.

MERAD, ALI. 1978. "Islah". *The Encyclopaedia of Islam*, New Edition, vol. IV, Leiden: Brill.

MITCHELL, TIMOTHY. 1988. *Colonising Egypt.* Cambridge: Cambridge University Press.

MORTIMER, EDWARD. 1981. "Islam and the Western journalist". *Middle East Journal*, 35:493–505

MOUSSALLI, AHMED. 1992. *Radical Islamic Fundamentalism: The Ideological Discourse of Sayyid Qutb.* Beirut: American University of Beirut Press.

MOWLANA, HAMID. 1990. "Communication and international relations".

Culture and International Relations, ed. Jongsuk Chay. New York: Praeger.

NORA, PIERRE. [1972] 1974. "Le Retour de l'événement". *Faire de l'histoire*, ed. Jaques Le Goff et Pierre Nora. Paris: Gallimard.

NORRIS, CHRISTOPHER. [1982] 1991. *Deconstruction. Theory and Practice*. London and New York: Routledge.
—1992. *Uncritical Theory: Postmodernism, Intellectuals and the Gulf War*. London: Lawrence and Wishart.

NOTH, ALBRECHT. [1987] 1994. "Früher Islam". *Geschichte der arabischen Welt*, ed. Ulrich Haarmann. München: Beck.

O'FAHEY, R. S. and RADTKE, BERND. 1993. "Neo-Sufism reconsidered". *Der Islam*, 70:52–87.

PALMER, MONTE. 1973. *The Dilemmas of Political Development*. Itasca, Ill.: Peacock.

PETERS, RUDOLPH. 1984. "Erneuerungsbewegungen im 18. und in der ersten Hälfte des 19. Jahrhunderts". *Der Islam in der Gegenwart*, ed. Werner Ende and Udo Steinbach. München: Beck.
—1990. "Reinhard Schulze's quest for an Islamic Enlightenment". *Die Welt des Islam*, 30:160–62.

PISCATORI, JAMES ed. 1983. *Islam in the Political Process*. Cambridge: Cambridge University Press.

AL-QARADAWI, YUSUF. [1974] 1977. *Al-hall al-islami farida wa darura*. Cairo: Maktaba Wahba.
—1982. *Al-sahwa al-islamiyya bayna al-juhud wa-l-tatarruf*. Qatar: Matabi' al-Dawha al-Haditha.
—[1982] 1987. *Islamic Awakening Between Rejection and Extremism*. Herndon, Va: International Institute of Islamic Thought.
—1988. "Al-itar al-'amm li-l-sahwa al-islamiyya al-mu'asira". *Al-sahwa al-islamiyya wa humum al-watan al-'arabi*, ed. Sa'd al-din Ibrahim. 'Amman: Muntada al-Fikr al-'Arabi.
—[1990] 1992. *Al-sahwa al-islamiyya bayna al-ikhtilaf al-mashru' wa-l-tafarruq al-madhmum*. Cairo: Dar al-Sahwa li-l-Nashr wa-l-Tawzi'.

RADTKE, BERND. 1994. "Erleuchtung und Aufklärung: Islamische Mystik und europäischer Rationalismus". *Die Welt des Islams*, 34: 48–66.

RIDA, RASHID M. [1922] 1988. *Al-khilafa.* Cairo: al-Zahra' li-l-I'lam al-'Arabi.

RIESEBRODT, MARTIN. 1990. *Fundamentalismus als patriarchalische Protestbewegung.* Tübingen: Mohr.

ROBERTSON, ROLAND. 1971. "Sociologists and secularization". *Sociology,* 5:297–312.
—1989. "Globalization, politics, and religion". *The Changing Face of Religion,* ed. James Beckford and Thomas Luckmann. London: SAGE.
—1990. "Mapping the global condition: globalization as the central concept". *Theory, Culture and Society,* 7:15–30.
—1992. *Globalization: Social Theory and Global Culture.* London: SAGE.

RODINSON, MAXIME. 1966. *Islam et capitalisme.* Paris: Seuil
—1980. *La Fascination de l'Islam.* Paris: Maspero.

ROFF, WILLIAM R. 1987. "Islamic movements: one or many?" *Islam and the Political Economy of Meaning,* ed. William R. Roff. London: Croom Helm.

ROSEN, LAWRENCE. 1989. "Responsibility and compensatory justice in Arab culture and law". *Semiotics, Self and Society.* ed. Benjamin Lee and Gregg Urban. Berlin and New York: Mouton de Gruyter

ROSEN, STANLEY. 1987. *Hermeneutics as Politics.* New York and Oxford: Oxford University Press.

ROSENTHAL, FRANZ. 1973. "In memoriam: Gustave E. von Grunebaum, 1909–1972". *International Journal of Middle East Studies,* 4:355–58.
—1983. *Sweeter than Hope: Complaint and Hope in Medieval Islam.* Leiden: Brill.

ROUSSILLON, ALAIN. 1985. "Les 'Nouveaux fondamentalistes' en colloque. 'Authenticité et modernité': les défis de l'identité dans le monde arabe". *Maghreb–Machrek,* janvier–février–mars, 5–22.
—1990. "Intellectuels en crise dans l'Egypte contemporaine". *Intellectuels*

et militants de l'Islam contemporain, ed. Gilles Kepel and Yann Richard. Paris: Seuil.
—1991. "Entre al-jihad et al-rayyan: phenomenologie de l'islamisme égyptien". *Modernisation et mobilisation sociale I, Égypte–Brésil*, Cairo: Dossiers du CEDEJ.

ROY, OLIVIER. 1990. "Les Nouveaux Intellectuels islamistes: essai d'approche philosophique." *Intellectuels et militants de l'Islam contemporain*, ed. Gilles Kepel and Yann Richard. Paris: Seuil.
—1992. *L'Echec de l'Islam politique*. Paris: Seuil.

SADOWSKI, YAHYA. 1993. "The new Orientalism and the democracy debate". *Middle East Report*, July–August, 14–21.

SAID, EDWARD W. 1970. "The Arab portrayed". *The Arab–Israeli Confrontation of June 1967: An Arab Perspective*, ed. Ibrahim Abu-Lughod. Evanston, Ill.: North-Western University Press.
—1976. "Arabs, Islam, and the dogmas of the West". *The New York Times Book Review*, 31 October.
—1978. *Orientalism*. London: Routledge and Kegan Paul.
—1981. *Covering Islam: How the Media and the Experts Determine How We See the Rest of the World*. London: Routledge and Kegan Paul.
—1983. *The World, the Text, and the Critic*. London: Faber and Faber.
—1986. "Orientalism reconsidered". *Literature, Politics and Theory: Papers from the Essex Conference 1976–1984*, eds. Francis Barker *et al.* London and New York: Methuen.
—1988. "Orientalism Revisited". *Middle East Report*, January–February, 32–6.

SALVATORE, ARMANDO. 1991. *Ruolo egemonico e modernizzazione in "Medio Oriente". Il dilemma degli aiuti economici americani in Egitto.* Napoli: Ferraro
—1995a. "Fundamentalization of life conduct and islamization of the public space: a theoretical approach", unpublished paper, MESA Meeting, Washington, 6–10 December.
—1995b. "The rational authentication *of turath* in contemporary Arab thought: Muhammad al-Jabiri and Hasan Hanafi". *The Muslim World*, 85:191–214.
—1996. "Beyond Orientalism? Max Weber and the displacements

of 'essentialism' in the study of Islam". *Arabica. Revue d'Etudes Arabes*, 43: 412–33.

SCHELSKY, HELMUT. 1975. *Die Arbeit tun die anderen*. Opladen: Westdeutscher Verlag.

SCHLUCHTER, WOLFGANG. 1987. "Einleitung. Zwischen Welteroberung und Weltanpassung: Überlegungen zu Max Webers Sicht des frühen Islams". *Max Webers Sicht des Islams*, ed. Wolfgang Schluchter. Frankfurt: Suhrkamp.

SCHULZE, REINHARD. 1982. "Die Politisierung des Islam im 19. Jahrhundert". *Die Welt des Islams*, 22:103–16.
—1985. "Islamische Kultur und soziale Bewegung". *Peripherie*, 5:62–74.
—1987. "Mass culture and Islamic cultural production in 19th century Middle East". *Mass Culture, Popular Culture, and Social Life in the Middle East*, ed. Georg Stauth and Sami Zubaida. Frankfurt: Campus.
—1990a. "Das islamische Achtzehnte Jahrhundert: Versuch einer historiographischen Kritik". *Die Welt des Islams*, 30:140–59.
—1990b. *Islamischer Internationalismus im 20. Jahrhundert: Untersuchungen zur Geschichte der Islamischen Weltliga*. Leiden: Brill.
—1992a. "Islam und Herrschaft. Zur politischen Instrumentalisierung einer Religion". *Der Islam im Aufbruch? Perspektiven der arabischen Welt*, ed. Michael Lüders. München: Piper.
—1992b. "Einführung zum Vortrag von Prof. Dr. Hanafi". *Gesichter des Islam. 2. Orient-Tagung im Haus der Kulturen der Welt*, Berlin: Das Arabische Buch.
—1993. "Muslimische Intellektuelle und die Moderne". *Feindbild Islam*, ed. Jochen Hippler and Andrea Lueg. Hamburg: Konkret.
—1994. *Geschichte der islamischen Welt im 20. Jahrhundert*. München: Beck.

SCHWAB, RAYMOND. 1950. *La Renaissance orientale*. Paris: Payot.

SCHWARTZ, BENJAMIN I. 1975. "The age of transcendence". *Daedalus*, 104:1–7.

SELIGMAN, ADAM B. 1992. *The Idea of Civil Society*. New York: The Free Press.

SHAHEEN, JACK G. 1984. *The TV Arab*. Bowling Green, Ohio: Bowling Green State University Popular Press.

SHEPARD, WILLIAM E. 1987. "Islam and ideology: towards a typology". *International Journal of Middle East Studies*, 19:307–36.

SMITH, WILFRED CANTWELL. 1962a. *The Meaning and End of Religion*. New York: Macmillan.
—1962b. "The historical development in Islam of the concept of Islam as an historical development". *Historians of the Middle East*, ed. Bernard Lewis and P. M. Holt. London: Oxford University Press.

SPERBER, DANIEL. 1985. *On Anthropological Knowledge*. Cambridge: Cambridge University Press.

STARRETT, GREGORY. 1995. "The Political Economy of Religious Commodities in Cairo". *American Anthropologist*, 97:51–68.

STAUTH, GEORG. 1987. *Civilizing the Soul: German Orientalists*. University of Bielefeld, working paper.
—1991. "Revolution in spiritless times: an essay on Michel Foucault's enquiries into the Iranian revolution". *International Sociology*, 6:259–80.
—1993. *Islam und westlicher Rationalismus: Der Beitrag des Orientalismus zur Entstehung der Soziologie*. Frankfurt and New York: Campus.

SULLIVAN, DENIS J. 1994. *Private Voluntary Organizations in Egypt: Islamic Development, Private Initiative, and State Control*. Gainesville, Fl.: University Press of Florida.

SZAKOLCZAI, ARPAD. 1993a. *From Governmentality to the Genealogy of Subjectivity: On Foucault's Path in the 1980s*. Florence: European University Institute, working paper.
—1993b. *Nietzsche's Genealogical Method: Presentation and Application*. Florence: European University Institute, working paper.
—1996. *Durkheim, Weber and Parsons, and the Founding Experiences of Sociology*. Florence: European University Institute, working paper.

TARABISHI, JORJ. 1991. *Al-muthaqqafun al-'arab wa-l-turath*. London: Riad El-Rayyes.

TAYLOR, CHARLES. 1992. *The Ethics of Authenticity*. Cambridge, Mass.: Harvard University Press.

TENBRUCK, FRIEDRICH H. 1993. "Die Religion im Maelstrom der Reflexion". *Religion und Kultur*, ed. Jörg Bergmann *et al.* Opladen: Westdeutscher Verlag.

TIBAWI, A. L. 1964. *English-speaking Orientalists: A Critique of Their Approach to Islam and the Arabs.* London: The Islamic Cultural Centre.

TIBI, BASSAM. 1981. *Die Krise des modernen Islams: Eine vorindustrielle Kultur im wissenschaftlich-technischen Zeitalter.* München: Beck.
—1983. "The renewed role of Islam in the political and social development of the Middle East". *The Middle East Journal*, 37:3–13.
—1985. *Der Islam und das Problem der kulturellen Bewältigung des sozialen Wandels.* Frankfurt: Suhrkamp.
—1988. *The Crisis of Modern Islam: A Preindustrial Culture in the Scientific-Technological Age.* Salt Lake City: University of Utah Press.
—[1981] 1991. *Die Krise des modernen Islams: Eine vorindustrielle Kultur im wissenschaftlich-technischen Zeitalter. Erweiterte Ausgabe. Mit einem Essay: Islamischer Fundamentalismus als Antwort auf die doppelte Krise.* Frankfurt: Suhrkamp.
—1992. *Islamischer Fundamentalismus, moderne Wissenschaft und Technologie.* Frankfurt: Suhrkamp.

TOMICHE, N. 1993. "Nahda". *The Encyclopaedia of Islam.* vol. VII, Leiden and New York: Brill.

TOURAINE, ALAIN. 1992. *Critique de la modernité.* Paris: Fayard.

TUCKER, JUDITH E. 1990. "Taming the West: trends in the writing of modern Arab social history in anglophone academia". *Theory, Politics and the Arab World*, ed. Hisham Sharabi. New York and London: Routledge.

TURNER, BRYAN S. 1974. *Weber and Islam: A Critical Study.* London and Boston: Routledge and Kegan Paul.
—1984. "Gustave E. von Grunebaum and the mimesis of Islam". *Orientalism, Islam and Islamists*, ed. Asaf Hussein *et al.* Brattleboro, Vermont: Amana Books.
—1990. "The two faces of sociology: global or national?" *Theory, Culture and Society*, 7:343–58.
—[1983] 1991. *Religion and Social Theory.* London: SAGE.

—1994. *Orientalism, Postmodernism and Globalism*. London and New York: Routledge.

VATIKIOTIS, P. J. [1969] 1991. *The History of Modern Egypt: From Muhammad Ali to Mubarak*. Baltimore: The Johns Hopkins University Press.

VOLL, JOHN. 1994 [1982]. *Islam. Continuity and Change in the Modern World*. Syracuse, NY: Syracuse University Press.

VON GRUNEBAUM, 1964a [1961]. "An Analysis of Islamic Civilization and Cultural Anthropology". *Modern Islam*, New York: Vintage Books.
—1964b [1960]. "Islam: its inherent power of expansion and adaptation". *Modern Islam*, New York: Vintage Books.
—1964c [1962]. "The concept of cultural classicism". *Modern Islam*. New York: Vintage Books.

VON KÜGELGEN, ANKE. 1994. *Averroes und die arabische Moderne. Ansätze zu einer Neubegründung des Rationalismus im Islam*. Leiden: Brill.

WAARDENBURG, JEAN JACQUES. 1963. *L'Islam dans le miroir de l'occident*. Paris et La Haye: Mouton.

WAINES, DAVID. 1975. "Cultural anthropology and Islam: the contribution of G. E. von Grunebaum". *Review of Middle East Studies*, 1:113–23.

WALKER, R. B. J. 1990. "The concept of culture in the theory of international relations". *Culture and International Relations*, ed. Jongsuk Chay. New York: Praeger.

WARNER, MICHAEL. 1992. "The mass public and the mass subject". *Habermas and the Public Sphere*, ed. Craig Calhoun. Cambridge, Mass.: The MIT Press.

WEBER, MAX. 1922. (RS) *Gesammelte Aufsätze zur Religionssoziologie*, I. Tübingen: Hans Mohr.
—1976. (WG) *Wirtschaft und Gesellschaft. Grundriß der verstehenden Soziologie*, ed. Johannes Winckelmann. Tübingen: Hans Mohr.

WEINTRAUB, JEFF. 1992. "Democracy and the market: a marriage of inconvenience". *From Leninism to Freedom: The Challenges of Democratization.* ed. Margaret Latus Nugent. Boulder, Colo.: Westview.
—1996. "The theory and politics of the public/private distinction". *Public and Private in Thought and Practice: Perspectives on a Grand Dichotomy.* ed. Jeff Weintraub and Krishnan Kumar. Chicago: University of Chicago Press.

WIELANDT, ROTRAUT. 1982. "Zeitgenössische ägyptische Stimmen zur Säkularisierungspolitik". *Die Welt des Islam,* 22:117–33.

AL-ZAHRANI, ABDULAZIZ ATIYAH. 1988. *US Television and Press Coverage of Islam and Muslims.* Ph.D. thesis, University of Oklahoma.

ZARTMAN, WILLIAM. 1976. "Political science". *The Study of the Middle East. Research and Scholarship in the Humanities and the Social Sciences,* ed. Leonard Binder. New York: John Wiley and Sons.
—1992. "Democracy and Islam: the cultural dialectic". *The Annals of the American Academy of Political and Social Science,* 524, 181–9.

ZUBAIDA, SAMI. 1988. "Islam, cultural nationalism and the left". *Review of Middle East Studies,* 4:1–32.
—1989a. "Introduction". *Islam, the People and the State: Essays on Political Ideas and Movements in the Middle East.* New York and London: Routledge.
—[1987] 1989b. "The quest for the Islamic State: Islamic fundamentalism in Egypt and Iran". *Islam, the People and the State: Essays on Political Ideas and Movements in the Middle East.* New York and London: Routledge.
—1989c. "The nation state in the Middle East". *Islam, the People and the State: Essays on Political Ideas and Movements in the Middle East.* New York and London: Routledge.

ZUBAIDA, SAMI. 1992. "Islam, the state and democracy: contrasting conceptions of society in Egypt". *Middle East Report,* no. 179, 2–10.

INDEX